THE WHOLE
MOTION

THE WHOLE MOTION

COLLECTED POEMS
1945 - 1992

JAMES DICKEY

WESLEYAN UNIVERSITY PRESS

Published by University Press of New England / Hanover and London

WESLEYAN UNIVERSITY PRESS

Published by University Press of New England, Hanover, NH 03755
Printed in the United States of America 5 4 3 2 1
CIP data appear at the end of the book

Acknowledgments appear on page 477

to my wife Deborah
    and our daughter Bronwen

        and

to my first wife Maxine
    and our sons Christopher and Kevin

CONTENTS

Summons

Into the Stone

Drowning with Others

Helmets

Buckdancer's Choice

Falling, May Day Sermon, and Other Poems

The Eye-Beaters, Blood, Victory, Madness, Buckhead and Mercy

The Zodiac

The Strength of Fields

Head-Deep in Strange Sounds: Free-Flight Improvisations from the unEnglish

Six from Puella

The Eagle's Mile

Double-tongue: Collaborations and Rewrites

SUMMONS

THE PLACE OF
THE SKULL

The Baggage King

There in New Guinea, by the grounded metal
And the birds' free flight,
Under their cries, far under:
Under them at the level of the ocean
We came from the rusted freighter

With a thousand bags, duffel,
Kit-bags, B-4's, A-3's,
Barracks bags, handbags,
Kits, "personal bags," musette bags,
Parachutes, kith and kin,
And were left, there,
The recruits,
The never-failing replacements

As the ship drew out in darkness to the sea.
There the trucks came,
Or were supposed to come
Out of combat,
Moaning like the wounded,
Like the enemy and friend
Of life, to take us to the tents
Where the boys who came a week earlier

Lay in a cold sweat,
Or their ghosts lay, sweating
In a small tepid fog from the ground.
This was done, but I could not find
My bag, my flying gear, my books,

And so would not leave
The mountain of baggage.

When the last truck deserted, groaning
Through the great, beseiging mud,
I saw the mound of baggage
Begin to sink through the clay
Like the hill of a dead king
Beleaguered by mosquitoes and flies
Losing their way in the dark.
Not knowing what this thing was

That at last I climbed aboard, clambering over
The musette bags which crunched
Like eggs, the long case
Where the guitar was straining its breast,
Up the long, crumbling slope of baggage
I sat in trashy triumph at the top,
Knowing my own equipment, my own link
With the past was buried beneath me, or lost,

And not caring, not at all,
But only knowing that I was there,
Drenched in sweat, my shirt open down to my balls,
Nineteen years old, commanding the beach
Where life and death had striven, but safe
At the top of the heap, in the dark
Where no lights came through
From the water, and nothing yet struck.

Patience: In the Mill

Through a place in the roof the sun came down
Where in a hall of light Mike Cole sat up,
His menial harness broken on his arms.
It shed a circle upon him,
As if he certainly were blessed, to be filling the cockpit with blood
Blushed eagerly from his face,
And laid on the sunburst of dials with glowing hands.

He could not look, but did,
And saw a smear, like egg, on the ragged panel wiped.
It was his other eye, which last had looked
In seeing his engine die from a vibrant disk
To four great innocent sails.

Through his own incredible sternness
Of pain, he heard the sirens flare
On the gunned dust of the strip,
And motes from the stacks of sugar whirled
And unsupported slept upon the air, beside his props
Like petals carved from off the basined floor.

A tooth lodged in his throat.
He did not speak of it, but a loft of children
In the light he had let in
Were standing and piping. He could not sing with them,
And almost wept,
     but like a child, forgot,

And wandered, lost, among their faces,
Opening the bags, tasting the slanted sugar as he would.

The Liberator Explodes

There, in the order of traffic
Of aircraft. Where one of them once
Was moving, in a clumsy hover,
It is like a blow through the sky
That does not move.

Why would you watch it
Before it becomes of fire?
There are many arranged on the air.
This one you might be watching,
Held in a fear

That contains no fear, but boredom, or fascination,
As it turns on the final approach.
Or you might be watching another
That does not fall.

If it is this one, you see
For an instant, nothing special. It is hanging down
As it would, the big wheels not spinning,
And now are fire:

One shot, a great one,
By accident takes place where the plane is:
The plane was. All of it is gone
Save the part that goes in on one wing,
There, off the end of the runway.

Then comes the shape
Of a silence made of an army
In one breath all watching wildly.
Things move out, and toward
Where it must have come down

There, off the end of the runway,
Still alive with a little of fire.
Here is the purest of fact
That took place like the purest of symbols.
The mind fires over and over

An aircraft that has blown away distance,
But cannot fetch that fact,
Or remember or know or imagine
What the faces of those must have felt
There in the brief shot of light,

And so must lie down again, and again,
Below the ground moved by palm-leaves
Of the mind of that time, and let that fade,
And lie in the luck of salvation
In the cities,
In the suburbs of time, until

There cracks across the simplest of the mind's
Eyes, that purchase of terror on the air,
The burst of light within flame,
Magnificent, final, and you behold your own
Unmirrored face freely explode,
And face, beyond faces,
Your brother of parallel fire.

The Place of the Skull

—1945—

I used to get up, in the tent,
In the canvas sewn over the stroke
And shimmer of the inside of an orange,
And from my banged canteen the cup
Tip full of a curve of water, and pour it out on my head,
The air would be breathless; the other would

Be breathing it, all asleep.
Across the downed gilt of the canvas, the shadow of a fly
In the outside world would go
Like a bullet, saying, "Maze."
I would dry my hands, and pick up the poetry books

And walk through the area, out,
Over the rise with the crumbled machine-gun pit,
In the licked, light, chalky dazzle
Kicking the laces of my shoes along,
Until sea blue from under my belt

Trembled up, as down
To a bench in the stillest side
Of height, I came, to meet my holy masters in the Word
Above the gauze- and powder-burning bay.

I would sit all morning and read
In the sun, the page coming off my eye
More quivered-in than all the blue danced-up
By the miles of centerless waves, that spread to say
If I reached off the book, my hand would die

In the sea, of fire, with Shelley and with Crane,
And never touch the ships that anchored there.
The Spirit moving on the face of print
Left out the nights, when past the honest sleepers of the fleet

I rose in starry harness on the air,
And in my rubber mouth, from out the slender breeze
Of oxygen, I made a song of what I meant to kill
Before I poured my hanging head

From a can of water, and sat
Again above the bay, which loved the Word, and caught

My country's ships in such a full
And furious holocaust of soul,
The lines of ashen text marked off the graves
Where all my men, who sailed the ships, must die
For lack of Good, that I drew off the page.
I bit the silent tongue

Of men and angels, reading on
In the sound of engines run-up on the strip,
A grizzle of fly-wings, saying,
"Who asks for Truth as a time like this
Is shut from pity, and will slay his own
Whose vision kills the meaning of his view:

Only the larger war, with God,
Half-knows such seeming peace."

Obstructions

Things placed there

First a cornfield
Where you wandered, drunk on your own afterbirth,
Weaving and crying.
The ears on the stalks were blackened
Two clouds went over the sun
Like lop-ears, and when they passed, you could see
That the rows of corn each made
A little road; down one
Of these you stumbled, and where you came out
A deer was eating the rotten shucks

Beyond that

Men, boys almost men,
Stood before a goal,
And you dressed in plastic and leather,
Carrying something in your arm,
And fled into the midst

Into the grunting midst of them.
They opened like rows of corn,
And you plunged through

Into a motel

In Fresno, California
Where a girl with a face you'd forget
Lay tangled in sheets.
In the early morning you rose,
In the gray, still light,
And tumbled into the swimming pool
Whose waters lapped and tingled
With the mighty rhythm of cottages
Where the pilots lay with their girls

Drunk on that water

You crawled barefooted over
A rusted aircraft engine,
A Pratt and Whitney
Pulled out of the ocean and junked,
Crusted with barnacles,
The cylinders fused into the block
From too much water-injection.
Past that it was moonlight

Shining over the island,

The graves out of sight
Every which way you could swivel.
Naked, you got ready, and set out
With a canteen of bourbon
And grapefruit juice,
Through the graves that opened in fans
Of infinite, knee-high perspectives,
Shifting like spokes of the wheel
That turned Okinawa through sea-foam.

Various ships took you away

To schools, to peacetime France,
And at last into the lap
Of students, each looking at you

With the stone question
In the heads of Greek statues
Who ask where their arms
And legs and the tips of their noses
Have gone. Your two sons took you

Under the arms, out through

The students, aging themselves,
And brought you to a broad field,
Green turning paler with dusk.
You pulled a cane from a bush
And sat there, looking at nothing
But how it all whitens and darkens,
Bourbon and beer still fasting,
Still tasting of ghosts, who all like it.

The Confrontation of the Hero

—April, 1945—

Claw-hammer, hay, and grease,
We club the engine from its crate,
Swinging, and harness the nacelle.
The dog's head blown from earth
By propeller blast, then buried, then
Stencilled to hem the nosewheel in its jaws,
Looks off between us at quiet,
Increasing, until there is a sound.
I drag on the hemp and chain of the pulley,
But the engine grinds into coral.
Line astern through a smoked first sketch
For swans, the craft come over.

You place your foot, still, forward
Sleeping in its flesh, road by road
Into the island, and the coral shudders,
Gives way, turns easily, a zodiacal wheel,
And the beasts step from their stars over you
And disappear in the sea and earth of noon.
For a second you seem to move among them,

Sewn as a flower on the Ram's light horn.
You grow, then soar from the matted head
And stretch toward night, swelling and foaming
Into sparks, your leg-bone traversed
By an incandescent angle of the pattern,
Blue-white and fixed. The rest drops off.
Down the long road where the aircraft break
From dust, and wedge their wheels,
There is no violence, and under the stumps
Of the plantain wood you turn like stars,
And a spring forces suddenly open,
Shining and groaning, at your ear.
A bulldozer moves with the sun downhill,
Mice racing softly before the blade.
In, where wire-meshed bulbs are set,

I hear the right hand of the sky
Purl, withheld. Searchlights brim through heads
Of horses masked and run in a field of flowers
To the knife, on the shell of canvas:
Men running, wading the leaves of shadow
Strongly with their eyes. From hour to hour
Medics bandage-roll and thread my calf
Into the sea. Their needles buckle, slash,
And hold to count; my nostril jerks at its hose;
Light fastens to my shin. His blade
Strikes on the sun let down through walls
A man is putting up leaf by leaf.
His whirring feathers fill my ears;
His wolf-hound's skull lights up
Around my serum; he swings his shield
Flashing and streaming down the aisle of beds
To cut his sight from mine, but I rise
From cotton, aluminum, rubber, gauze, tin,
And creep out on a leg like a double exposure's:
Out, as the wind dives still,
And the light from the high sword falls
To the roads through my leg
In dim and complex joy. My foot breaks
New, as with throat-heat, down smashing the records
Shed, slamming into tents, over bunkers.

He dances like dust, low in the chalk fields
As I sprint the beach past landing-craft,
Fuel drums, crates, revetments, stars
Waiting in delicate rain to fix my form at night
To the north. In gold flats of sun, he hangs,
Not sure, because of the speed that takes my head
Lashing from side to side on guano'd rocks.
My eyes close in unforgiving pity

On his dwindling shield. I sleep
And wake. My loins draw in: I relax
And stream all day and night
As rocks, sea, sun, above the landing beach.
A truck blasts through with a load of coral.
About that spirit burning emptily
Darkness lowers the coals into the nut grove,
Where we blew on the soil, and licked with flame,
Mud, from the fortified tombs. Looped with cartridges,
With foresters' gear, dug in, I sprawled
In the enfilade: the urn-shaped gun-pits rocketed
Through my sights, and the island sang
Glory for glory into my shadow,
For the field lay clear to the sea,
And the aircraft rose. I woke and knelt

Over the ward, then crept, knee, fist, and stump,
Into a crab-grassed, brambled gulley
Where was a cow. Its eyes rolled
And fell back. For a while I lay with my side
Touching in and out of the earth,
Until the dark boys formed in ranks around,
And from above, as at a sign, all raised to their lips
Thistle, and blew a long soft mirror-clouding breath
In which something shook to come back,
Or to go on, but could not, in the huge light snow
Like a face advancing to its counterparts:
The mouth toward hunger to be made serene,
The eyes to enchanted marble, the ears, the sea,
All through my eyeholes floating still.
In my horns I held the short-haired
Or crab-back-thorned sun, far off,

Listening. Round metal cleared.
My grinning serpents flew at his feathered heels,
Beat down, and Spring tore off their skins.
He placed his armor on the stair of light
And bent to take my yellowed head,
His muscles gliding naked in the mirror
Of the air, his face warm as a man's
Who shall hold at his breast the look
To freeze his peaceful cities to the stone
Lamp of every room, though over plotted graves
He bear it in trembling gentleness, till it be richened
With the stars between the ships of all the bays,
And nail it to the ground in secret weeping.

The Courtship

Though lumber was scarce, we found it,
    Trading with rations of whiskey,
    And began to build on the clifftop
    Not a tent with a floor, but a house
Above the ragged island which had changed
    To peace one night while we slept:
    A three-room house with a view,
    A porch, two rugs, and a kitchen.
        All ends in gentleness.

It was not a place to bring girls
    We would marry, but we liked
    To think of bringing others:
    Perhaps those, in the flesh,
    Cut out of polished magazines
And smiling like a harem from our walls.
    Each fluttered on her four nails
As we cut windows near her in the wind.
        All ends in gentleness.

The live slats under our camp chairs
    Rocked, as we drank tea, becalmed,
    Our missions done, seeing the earth
    No longer from aircraft, but a porch

We had built for idling upon.
In shorts and unmartial attire
We kept the high house for officers
And gentlemen, and dozed for weeks.
All ends in gentleness.

Yet strange claims settled upon us
For this was becoming home.
Each thought for the first time of children
By an unknown woman he should love
Enough to go back to war for,
Who kept this house by unlikeness
To the slick girls who trembled and chattered
All day and night on our walls.
All ends in gentleness.

Before we moved out, our girls,
Their immortal skin in tatters,
Flaked strangely away, still smiling,
And while we awaited that day
A captain went down the cliff
On a rope, each dangerous evening,
To bring back blue, foreign flowers
For no one, to place on the table.
All ends in gentleness.

A Morning

A dog surroundingly howls.
Painfully he is changing
His voice from a voice for the moon

To the voice he has for the sun.
I stoop, and my hands are shining;
I have picked up a piece of the sea

To feel how a tall girl has swum
Yesterday in it too deeply,
And, below the light, has become

More naked than Eve in the garden.
I drop her strange body on cobbles.
My hands are shining with fever,

And I understand
The long, changing word of the dog
With the moon dying out in his voice,

And the pain when the sun came up
For the first time on angel-shut gates,
In its rays set closer than teeth.

Drifting

—for Al Braselton

I

It is worth it to get
Down there under the seats, stretched believingly out
With your feet together,

Thinking of nothing but the smell of bait and the sky
And the bow coming
To a point and the stern squared off until doomsday;

It is good to go for hours
With the wind down the lake in some unhindered direction
And feel the stem of one weed

Rise somewhere unseen, near land, and stop you dead.
It is also good to sense
The wind die, and the boat move gravely, without it,

Back onto the depths,
And to sail, positioned for burial, broadly smiling,
Until the center is reached,

The bones form a teeming new order, the boat does not
Sail, but spins, not going
Down, too light for the maelstrom's grand passion,

And the embodied hull
Sheds perfect rings outward, messageless, always received,
For there is time.

II

Once in a lifetime a man must empty his pockets
On the bank of a river,
Take out two monogrammed handkerchiefs and tie them

To the oars stuck in the sand:
These mark the edge of the known; he will sail from here
On the grains of the mountain,

Ground fine, on the sea's winding, unappeasable call
Sent through his blood-curves,

On thousand-pound boulders that sensitize the water

Like a skin, like banner-cloth,
And scrape with the weight and authority of the dead
On the floor of the human house,

And in his relaxed biceps will comprehend how the snake's
Body is one with the heart
Of the current, and how his abandoned oars must stand

Signifying a triumph,
So that he can roll, in a long mind-motion, the river
Up like a bolt of cloth,

Snipping it off at the sea, and store it on land
In a camphored clothes closet
In its huge red impure length of blazing mud and movement,

Bronze suns, dim clouds
Of rocks, and all the surprising flashes of things that never
Cease to stream,

And thus, a rare hand dropped off the balancing chair side
As on a snake's back,
Feeling the world go unopposedly where it will, may sit

In an uncontrollable
And wholly justified dance of pure acceptance
On the grains of the mountain,

Drifting round and round a great foaming banner, unfurled
On all four walls
While two named handkerchiefs flutter at his surpassed frontier.

Adam in Winter

This road is a river, white
Of its slow-frozen light.
Not treading on earth, I walk
The turnpike of a dream,
Pursuing the buried stream
The fell beneath the snow.
I feel its waters grow

Thick ice to bear me up,
   But now I have knelt down.

But now I have knelt down
As if I swam out of the sky,
Or fell with tremendous force
Of gentleness, like snow,
Toward a thing I know.
Last night I turned and found
I lay with a rifled wound.
That bone completes me; I
   Must kneel with the gentle snow.

Some hand has entered the snow
To rummage me where I lay.
My rib has been plucked away
And taken to Heaven, or
Flung down on the icy floor.
A voice said, "Follow the river."
I have followed; now I hover
Near something the flakes half-hide
   That has come from my sleeping side.

It has come from my sleeping side,
Some being that could not be
Made of anything other than me:
Whose curve my heart fits in.
I lift the light bone in my palm
And feel my whole body grow warm.
Exhaling my soul out, bare,
My lungs take shape in the air.
   My rib moves in my hand.

My rib moves in my hand,
And all my other ribs move.
I whisper the warning of love.
A great image stirs in my breath,
Denying the body of death.
She stands in the shape of my lungs.
My heart beats like her wings,
Yet breath fades from my sight.
   My mouth no longer sheds light.

My mouth no longer sheds light,
Though I laugh with a magical sound
That heals my amazing wound.
All things grow warm in this place.
The green river trembles its ice.
She comes to me weeping, as if
She came to return my life,
Though purity dies, and I feel
    The ice turn sick at my heel.

Lazarus to the Assembled

It is you who have made light crawl
And become the hot, caved-in brightness
Where I lie without shadow or weight
Inside the whole weight of the hill,
Now, thinking, "Alive. Alive shortly.
I cannot stay here with this."
    As the stone rolled away

I heard you frightenedly speak
As though you had hidden the dead.
I can, you cannot know
That this cannot be done.
I move; you try to be still,
But now I begin to feel
    Your movement set in, like a forest

By a miracle touched at the roots.
My life, coming back, runs through
Body after body among you,
And as far as the heart of the city.
In the dark of a jar in the market
Clear water as helplessly shakes.
    By stirrings such as these I return.

I am the dead new-born.
From the mouth of the cave, the sun
Comes into my mouth,
And I can devour all light.
The water in wells

Is ringing like cymbals.
The doors of the houses fly open.

"Bring out your dead," I cry,
And how this must be done
You can, I cannot know.
Instead, I lie here feasting
On your habitual dust
Of sunlight. Slowly I bend
And sit upright like a man

Who does a hard exercise
That must be good for him.
How long have I been gone?
My failed face shines and stares.
The hill falls off me, and I
Step out, beholding my people
Who have waited in blinding clothes.

As the stone rolled away
Your movement set in like a forest.
By stirrings such as these I return.
The doors of the houses fly open
And I stand upright like a man
You can, I cannot know
Who has waited in blinding clothes.

You move; I try to be still,
By a miracle touched at the roots.
And now I begin to feel
Body after body born among you.
I cannot stay here with this!
The sun comes into my mouth.
"Bring out your dead," I cry.

Paestum

One cloud in the sky comes from Greece.
The sun, set at noon, moves toward it
And is ready to change into rain.

Around a lemon tree throwing
A still shadow easily drawn
From the depths of Italian rock,
All things drop off their names
And softly stand in the warm
Speechless ruin of their being, and pride.
A wave falls, back of some trees.
Sound blooms as from a seed;
The human face wears for an instant
A white flash, vital and mortal,

Like the star on a horse's brow.
A man puts cautiously down
The blue-eyed floating of his soul
Over the ruins, around
The eternal youth of well-water.
Down a road a thousand years old
Growing dazedly through the oats,
Awe comes into the city
As into a dead artist's home,
Where the stone and the unpicked lemon

Give the same hand-burning power
As to the curved palm
Of a genius sculpting.
Brightness goes under the fields
Travelling like shadow

Through the well-stones and brier-roots;
Dead crickets come back to life;
Snakes under the cloud live more
In their curves to move. Rain falls
With the instant, conclusive chill

Of a gnat flying into the eye.
Crows fall to the temple roof;
An American feels with his shoulders
Their new flightless weight be born
And the joy of the architect
Increase, as more birds land.
He remembers standing in briers
Ten minutes ago, in the sun,

As cast among tiny star-points
That cramped and created his body

By their sail-shapes' sensitive clinging,
Making him stand like a statue
With its face coming out of the stone
From the thousand shrewd perilous scars
Left by the artist on marble.
The chipped columns brace in the rain-rays
For the crucial first instant of shining.
At the far edge of cloud, the sun
Arrives at its first thread of light.
Unpacking them slowly, it lays

Itself at the door of the temple.
Shining comes in from the woods,
Down the road at a walking pace
Like a thing that he owns and gets back.
Crows open their wings and rise
Without wind, by the force of new light.
Every woman alive in the ruins
Becomes a virgin again.
His nose, broken badly in childhood,
And the brier's coiled scratch on his wrist

Begin to hurt like each other.
A wave of water breaks inward
And a wave of grain lifts it up
And bears it toward him,
A crest he must catch like a swimmer,
Just as it breaks, to rise
Up the stairs of the temple.
The image of a knife bronze-glitters
With the primal, unshielded light
Of a bald man's brain

As he climbs to the place of sacrifice
Where the animals died for the gods
And cried through the human singing.
Crows set their wings to glide
In with him through the portals
But rise without will to the roof.

The shimmering skin of his head
Sheds a hero's blond shade on the ground.
He stares at the drops on his wrist
As at animal blood

That has power over Apollo.
His smile is brought slowly out
Of his unchanging skull by the sun;
He feels its doomed fixity turn
Uncertain and strange in the space
Where a wave shall break into light,
A crow feather whirl upon stone
And the brow-stars of horses shall flicker,
Gone bodiless, in the dark green
Middle limbs of the pine wood

Seeking human and stone broken faces:
Where a wave shall catch the noon sun
In a low, falling window and break it
And a statue shall break its nose off
Revealing a genius's smile

And the great fleet of thorns in the weeds
Shall sail for Piraeus
Bearing a man shaped by nettles
Like a masterpiece made by a bush
In the sculptor's absence:

Where the sails shall set course
By the star on a stallion's brow
And bear him, upright, in a track
Like the ram's horn etched on his wrist,
Inward, all night in an aching
Creative, impossible position
With a crow on his shoulder,
With his arms and his nose breaking off,
Till he wakes at the heart of Greece,
Steps down, is whole there, and stands.

Via Appia

Going through me, the Roman sun
Leaves the seeds of wings in my shoulders.
Two women are shining also.

We are watching the Roman stone
We sit on, float through the grass.
Beneath it a soldier is lying.

Moment by moment his lungs
With flowers are filling more deeply,
And his shield, with the lichen of rust.

If we were to step from his grave
We would fall through this earth as through water.
We would lie in the full weight of armor,

In the ponderous death of all Rome.
Yet now I am thinking of children,
Of the two ways to go after death.

With the blond, heavy girl, I can shed
This very sun down through the years
On my grandchildren's coarse, blinding hair;

With the dark, other one, I could twist
Black, vine-scented curls on their foreheads.
I choose the bright woman, and touch her.

I see that she looks more deeply
Into death, to watch life arise.
She could crack this stone with a smile.

Yet I think of the dark woman's children,
All spirit, and great-eyed with singing
In another world, waiting to come.

When I turn the blind sides of myself,
Like armor or gold water flashing,
And come back from death as another,

Unremembered, descending the sun,
Or drifting my dust through the smile

Of the stone love breaks like a wafer,

I shall come for my chorus of children
Kept from life by those that I shall
Have known in my present body.

Dark choir behind the huge light,
Thin voices with flowers for lungs,
I still can make you. I am coming.

Wall and Cloud

The white cloud bearing to me the darkness of my mind
   Is coming in from the sea, a hundred feet out
      Where it is darkening the water and passing from it.
         Now it sails upon land, leaving the ocean brighter.
      Where we live, the wind is also timed, and set
         To come as the blood stands still.

To help what shall happen to me, I walk down the hill
   Where a useless brown wall moves through a stand of pines.
      I put my hand on its stone and feel the shade fall
         Up the other side and the sun cease shining there.
      Now I no longer have to help hold up the light;
         The cloud descends like the shadow of my brain.

As all grows dark around it, I can see what is in my mind
   Magically freed to glow of itself and its meaning.
      For example, I see my love, whose blond hair changes to black
         As she comes through a gate in the wall bearing flowers
      Milked of their color and just before getting it back.
         The wind arrives upon us when it should.

Slowly we fill up with light, and the flowers take on
   The painful red of their life, and hurt to look at
      As the sun shines freshly into our brains, and the wall
         Casts from the other side a new shadow that cannot climb
            After us walking upward to the house, that stilly sharpens
               Into more and more reality, set deep in the light of the world.

The Rafters

My father never finished
The ceiling, but light would stop

At the eight-foot level, knowing
How far it could go and be light.
Pure darkness held up the roof
And pine rafters wandered through that.
My sister and my dead brother,

Not dead then, would climb
Into them after supper,

Taking off from the sprained brass bedstead
Into great wheels and flowers
Of spider webs; gray sucked-dry moths,
Hanging head-down, saw us coming
As the lamp went away at the speed

Of light, standing finally firm
Deep down in the living room,

A small star not giving up
Until we fell, and the four
Shining balls of the bedstead snapped
Their scratched lights off around us.
We knew all the dirt on those beams,

Scrambling forward just after the mice
(A mouse we dislodged fell all

One afternoon through the four-legged void
To arrive just in time for dinner
In the rice-and-potato soup.)
With the dark staying good around us,
We sometimes went all the way up

To the top of the narrowing roof.
To the odd inner peak of our life,

Where we could hear, very low,
The night wind come to a point.
That was the place we went

When strangers came, all of us shy
Out of our country minds:

When my father had city men in
To look at gamecocks, we

Took off, straight up from the bed-bars
Flaring with tarnish and brass
And crossed, with a knowing shudder,
The not-finished ceiling of light,
And hid there, watching my father

Pour corn liquor out of glass bell-jars.
All during my childhood, no stranger

Ever looked up and saw anything—
A pale, moth-gray, heel-hanging
Sucked-dry small vivid face—
But all felt that something was there,
And kept looking up, as the wind

Drew down to a point overhead.
The most loved thing I still hear

My father say from his seat
In the low, self-sealing light,
From the distant one star of our house,
Is "Sure; they used to be mine,
But now they just haunt the place."

The Sprinter at Forty

Knowing that nothing is in it,
I walk late at night out and down
Toward the glimmering mail box
Where it sits among houses whose windows
Throw light without trouble or searching.
Under the street lamp I pause

With my hand on the dew of my name
Hammered strongly in metal and urgent,
And find that my body is shaking
Out the old, longest muscles of its thighs.

As light after light in the houses
Snaps out all around me for acres,

I receive the wish to live more
Which nothing but motion can answer.
I touch down my fingers to pavement
And rise, and begin to run
Up the curved, crucial lane of the asphalt
Passing under the street lamps

And between the dark houses where men,
Grown suddenly light with amazement,
Cry out for their youth among nightmares
Of debt, and turn to their women.
Like a choir, something rises about me
And I try for the finish until

I am doing all I can do.
I tell you, sleepers, a thing
You know without having to move
From the shook, nailed blocks of your beds:
That wide-open running at forty
Is best done alone after midnight,

Seeing your shadow run with you
Maned with locked light under lamps
Where it sharpens and fades and renews,
Where gold after gold takes it up
Like the members of a relay team
Passing hope from hand into hand,

You know that youth occurs
In bursts, many times in a life,
And fades, and strains and comes.
Such a shade is now covering ground.
I see my thin hair shine
Again and again, and the earth

Between your houses be changed
And charged with successive golds
As I stomp there. The fat on my body leaps

In joy, and the past has exactly returned
From the dead, at dead of night,
In violent motion, sliding on cement.

Walking the Fire Line

Dead on one side
Or the other, I walk where fire gave out
Of its marvelous insanity, and sank

Underfoot in the wood
and died in the rain in the dark.
At odd times the natural border

Between life and death
Shows clearly; when you reach it, do not
Cross it back and forth, or favor

One side or the other
Or become dead black or bright green.
Stay on the line like a child

Stays on a crack
In the pavement until it gets home
And wing-walk between smoky rocks

And white, between ashes
And weeds. In sleep, you say, when the fire
Rises again from the earth where you balanced

And stands like the wall
Of an eternal city founded on this ground,
You will come back and painlessly pass

From the living to the dead
And back again through the flame
And know in a flash how the rain chooses

To stop it just here
In the dark, and why a man dies when he does
And wanders into burnt blackness

Going past the flower
Still living an inch from its death,
Saved when the dark water fell.

Some night the walker
Shall rise to walk the line
Like a miracle man, knowing wholly

Not only how death
Stops and life begins and thrives
Just here, but why, or nearly why.

Seeking the Chosen

It is good, when leaving a place
Forever, to crawl in it
A little. So many times in that yard
I had been hit on the head
By an acorn, my brain was full
Of trees that struck me like lightning
Out of one almighty oak.
When I left that house I went down on my knees

And fell with the acorns
Rotting in the grass
To try to find out which of us would get
Up again from the ground
And go through the trouble of rebirth.
Nuts pelted my bestial form
All afternoon, some dying
In flight, some dying of my skull

And back and shoulderblades
But all day I went on all fours
Up down and around the same path
I followed when mowing the lawn,
Moving like a hog among the shells
Of powerless acorns, looking for the few
Trees that would come of the deluge
Of hulls: what few of the living

From the dead lying everywhere
Unchanged. That was farewell,
And I imagine now two things that touch the top
Of my head with thought, unexpected as lightning
Out of leaves. One is that the yard is
Choked with trees, and that I would smother
On chlorophyll before I could
Knee-walk to the house. The other is that

This lawn is still crawlable, and that a simple
Shoot I found with a split of green
And one pigtail of a root I was lucky
Enough to hold in my hand and put back
To clutch again the essential of earth
Where it was meant to be held,
Took hold, that it now would hold
Me, that I still could achieve it, still rise.

The Angel of the Maze

I. THE MAZE

At mid-morning her wheel-chair seems to rock
Softly, plaited and varnished, free
Of the light held thick with clearness
Under the sill. The lawn of ivy rustles.
As he sits and reads, hand on wicker table,
Light passing over his wrist and sleeve
And fingers composedly trembling
As if raised, not sure, nor yet in appeal
From an animal partially withdrawn,
Ivy moving together in one heaped, gently
Flaking sound, an angel comes to pay
Him for his wife. He knows with what
Inflections the spirit relievedly smiles
Through the braced shuttle of the blind
Hung with its side-faced and deepening coin.
He feels his palm glance into the small
Cambricked light, and the other burns off,
Not seen, past the window: the stripes turn

For one closed furious shock of sun, black,
Or solid light, and behind them something runs,
Pattering rapidly over the ivy leaves,
Then stands.

           He takes his cap and cane
And goes out the bright door, down
The three stairs into the garden,
For a moment looking up at the house
Like a cliff, forty years old, white,
The back as pretty as the front.

In the summerhouse mired in roses
He pins a rose-leaf with his cane,
And hears the intricate circle glide
Form within form toward perfect
Silence, order, place, and sun.
Here, he imagines the statue of a boy,
Or a girl, it is sexless with youth,
On a pedestal: just the warm head
And unfinished shoulders. Leaves,
The small-squared light, shower it
With motion, and lay the shadows
Bare against the hesitant sweet mouth.
He wraps his fingers on the cane, shifts,
And tries to think. Beside, before
His trying, inside the hedges, the green
Lattice-work, on gravel, the head stands,
A cloud breathed dazzling about its unknown
Rain, conceived like thirst, not moving,
Never giving up, fiercer, more perfect—
Unchanged. Toward the slender lips, his voice
Brims like a harp, and is still.

Day after day, the edges of the mouth
Hold more, to keep the smile the same,
As though the sculptor, having placed a hand
In the clean spring of his childhood,
With the other flowered stone to dream
His mother's face. It is healed forever
Into shadows: it need not speak,
It need not lift into noon, nor to his face:

He has nothing but to believe
In the silver light coming through it,
And out of the harmless wild of the eyes
Altering, and altering back
So fast there is no change, and he must run
Still and deep to his gaze as stone
To make the bright rooms stop
Upon him here, their flowers close
Him down among the cut paths of the sun.

At night each leaf of ivy trembles
As though it grew sharply, lightly,
Over a mouth. All night, upstairs,
He thinks of wandering, lifting his hand
Upon his chest, feeling it solidly
Hold him there, as he turns in the leaves
And corners of the paths of the centerless
Garden. *Subtly the hedges are changed
Out of a mind exhaustless, clear, struck whole
Into its open gaze prefigured deviously
In crossing wheels and limits of the sight
Through fire, in forests grown amazed and mild
About recurrent passage.* The ivy scatters,
Bending to moon-white, as a low wind breasts.
*Scott? Falcon? Falcon Scott? Such cold
To hover trackless, for miles, he did not wish—
He came again upon*
                       his dead soul,
Leaning forward out of the air
Of the circle, touches him, and the circle parts
To his lifted hand at the same place,
But the place itself is changed
Over with suns through different, more
Radiant brush, perfect, beginning again,
Marvelling painlessly—
                         for a moment
He is confused by a stone figure
Of his mother's: a boy with a straw
Marble hat. He grins into the dark
Like an old young man, and the timbers
Of a fiery wood fall dead together

About him, into his cool-breathing house,
And he sleeps, and the angel wakes.

II. THE ANGEL

Steadily in the thinning dark
His sleep forms on the pane,
Delicate, blurred into one
Renewing continuous white
Stride of breath toward morning.
The broad walls of his room
Swim in tentative flowers.

As he wakes, as his gray mind cramps
Drowning on the unshaped weight
Of air, I am deeper into marble
Fractured, again and again
Broken back to hold his waning head
In conclusive mystery he feels
As awe, as something properly done
He cannot grasp, appointing entire
The low siege of ivy, brush,
Roses like two hands caught
Together and seen through an artery,—
Beginning to hold out of air
Features mask-like and bearable,
Humbly smiling, prettily forlorn.
Down the white seethe of marble
The sun is limed upon my breast;
The particles boil coldly
Circling into place, and
The ancient summer closes
In a storm of corruptible leaves
Upon the ruins of heaven.
The sun kills his breath through glass.
From the blue print of sunlight
On his page, he bends to walk
After the dazzling solitude of wings
He cannot think, or that he would,
If he could, believe as trailing
Awkwardly underfoot, like oars,

And sits where their snow-graved feathers
Warmly danced over by depth
Fold tremorless into the child.
His gaze falls earnestly,
Changing through my head
Into the earth, whereon I lie,
A virgin, still in the slender hall
Of roses, wedded to die
Again, be broken eagerly
Across the altar scented
Of rockery stone and fern,
And the dumb, first breath
Of the entering angel plays,
Deepening, unsteady,
With stumbling force blares
Heavily, silently, until the child
Rises to the gold and humming
Of the leaves. Here, where purity
Sharpened upon my age, and, scraped
By cloth to bleed, one eye
Pulled empty by the lights
Of every room, the other burning
Near a snow, a stone, a child
Weeping into its teeth, I struck
Into the bent and whirling spokes
To labor down your halls
Onto the porch, and see the garden
Made, Ervin, you sit steadily
Holding the great crushed bow
Of your blood, among the grasses,
In the soft deadfall of sun
Where the white image grinds with fury
Of life to make your mortal limits
One, draw in, be near. Breathe,
Nod, Ervin. Your peace is inescapable:
Each moment brings to leaf
A deepening order of change
Perpetually renewed
In decisive, unattainable
Ceremony, which is the dead.

Blowgun and Rattlesnake

I

Some fires are heard most truly
Among dry rocks
On the sunward side of a hill.
The sound that comes from the leaves there
Is the lifted burning
Away of an angry tail.

II

There is a long dazzling pipe
That can be brought to bear.
The sun's intensest point
Tilts up and back down on it
Like the air in a carpenter's level.
A skin diver's mouthpiece
Fits the inside expression of the lips:
A plastic cone fits cleanly
The inside expression of the pipe,
And, taped to the cone
Is a knitting needle
Or a section of coat hanger
Sharpened on pavement.

III

The snake's watching head must be seen,
Retreating, retreating until
It can back up no more.
Gradually you can tell
Where the rings emerge from the bush
Without moving, a camouflage
—the diamond-dust-cut back—
Losing its secrecy.
You will never see the tail,
Dissolving louder and louder.

IV

Hold the sun still on the pipe
And build your breath like a basement.
Sight down into the head,
Into one eye if you can.
Hold the eye, mythical stone
Of the bird-charmer,
The thing that birds believe
Is the sun come near them,
Bringing, bringing.

V

He very likely expects
Almost anything,
But not, surely, this:
The sun like a bubble trued,
A man, unnaturally still,
Exploding in sunlight,
A coat hanger, sharpened by scraping
On a suburban driveway,
Aimed from the lungs.

VI

Put down your aluminum tube,
One end to the ground, like a dazzling
Staff towering over your head.
Lean on it, and watch
As though the tumultuous bush
Were thrashing with unspoken fire
About to break out, and you
A shepherd and prophet
Whose pasture is desert.

VII

His death has looped him into
Each intimate branch of the bush.
The head dangles clear, and through it
Is the intimate force of your breath,

Black, red, and still,
Shed twelve feet away.

VIII

Cut the rattle loose, and scrub
The long one drop of blood
From the unbent shaft.
Insert the needle back
Into your last breath
That feels as if it would sing
And blow these rocks into sand
And that sand up into storms
And whirlwinds with voices
Giving commandments.

IX

Go up the hill, keeping always
The sun balanced on your shoulders.
Listen. Listen,
All the time preparing,
Inside your face, the smile
To fit the mouthpiece
Unseen: some constricted
Expression inside a smile:
That of a man who wishes
Only utmost and holy reply
To reach him
From red rock and greasewood,
Ready once more
To dam himself up with his lips,
To put himself into a tube
Like a desert scroll—
A last word lasting forever
In the brain of serpents—
And then on a shimmering hillside
To explode, and listen again
For something else.

At the Home for Unwed Mothers

Gradually it is
From all sides coming,
Out of the effortless sky,
Out of all water and earth,
Out of whatever is there.
She settles, closely keeping,
In a lath-and-canvas chair,
The only secret of time,
Silent, alone, growing
In greenness with it.

There is nothing so well
This summer hidden
As the hovering child's
Blind thinking it is Joy
Where its mother rests,
Half shadow, half stone,
Aware that the father could be
One out of many,
But then being sure,
Almost, that he is the one

She hates and loves with the same
Expanding helplessness.
He is smiling; he is far
Away, he does not know,
He does not care,
God-like, indifferent,
Unreachably smiling
Like the child's dazzled thought
That it is the process of love:
Like the child's great idea

Of her great joy.
And there are times
She feels, against her will,
Her whole body smile
With the unborn,
With the guiltless smile

Of the possible father,
Far away, untouched,
And she sets her face
In her most impossible frown,

But changing goes on, goes on,
And she can only be
Unhappy all summer,
Trying her best to believe
That the one she hates
And loves is the only father
Of the child, who moves
At night in the pure blindness
Of absolute being and joy,
Believing it must be hers.

Until at last she rises,
Undoing her face
From the frown of death,
And stands in the window
In the full moon
Mild upon pregnant women,
And smiles as she will,
Smiles gradually,
Smiles on all sides,
Smiles on whatever is there.

Reading Genesis *to a Blind Child*

I am hiding beside you to tell you
What the world itself cannot show,
That you walk with an untold sight
Beyond the best reach of my light.
Try as you can to bear with me
As I struggle to see what you see
Be born of the language I speak.

Claw, feather, fur, and beak,
The beasts come under your hand
As into the Ark, from a land
That a cloud out of Hell must drown,

But for you, my second-born son.
The sheep, like your mother's coat,
The bear, the bird, and the goat

Come forth, and the cunning serpent.
I am holding my right arm bent
That you may take hold of the curve
Of round, warm skin that must serve
For evil. Now, unbreathing, I take
A pin, for the tooth of the snake.
You gravely touch it, and smile

Not at me, but into the world
Where you sit in the blaze of a book
With lion and eagle and snake
Represented by pillow and pin,
By feathers from hats, and thin
Gull-wings of paper, loosed
From pages my fingers have traced

With the forms of free-flying birds;
And these are the best of my words.
If I were to ask you now
To touch the bright lid of my eye
Might I not see what you see?
Would my common brain not turn
To untellable vision, and burn

With the vast, creative color
Of dark, and the serpent, hidden forever
In the trembling right arm of your father,
Not speak? Can you take this book
And bring it to life with a look?
And can you tell me how
I have made your world, yet know

No more than I have known?
The beasts have smelled the rain,
Yet none has wailed for fear.
You touch me; I am here.
A hand has passed through my head,
And this is the hand of the Lord.
I have called forth the world in a word,

And am shut from the thing I have made.
I have loosed the grim wolf on the sheep;
Yet upon the original deep
Of your innocence, they lie down
Together; upon each beast is a crown
Of patience, immortal and bright,
In which is God-pleasing delight.

Your grace to me is forbidden,
Yet I am remembering Eden
As you sit and play with a sword
Of fire, made of a word,
And I call through the world-saving gate
Each word creating your light:
All things in patient tones,

Birds, beasts, and flowering stones,
In each new word something new
The world cannot yet show.
All earthly things I have led
Unto your touch, have been fed
Thus on the darkness that bore them,
By which they most mightily shine,

And shall never know vision from sight,
Nor light from the Source of all light.
The sun is made to be hidden,
And the meaning and prospect of Eden
To go blind as a stone, until touched,
And the ship in a greenwood beached
Not rise through the trees on a smoke

Of rain, till that flood break,
The sun go out in a cloud
And a voice remake it aloud,
Striving most gently to bring
A fit word to everything,
And to come on the thing it is seeking
Within its speaking, speaking.

Walter Armistead

    Remember: not making
Memory climb the mind, as he
The half-dead rustling-still of summer tree,
But come, amazed with love, to stand, this hour dissolved

Upon him years away,
The axe lashed to his wrist.
Upright and braced in my head
Two hundred yards from me, as then,

He sets the tingling arches of his feet
On two great boughs, and swings.
I hear the dead limbs fall, and,
At every stroke, like Time to cut him down,

An axe within the wood knock back.
Those were the years we thought of being men,
And we must labor for it, hauling ourselves up ropes,
Running long hours in the woods,

Swinging our mauls and axes till we shook,
And afterwards, our muscles stunned with blood,
Coming back to the summer of the house, and the room
Where, in a harp of light, the great harp leant.

Then he would play
Parts of the missing music
Of the dead limbs on the lawn. It was a thing
I since have made him say: would not have thought of, then,

Hearing the sad rippled humming-forth, and forth.
Remember, remember
(How many years since his death
Exploded in air, whose body the earth never reached?)

Not so much the knocking of the axe
Inside the trunk, the answering one,
Or the stricken tree that cut the sun
Apart, and strewed it powerfully, shook, upon his head,

But the loom of rain he held between his hands,
The strings, the winter of the leaves.

For Richard Wilbur

    In such a tremendous window
Seated, the whole rich dark came through,

And the Arno most, we watched and talked

And the traffic roared through the vital ruins of Florence
Beneath, on a narrow street;
The river trembled in golden paints.

I thought that either you or I,
Or both, could rise from the mossy casement,
And from a standing start
Could clear the whole wild shaken street
To the river, where light felt for its shape.

It was a thing to think of: we could do it.
But here in the aftermath,
In the other heart of traffic, I sit
In the opening American night, and, through you, remember
That the great wild thing is not seeing
All the way in to the center,
But holding yourself at the edge,
Alive, where one can get a look.

For Robert Bhain Campbell

Unwandering, I can move
One hand, then both,
But not the hand to write what you can hear.
Young poet asleep within cancer,
I feel you changing with
I feel you changing my language.

Here is the place where I sit,
In-breathing the childhood sea,
But still a city man moves here
As under traffic bridges.
For him, there is no death so far,
So out and down, as yours.

Here in the sail-set sundown,
As though God were moved by His wind,
A man like a ghost may walk.
I have no picture, or memory,
But a tall sick man, and some words.

I like him; I love him,
I shall soon sit cold in an office,
Hearing the sea swing, the dead man step:
The sun at sunset in the mind
Never falls, never fails.

There is Berryman's poem, where you were a bird.
And I, an unsocial man,
Live working for some kind of living
In a job where there is no light. But
I can summon, can summon,
And your face in my mind is hid
By a beard I read you once grew.

Listen: the people in their parks
Think nothing, think of nothing.
But not for them I remember
Or invent or wish for memory
With a man from poems reconstructed.

But not so well, Bhain Campbell.
But not in your own flesh,
Young poet asleep within cancer.
I open your book again. If it were gone,
Where could I get another?
It is the place
That with yourself you have made, you say,

Deeper than the falling of the sun,
You say, you are saying.
And all and steadily deep
From that ultimate place where you speak, and I
In my office death-wish, must hear.

INTO THE STONE

Sleeping Out at Easter

All dark is now no more.
This forest is drawing a light.
All Presences change into trees.
One eye opens slowly without me.
My sight is the same as the sun's,
For this is the grave of the king,
Where the earth turns, waking a choir.
    All dark is now no more.

Birds speak, their voices beyond them.
A light has told them their song.
My animal eyes become human
As the Word rises out of the darkness
Where my right hand, buried beneath me,
Hoveringly tingles, with grasping
The source of all song at the root.
    Birds sing, their voices beyond them.

    Put down those seeds in your hand.
These trees have not yet been planted.
A light should come round the world,
Yet my army blanket is dark,
That shall sparkle with dew in the sun.
My magical shepherd's cloak
Is not yet alive on my flesh.
    Put down those seeds in your hand.

    In your palm is the secret of waking.
    Unclasp your purple-nailed fingers
    And the wood and the sunlight together
    Shall spring, and make good the world.
    The sounds in the air shall find bodies,
    And a feather shall drift from the pine-top
    You shall feel, with your long-buried hand.
    In your palm is the secret of waking,

For the king's grave turns him to light.
A woman shall look through the window
And see me here, huddled and blazing.
My child, mouth open, still sleeping,

Hears the song in the egg of a bird.
The sun shall have told him that song
Of a father returning from darkness,
 For the king's grave turns you to light.

 All dark is now no more.
 In your palm is the secret of waking.
 Put down those seeds in your hand;
 All Presences change into trees.
 A feather shall drift from the pine-top.
 The sun shall have told you this song,
 For this is the grave of the king;
 For the king's grave turns you to light.

The Underground Stream

I lay at the edge of a well,
And thought how to bury my smile
Under the thorn, where the leaf,
At the sill of oblivion safe,
Put forth its instant green
In a flow from underground.
I sought how the spirit could fall
Down this moss-feathered well:
The motion by which my face
Could descend through structureless grass,
Dreaming of love, and pass
Through solid earth, to rest
On the unseen water's breast,
Timelessly smiling, and free
Of the world, of light, and of me.
I made and imagined that smile
To float there, mile on mile
Of streaming, unknowable wonder,
Overhearing a silence like thunder
Possess every stone of the well
Forever, where my face fell
From the upper, springtime world,
And my odd, living mouth unfurled

An eternal grin, while I
In the bright and stunned grass lay
And turned to air without age.
My first love fingered a page
And sang with Campion.
The heart in my breast turned green;
I entered the words afresh,
At one with her singing flesh.
But all the time I felt
The secret triumph melt
Down through the rooted thorn,
And the smile I filtered through stone
Motionless lie, not murmuring
But listening only, and hearing
My image of joy flow down.
I turned from the girl I had found
In a song once sung by my mother,
And loved my one true brother,
The tall cadaver, who
Either grew or did not grow,
But smiled, with the smile of singing,
Or a smile of incredible longing
To rise through a circle of stone,
Gazing up at a sky, alone
Visible, at the top of a well,
And seeking for years to deliver
His mouth from the endless river
Of my oil-on-the-water smile,
And claim his own grave face
That mine might live in its place.
I lay at the edge of a well;
And then I smiled, and fell.

The String

Except when he enters my son,
The same age as he at his death,
I cannot bring my brother to myself.
I do not have his memory in my life,

Yet he is in my mind and on my hands.
I weave the trivial string upon a light
Dead before I was born.

Mark how the brother must live,
Who comes through the words of my mother.
I have been told he lay
In his death-bed singing with fever,
Performing with string on his fingers
Incredible feats of construction
There before he was born.

His Jacob's Coffin now
Floats deeply between my fingers.
The strings with my thin bones shake.
My eyes go from me, and down
Through my bound, spread hands
To the dead, from the kin of the dead,
Dead before I was born.

The gaze of genius comes back.
The rose-window of Chartres is in it,
And Euclid's lines upon sand,
And the sun through the Brooklyn Bridge,
And, caught in a web, the regard
Of a skeletal, blood-sharing child
Dead before I was born.

I believe in my father and mother
Finding no hope in these lines.
Out of grief, I was myself
Conceived, and brought to life
To replace the incredible child
Who built on this string in a fever
Dead before I was born.

A man, I make the same forms
For my son, that my brother made,
Who learnt them going to Heaven:
The coffin of light, the bridge,
The cup and saucer of pure air,
Cradle of Cat, the Foot of a Crow
Dead before I was born.

I raise up the bridge and the tower.
I burn the knit coffin in sunlight
For the child who has woven this city:
Who loved, doing this, to die:
Who thought like a spider, and sang,
And completed the maze of my fingers,
Dead before I was born.

The Vegetable King

Just after the sun
Has closed, I swing the fresh paint of the door
And have opened the new, green dark.
From my house and my silent folk
I step, and lay me in ritual down.

One night each April
I unroll the musty sleeping-bag
And beat from it a cloud of sleeping moths.
I leave the house, which leaves
Its window-light on the ground

In gold frames picturing grass,
And lie in the unconsecrated grove
Of small, suburban pines,
And never move, as the ground not ever shall move,
Remembering, remembering to feel

The still earth turn my house around the sun
Where all is dark, unhoped-for, and undone.
I cannot sleep until the lights are out,
And the lights of the house of grass, also,
Snap off, from underground.

Beneath the gods and animals of Heaven,
Mismade inspiringly, like them,
I fall to a colored sleep
Enveloping the house, or coming out
Of the dark side of the sun,

And begin to believe a dream
I never once have had,

Of being part of the acclaimed rebirth
Of the ruined, calm world, in spring,
When the drowned god and the dreamed-of sun

Unite, to bring the red, the blue,
The common yellow flower out of earth
Of the tended and untended garden: when the chosen man,
Hacked apart in the growing cold
Of the year, by the whole of mindless nature is assembled

From the trembling, untroubled river.
I believe I become that man, become
As bloodless as a god, within the water,
Who yet returns to walk a woman's rooms
Where flowers on the mantel-piece are those

Bought by his death. A warm wind springs
From the curtains. Blue china and milk on the table
Are mild, convincing, and strange.
At that time it is light,
And, as my eyelid lifts

An instant before the other, the last star is withdrawn
Alive, from its fiery fable.
I would not think to move,
Nor cry, "I live," just yet,
Nor shake the twinkling horsehair of my head,

Nor rise, nor shine, nor live
With any but the slant, green, mummied light
And wintry, bell-swung undergloom of waters
Wherethrough my severed head has prophesied
For the silent daffodil and righteous

Leaf, and now has told the truth.
This is the time foresaid, when I must enter
The waking house, and return to a human love
Cherished on faith through winter:
That time when I in the night

Of water lay, with sparkling animals of light
And distance made, with gods
Which move through Heaven only as the spheres

Are moved: by music, music.
Mother, son, and wife

Who live with me: I am in death
And waking. Give me the looks that recall me.
None knows why you have waited
In the cold, thin house for winter
To turn the inmost sunlight green

And blue and red with life,
But it must be so, since you have set
These flowers upon the table, and milk for him
Who, recurring in this body, bears you home
Magnificent pardon, and dread, impending crime.

The Enclosure

Down the track of a Philippine Island
We rode to the aircraft in trucks,
Going past an enclosure of women,
Those nurses from sick-tents,
With a fume of sand-dust at our backs.
We leapt to the tail-gate,
And drew back, then,
From the guards of the trembling compound,

Where the nailed wire sang like a jew's-harp,
And the women like prisoners paced.
In the dog-panting night-fighter climbing,
Held up between the engines like a child,
I rested my head on my hands;
The drained mask fell from my face.
I thought I could see
Through the dark and the heart-pulsing wire,

Their dungarees float to the floor,
And their light-worthy hair shake down
In curls and remarkable shapes
That the heads of men cannot grow,
And women stand deep in a ring
Of light, and whisper in panic unto us

To deliver them out
Of the circle of impotence, formed

As moonlight spins round a propeller,
Delicate, eternal, though roaring.
A man was suspended above them,
Outcrying the engines with lust.
He was carried away without damage,
And the women, inviolate, woke
In a cloud of gauze,
Overhearing the engines' matched thunder.

Then, the voice of the man, inmixed,
Seemed to them reassuring, unheard-of,
Passing out softly into the hush
Of nipa-leaves, reeds and the sea,
And the long wind up from the beaches,
All making the nets to be trembling
Purely around them,
And fading the desperate sound

To the whine of mosquitoes, turned back
By the powdery cloth that they slept in,
Not touching it, sleeping or waking,
With a thing, not even their hair.
The man sat away in the moonlight,
In a braced, iron, kingly chair,
As the engines labored
And carried him off like a child

To the west, and the thunderstruck mainland.
It may have been the notion of a circle
Of light, or the sigh of the never-thumbed wire,
Or a cry with the shape of propellers,
Or the untouched and breath-trembling nets,
That led me later, at peace,
To shuck off my clothes
In a sickness of moonlight and patience,

With a tongue that cried low, like a jew's-harp,
And a white gaze shimmered upon me
Like an earthless moon, as from women
Sleeping kept from themselves, and beyond me,

To sweat as I did, to the north:
To pray to a skylight of paper, and fall
On the enemy's women
With intact and incredible love.

The Jewel

Forgetting I am alive, the tent comes over me
Like grass, and dangling its light on a thread,
Turning the coffee-urn green
Where the boys upon camp-stools are sitting,
    Alone, in late night.

I see my coffee curving in a cup,
A blind, steeled, brimming smile
I hold up alive in my hand.
I smile back a smile I was issued,
    Alone, in late night.

A man doubled strangely in time,
I am waiting to walk with a flashlight
Beam, as a third, weak, drifting leg
To the aircraft standing in darkness,
    Alone, in late night.

Who packs himself into a cockpit
Suspended on clod-hopping wheels,
With the moon held still in the tail-booms,
Has taken his own vow of silence,
    Alone, in late night.

Across from him, someone snaps on
The faceted lights of a cabin.
There, like the meaning of war, he sees
A strong, poor diamond of light,
    Alone, in late night,

And inside it, a man leaning forward
In a helmet, a mask of rubber,
In the balance of a great, stressed jewel
Going through his amazing procedure,
    Alone, in late night.

Truly, do I live? Or shall I die, at last,
Of waiting? Why should the fear grow loud
With the years, of being the first to give in
To the matched, priceless glow of the engines,
Alone, in late night?

The Performance

The last time I saw Donald Armstrong
He was staggering oddly off into the sun,
Going down, of the Philippine Islands.
I let my shovel fall, and put that hand
Above my eyes, and moved some way to one side
That his body might pass through the sun,

And I saw how well he was not
Standing there on his hands,
On his spindle-shanked forearms balanced,
Unbalanced, with his big feet looming and waving
In the great, untrustworthy air
He flew in each night, when it darkened.

Dust fanned in scraped puffs from the earth
Between his arms, and blood turned his face inside out,
To demonstrate its suppleness
Of veins, as he perfected his role.
Next day, he toppled his head off
On an island beach to the south,

And the enemy's two-handed sword
Did not fall from anyone's hands
At that miraculous sight,
As the head rolled over upon
Its wide-eyed face, and fell
Into the inadequate grave

He had dug for himself, under pressure.
Yet I put my flat hand to my eyebrows
Months later, to see him again
In the sun, when I learned how he died,

And imagined him, there,
Come, judged, before his small captors,

Doing all his lean tricks to amaze them—
The back somersault, the kip-up—
And at last, the stand on his hands,
Perfect, with his feet together,
His head down, evenly breathing,
As the sun poured up from the sea

And the headsman broke down
In a blaze of tears, in that light
Of the thin, long human frame
Upside down in its own strange joy,
And, if some other one had not told him,
Would have cut off the feet

Instead of the head,
And if Armstrong had not presently risen
In kingly, round-shouldered attendance,
And then knelt down in himself
Beside his hacked, glittering grave, having done
All things in this life that he could.

The Wedding

During that long time, in those places,
Courage did no hard thing
That could not be easily lived-with.
There, as I watched them have it,
One of them leaned
Low in the bell-tent,
Sewing a tiger's gold head

To the scarred leather breast of his jacket.
Another pounded softly, with a hammer,
A Dutch coin, making a ring for his wife.
In the late afternoon, they placed
The mallet by the pole
Of the slack tent,
And put on the tiger's head, blazing

Over the heart. Among them I moved,
Doing the same, feeling the heavenly beast,
Without a body, attempt in pure terror to move
His legs, as if to spring from us,
His lips, as if
To speak for us,
As we rode to the black-painted aircraft,

And climbed inside and took off.
Many are dead, who fell battling
The gold, helpless beast that lay
Bodiless, on their breaths
Like an angel
In the air,
Who wore their silver rings upon

Their gloved, sprung little fingers,
So precious had they become,
So full of the thought of their wives
That the scratched, tired, beaten-out shining
Was more
Humanly constant
Than they. Years later, I go feeling

All of them turn into heroes,
As in the closed palm of my hand,
And am strangely delighted to find
That they are, to history also,
Heroes as well,
Though nameless,
As the tiger dies, folded over itself in the attic,

As the moon-glowing, center-bored rings
We made good before the dark missions,
Softly pounding our handful of money,
Have been given safely to children,
Or nothing,
Or to the sea,
The human silver, essential to hope in the islands,

Now never worn by woman in its life.

The Other

Holding onto myself by the hand,
I change places into the spirit
I had as a rack-ribbed child,
And walk slowly out through my mind
To the wood, as into a falling fire
Where I turned from that strength-haunted body
Half-way to bronze, as I wished to:

Where I slung up the too-heavy ax-head
And prayed to my thunderous ear-drums
That the deep sweat fall with the leaves
And raise up a man's shape upon me,
Come forth from the work of my arms
And the great, dead tree I hit down on:
That the chicken-chested form I belabored

Might swell with the breast of a statue
From out of the worm-shattered bole,
While I talked all the time through my teeth
To another, unlike me, beside me:
To a brother or king-sized shadow
Who looked at me, burned, and believed me:
Who believed I would rise like Apollo

With armor-cast shoulders upon me:
Whose voice, whistling back through my teeth,
Counted strokes with the hiss of a serpent.
Where the sun through the bright wood drove
Him, mute, and floating strangely, to the ground,
He led me into his house, and sat
Upright, with a face I could never imagine,

With a great harp leant on his shoulder,
And began in deep handfuls to play it:
A sail strung up on its spirit
Gathered up in a ruin in his arms,
That the dog-tired soul might sing
Of the hero, withheld by its body,
Upsprung like a magical man

To a dying, autumnal sound.
As I stood in the shadow-ruled clearing,
Wind died, all over a thicket.
Leaves stood everywhere within falling,
And I thought of our taking the harp
To the tree I had battered to pieces
Many times, many days, in a fever,

With my slow-motion, moon-sided ax.
Reason fell from my mind at a touch
Of the cords, and the dead tree leapt
From the ground, and together, and alive.
I thought of my body to come;
My mind burst into that green.
My brother rose beside me from the earth,

With the wing-bone of music on his back
Trembling strongly with heartfelt gold,
And ascended like a bird into the tree,
And music fell in a comb, as I stood
In a bull's heavy, bronze-bodied shape
As it mixed with a god's, on the ground,
And leaned on the helve of the ax.

Now, owing my arms to the dead
Tree, and the leaf-loosing, mortal wood,
Still hearing that music amaze me,
I walk through the time-stricken forest,
And wish another body for my life,
Knowing that none is given
By the giant, unusable tree

And the leaf-shapen lightning of sun,
And rail at my lust of self
With an effort like chopping through root-stocks:
Yet the light, looming brother but more
Brightly above me is blazing,
In that music come down from the branches
In utter, unseasonable glory,

Telling nothing but how I made
By hand, a creature to keep me dying
Years longer, and coming to sing in the wood

Of what love still might give,
Could I turn wholly mortal in my mind,
My body-building angel give me rest,
This tree cast down its foliage with the years.

Trees and Cattle

Many trees can stand unshaded
In this place where the sun is alone,
But some may break out.
They may be taken to Heaven,
So gold is my only sight.

Through me, two red cows walk;
From a crowning glory
Of slowness they are not taken.
Let one hoof knock on a stone,
And off it a spark jump quickly,

And fire may sweep these fields,
And all outburn the blind sun.
Like a new light I enter my life,
And hover, not yet consumed,
With the trees in holy alliance,

About to be offered up,
About to get wings where we stand.
The whole field stammers with gold;
No leaf but is actively still;
There is no quiet or noise;

Continually out of a fire
A bull walks forth,
And makes of my mind a red beast
At each step feeling how
The sun more deeply is burning

Because trees and cattle exist.
I go away, in the end.
In the shade, my bull's horns die
From my head; in some earthly way
I have been given my heart:

Behind my back, a tree leaps up
On wings that could save me from death.
Its branches dance over my head.
Its flight strikes a root in me.
A cow beneath it lies down.

Walking on Water

Feeling it with me
On it, barely float, the narrow plank on the water,
I stepped from the clam-shell beach,
Breaking in nearly down through the sun
Where it lay on the sea,
And poled off, gliding upright
Onto the shining topsoil of the bay.

Later, it came to be said
That I was seen walking on water,
Not moving my legs
Except for the wrong step of sliding:
A child who leaned on a staff,
A curious pilgrim hiking
Between two open blue worlds,

My motion a miracle,
Leaving behind me no footprint,
But only the shimmering place
Of an infinite step upon water
In which sat still and were shining
Many marsh-birds and pelicans.
Alongside my feet, the shark

Lay buried and followed,
His eyes on my childish heels.
Thus, taking all morning to stalk
From one littered beach to another,
I came out on land, and dismounted,
Making marks in the sand with my toes
Which truly had walked there, on water,

With the pelicans beating their shadows
Through the mirror carpet
Down, and the shark pursuing
The boy on the burning deck
Of a bare single ship-wrecked board.
Shoving the plank out to sea, I walked
Inland, on numb sparkling feet,

With the sun on the sea unbroken,
Nor the long quiet step of the miracle
Doing anything behind me but blazing,
With the birds in it nodding their heads,
That must ponder that footstep forever,
Rocking, or until I return
In my ghost, which shall have become, then,

A boy with a staff,
To loose them, beak and feather, from the spell
Laid down by a balancing child,
Unstable, tight-lipped, and amazed,
And, under their place of enthrallment,
A huge, hammer-headed spirit
Shall pass, as if led by the nose into Heaven.

Awaiting the Swimmer

Light fails, in crossing a river.
The current shines deeply without it.
I hold a white cloth in my hands.
The air turns over one leaf.
One force is left in my arms
To handle the cloth, spread it gently,
And show where I stand above water.

I see her loosed hair straining.
She is trying to come to me, here.
I cannot swim, and she knows it.
Her gaze makes the cloth burn my hands.
I can stand only where I am standing.
Shall she fail, and go down to the sea?
Shall she call, as she changes to water?

She swims to overcome fear.
One force is left in her arms.
How can she come, but in glory?
The current burns; I love
That moving-to-me love, now passing
The midst of the road where she's buried.
Her best motions come from the river;

Her fear flows away to the sea.
The way to move upon water
Is to work lying down, as in love.
The way to wait in a field
Is to hold a white cloth in your hands
And sing with the sound of the river.
Called here by the luminous towel,

My rib-humming breath, and my love,
She steps from the twilit water.
At the level of my throat, she closes
Her eyes, and ends my singing.
I wrap her thin form in the towel,
And we walk through the motionless grasses
To the house, where the chairs we sit in

Have only one force in their arms.
The bed like the river is shining.
Yet what shall I do, when I reach her
Through the moon opened wide on the floor-boards?
What can I perform, to come near her?
How hope to bear up, when she gives me
The fear-killing moves of her body?

On the Hill Below the Lighthouse

Now I can be sure of my sleep;
I have lost the blue sea in my eyelids.
From a place in the mind too deep
For thought, a light like a wind is beginning.
    Now I can be sure of my sleep.

When the moon is held strongly within it,
The eye of the mind opens gladly.
Day changes to dark, and is bright,
And miracles trust to the body,
 When the moon is held strongly within it.

A woman comes true when I think her.
Her eyes on the window are closing.
‘ She has dressed the stark wood of a chair.
Her form and my body are facing.
 A woman comes true when I think her.

Shade swings, and she lies against me.
The lighthouse has opened its brain.
A browed light travels the sea.
Her clothes on the chair spread their wings.
 Shade swings, and she lies against me.

Let us lie in returning light,
As a bright arm sweeps through the moon.
The sun is dead, thinking of night
Swung round like a thing on a chain.
 Let us lie in returning light.

Let us lie where your angel is walking
In shadow, from wall onto wall,
Cast forth from your off-cast clothing
To pace the dim room where we fell.
 Let us lie where your angel is walking,

Coming back, coming back, going over.
An arm turns the light world around
The dark. Again we are waiting to hover
In a blaze in the mind like a wind
 Coming back, coming back, going over.

 Now I can be sure of my sleep;
 The moon is held strongly within it.
 A woman comes true when I think her.
 Shade swings, and she lies against me.
 Let us lie in returning light;
 Let us lie where your angel is walking,
 Coming back, coming back, going over.

On the Hill Below the Lighthouse / 67

Near Darien

It may be the sea-moving moon
Is swayed upon the waves by what I do.
I make on the night no shade,
But a small-stepping sound upon water.
I have rowed toward the moon for miles,
Till the lights upon shore have been blown

Slowly out by my infinite breath,
By distance come slowly as age,
And at last, on the heart-shaken boards
Of the boat, I lie down,
Beginning to sleep, sustained
By a huge, ruined stone in the sky

As it draws the lost tide-water flat,
And the wind springs into the sea,
And for miles on the calming surface
The moon creeps into its image.
Inside the one flame of that stone
My breath sheds the light of the sun,

All water shines down out of Heaven,
And the things upon shore that I love
Are immortal, inescapable, there.
I know one human love,
And soon it must find me out.
I shall float in the mind of a woman

Till the sun takes its breath from my mouth,
And whispers to my wife upon the land,
Who, like this unbalancing light,
When the half-eaten stone in the sky
Pulls evenly, and the wind leaps out of its life,
Assembles upon this place,

And finds me exultantly sleeping,
My ear going down to the floor
Of the sea, overhearing, not fish,
Their gills like a bracken all swaying,
But man and wife breathing together.
I shall row from the sun to the beach,

Where she shall have risen from darkness,
From her vast, shining place in the moonlight,
Where a man slaved for hours to reach her
And lie in the quick of her image.
She shall stand to her knees in her shadow,
Gazing outward, her eyes unshaded,

As I ride blindly home from the sun,
Not wishing to know how she came there,
Commanded by glorious powers:
At night by the night's one stone
Laid openly on the lost waves,
By her eyes catching fire in the morning.

Into the Stone

On the way to a woman, I give
My heart all the way into moonlight.
Now down from all sides it is beating.
The moon turns around in the fix
If its light; its other side totally shines.
Like the dead, I have newly arisen,
Amazed by the light I can throw.
Stand waiting, my love, where you are,

For slowly amazed I come forward
From my bed through the land between,
Through the stone held in air by my heartbeat.
My thin flesh is shed by my shadow;
My hair has turned white with a thought.
No thing that shall die as I step
May fall, or not sing of rebirth.
Very far from myself I come toward you

In the fire of the sun, dead-locked
With the moon's new face in its glory.
I see by the dark side of light.
I am he who I should have become.
A bird that has died overhead
Sings a song to sustain him forever.

Elsewhere I have dreamed of my birth,
And come from my death as I dreamed;

Each time, the moon has burned backward.
Each time, my heart has gone from me
And shaken the sun from the moonlight.
Each time, a woman has called,
And my breath come to life in her singing.
Once more I come home from my ghost.
I give up my father and mother;
My own love has raised up my limbs:

I take my deep heart from the air.
The road like a woman is singing.
It sings with what makes my heart beat
In the air, and the moon turn around.
The dead have their chance in my body.
The stars are drawn into their myths.
I bear nothing but moonlight upon me.
I am known; I know my love.

DROWNING WITH OTHERS

The Lifeguard

In a stable of boats I lie still,
From all sleeping children hidden.
The leap of a fish from its shadow
Makes the whole lake instantly tremble.
With my foot on the water, I feel
The moon outside

Take on the utmost of its power.
I rise and go out through the boats.
I set my broad sole upon silver,
On the skin of the sky, on the moonlight,
Stepping outward from earth onto water
In quest of the miracle

This village of children believed
That I could perform as I dived
For one who had sunk from my sight.
I saw his cropped haircut go under.
I leapt, and my steep body flashed
Once, in the sun.

Dark drew all the light from my eyes.
Like a man who explores his death
By the pull of his slow-moving shoulders,
I hung head down in the cold,
Wide-eyed, contained, and alone
Among the weeds,

And my fingertips turned into stone
From clutching immovable blackness.

Time after time I leapt upward
Exploding in breath, and fell back
From the change in the children's faces
At my defeat.

Beneath them I swam to the boathouse
With only my life in my arms
To wait for the lake to shine back
At the risen moon with such power
That my steps on the light of the ripples
Might be sustained.

Beneath me is nothing but brightness
Like the ghost of a snowfield in summer.
As I move toward the center of the lake,
Which is also the center of the moon,
I am thinking of how I may be
The savior of one

Who has already died in my care.
The dark trees fade from around me.
The moon's dust hovers together.
I call softly out, and the child's
Voice answers through blinding water.
Patiently, slowly,

He rises, dilating to break
The surface of stone with his forehead.
He is one I do not remember
Having ever seen in his life.
The ground I stand on is trembling
Upon his smile.

I wash the black mud from my hands.
On a light given off by the grave
I kneel in the quick of the moon
At the heart of a distant forest
And hold in my arms a child
Of water, water, water.

Listening to Foxhounds

When in that gold
Of fires, quietly sitting
With the men whose brothers are hounds,

You hear the first tone
Of a dog on scent, you look from face
To face, to see whose will light up.

When that light comes
Inside the dark light of the fire,
You know which chosen man has heard

A thing like his own dead
Speak out in a marvelous, helpless voice
That he has been straining to hear.

Miles away in the dark,
His enchanted dog can sense
How his features glow like a savior's,

And begins to hunt
In a frenzy of desperate pride.
Among us, no one's eyes give off a light

For the red fox
Playing in and out of his scent,
Leaping stones, doubling back over water.

Who runs with the fox
Must sit here like his own image,
Giving nothing of himself

To the sensitive flames,
With no human joy rising up,
Coming out of his face to be seen.

And it is hard,
When the fox leaps into his burrow,
To keep that singing down,

To sit with the fire
Drawn into one's secret features,
And all eyes turning around

From the dark wood
Until they come, amazed, upon
A face that does not shine

Back from itself,
That holds its own light and takes more,
Like the face of the dead, sitting still,

Giving no sign,
Making no outcry, no matter
Who may be straining to hear.

A Dog Sleeping on My Feet

Being his resting place,
I do not even tense
The muscles of a leg
Or I would seem to be changing.
Instead, I turn the page
Of the notebook, carefully not

Remembering what I have written,
For now, with my feet beneath him
Dying like embers,
The poem is beginning to move
Up through my pine-prickling legs
Out of the night wood,

Taking hold of the pen by my fingers.
Before me the fox floats lightly,
On fire with his holy scent.
All, all are running.
Marvelous is the pursuit,
Like a dazzle of nails through the ankles,

Like a twisting shout through the trees
Sent after the flying fox
Through the holes of logs, over streams
Stock-still with the pressure of moonlight.
My killed legs,
My legs of a dead thing, follow,

Quick as pins, through the forest,
And all rushes on into dark
And ends on the brightness of paper.
When my hand, which speaks in a daze
The hypnotized language of beasts,
Shall falter, and fail

Back into the human tongue,
And the dog gets up and goes out

To wander the dawning yard,
I shall crawl to my human bed
And lie there smiling at sunrise,
With the scent of the fox

Burning my brain like an incense,
Floating out of the night wood,
Coming home to my wife and my sons
From the dream of an animal,
Assembling the self I must wake to,
Sleeping to grow back my legs.

The Movement of Fish

No water is still, on top.
Without wind, even, it is full
Of a chill, superficial agitation.
It is easy to forget,
Or not to know at all

That fish do not move
By means of this rippling
Along the outside of water, or
By anything touching on air.
Where they are, it is still,

Under a wooden bridge,
Under the poised oar
Of a boat, while the rower leans
And blows his mistaken breath
To make the surface shake,

Or yells at it, or sings,
Half believing the brilliant scan
Of ripples will carry the fish away
On his voice like a buried wind.
Or it may be that a fish

Is simply lying under
The ocean-broad sun
Which comes down onto him
Like a tremendous, suffusing
Open shadow

Of gold, where nothing is,
Sinking into the water,
Becoming dark around
His body. Where he is now
Could be gold mixed

With absolute blackness.
The surface at mid-sea shivers,
But he does not feel it
Like a breath, or like anything.
Yet suddenly his frame shakes,

Convulses the whole ocean
Under the trivial, quivering
Surface, and he is
Hundreds of feet away,
Still picking up speed, still shooting

Through half-gold,
Going nowhere. Nothing sees him.
One must think of this to understand
The instinct of fear and trembling,
And, of its one movement, the depth.

The Heaven of Animals

Here they are. The soft eyes open.
If they have lived in a wood
It is a wood.
If they have lived on plains

It is grass rolling
Under their feet forever.

Having no souls, they have come,
Anyway, beyond their knowing.
Their instincts wholly bloom
And they rise.
The soft eyes open.

To match them, the landscape flowers,
Outdoing, desperately
Outdoing what is required:
The richest wood,
The deepest field.

For some of these,
It could not be the place
It is, without blood.
These hunt, as they have done,
But with claws and teeth grown perfect,

More deadly than they can believe.
They stalk more silently,
And crouch on the limbs of trees,
And their descent
Upon the bright backs of their prey

May take years
In a sovereign floating of joy.
And those that are hunted
Know this as their life,
Their reward: to walk

Under such trees in full knowledge
Of what is in glory above them,
And to feel no fear,
But acceptance, compliance.
Fulfilling themselves without pain

At the cycle's center,
They tremble, they walk
Under the tree,
They fall, they are torn,
They rise, they walk again.

A Birth

Inventing a story with grass,
I find a young horse deep inside it.
I cannot nail wires around him;
My fence posts fail to be solid,

And he is free, strangely, without me.
With his head still browsing the greenness,
He walks slowly out of the pasture
To enter the sun of his story.

My mind freed of its own creature,
I find myself deep in my life
In a room with my child and my mother,
When I feel the sun climbing my shoulder

Change, to include a new horse.

Fog Envelops the Animals

Fog envelops the animals.
Not one can be seen, and they live.
At my knees, a cloud wears slowly
Up out of the buried earth.
In a white suit I stand waiting.

Soundlessly whiteness is eating
My visible self alive.
I shall enter this world like the dead,
Floating through tree trunks on currents
And streams of untouchable pureness

That shine without thinking of light.
My hands burn away at my sides
In the pale, risen ghosts of deep rivers.
In my hood peaked like a flame,
I feel my own long-hidden,

Long-sought invisibility
Come forth from my solid body.
I stand with all beasts in a cloud.

Of them I am deadly aware,
And they not of me, in this life.

Only my front teeth are showing
As the dry fog mounts to my lips
In a motion long buried in water,
And now, one by one, my teeth
Like rows of candles go out.

In the spirit of flame, my hood
Holds the face of my soul without burning,
And I drift forward
Through the hearts of the curdling oak trees,
Borne by the river of Heaven.

My arrows, keener than snowflakes,
Are with me whenever I touch them.
Above my head, the trees exchange their arms
In the purest fear upon earth.
Silence. Whiteness. Hunting.

The Summons

For something out of sight
I cup a grass-blade in my hands,
Tasting the root, and blow.
I speak to the wind, and it lives.
No hunter has taught me this call;
It comes out of childhood and playgrounds.
I hang my longbow on a branch.
The wind at my feet extends

Quickly out, across the lake,
Containing the sound I have made.
The water below me becomes
Bright ploughland in its body.
I breathe on my thumbs, and am blowing
A horn that encircles the forest.
Across the lake, a tree
Now thrums in tremendous cadence.

Beneath it, some being stumbles,
And answers me slowly and greatly
With a tongue as rasping as sawgrass.
I lower my hands, and I listen
To the beast that shall die of its love.
I sound my green trumpet again,
And the whole wood sings in my palms.
The vast trees are tuned to my bowstring

And the deep-rooted voice I have summoned.
I have carried it here from a playground
Where I rolled in the grass with my brothers.
Nothing moves, but something intends to.
The water that puffed like a wing
Is one flattened blaze through the branches.
Something falls from the bank, and is swimming.
My voice turns around me like foliage,

And I pluck my longbow off the limb
Where it shines with a musical light,
And crouch within death, awaiting
The beast in the water, in love
With the palest and gentlest of children,
Whom the years have turned deadly with knowledge:
Who summons him forth, and now
Pulls wide the great, thoughtful arrow.

In the Tree House at Night

And now the green household is dark.
The half-moon completely is shining
On the earth-lighted tops of the trees.
To be dead, a house must be still.
The floor and the walls wave me slowly;
I am deep in them over my head.
The needles and pine cones about me

Are full of small birds at their roundest,
Their fists without mercy gripping
Hard down through the tree to the roots
To sing back at light when they feel it.

We lie here like angels in bodies,
My brothers and I, one dead,
The other asleep from much living,

In mid-air huddled beside me.
Dark climbed to us here as we climbed
Up the nails I have hammered all day
Through the sprained, comic rungs of the ladder
Of broom handles, crate slats, and laths
Foot by foot up the trunk to the branches
Where we came out at last over lakes

Of leaves, of fields disencumbered of earth
That move with the moves of the spirit.
Each nail that sustains us I set here;
Each nail in the house is now steadied
By my dead brother's huge, freckled hand.
Through the years, he has pointed his hammer
Up into these limbs, and told us

That we must ascend, and all lie here.
Step after step he has brought me,
Embracing the trunk as his body,
Shaking its limbs with my heartbeat,
Till the pine cones danced without wind
And fell from the branches like apples.
In the arm-slender forks of our dwelling

I breathe my live brother's light hair.
The blanket around us becomes
As solid as stone, and it sways.
With all my heart, I close
The blue, timeless eye of my mind.
Wind springs, as my dead brother smiles
And touches the tree at the root;

A shudder of joy runs up
The trunk; the needles tingle;
One bird uncontrollably cries.
The wind changes round, and I stir
Within another's life. Whose life?
Who is dead? Whose presence is living?
When may I fall strangely to earth,

Who am nailed to this branch by a spirit?
Can two bodies make up a third?
To sing, must I feel the world's light?
My green, graceful bones fill the air
With sleeping birds. Alone, alone
And with them I move gently.
I move at the heart of the world.

For the Nightly Ascent of the Hunter Orion Over a Forest Clearing

Now secretness dies of the open.
Yet all around, all over, night
Things are waking fast,
Waking with all their power.
Who can arise

From his dilating shadow
When one foot is longing to tiptoe
And the other to take the live
Stand of a tree that belongs here?
As the owl's gaze

Most slowly begins to create
Its sight from the death of the sun,
As the mouse feels the whole wood turn
The gold of the owl's new eyes,
And the fox moves

Out of the ground where he sleeps,
No man can stand upright
And drag his body forth
Through an open space in the foliage
Unless he rises

As does the hunter Orion,
Thinking to cross a blue hollow
Through the dangers of twilight,
Feeling that he must run
And that he will

Take root forever and stand,
Does both at once, and neither,
Grows blind, and then sees everything,
Steps and becomes a man
Of stars instead,

Who from invisibility
Has come, arranged in the light
Of himself, revealed tremendously
In his fabulous, rigid, eternal
Unlooked-for role.

The Rib

Something has left itself scattered
Under a bush in the evening,
Not recalling what lay down at first
To make its claimed body for years
Disappear into air,

Or lay with its small bones desiring
To come slowly forth into twilight
Where the moon begins to raise up
A dead tree now at my side.
I pick up a rib

And something like what must be
The bite small animals die of
Encircles myself and the tree,
Coming round again, coming closer,
A breath forming teeth,

Warming the bones of my wrist.
That my radiant palm is unopened,
That my breast is still whole
When I feel it seized on and thrown down
By the madness of hunting

Is a miracle, like the dead moon
Creating black trees with stone fire.
Can it be that the wounds of beasts,

The hurts they inherit no words for,
Are like the mouths

Of holy beings we think of,
So strongly do they breathe upon us
Their bloodletting silence?
A rib in my right side speaks
To me more softly

Than Eve—the bidden, unfreeable shape
Of my own unfinished desire
For life, for death and the Other—
So that the wound in the air
And its giver

Far off in the brush, all teeth,
Hear me answer the patient world
Of love in my side imprisoned
As I rise, going moonward toward better
And better sleep.

The Owl King

I. THE CALL

Through the trees, with the moon underfoot,
More soft than I can, I call.
I hear the king of the owls sing
Where he moves with my son in the gloom.
My tongue floats off in the darkness.
I feel the deep dead turn
My blind child round toward my calling,
Through the trees, with the moon underfoot,

In a sound I cannot remember.
It whispers like straw in my ear,
And shakes like a stone under water.
My bones stand on tiptoe inside it.
Which part of the sound did I utter?
Is it song, or is half of it whistling?
What spirit has swallowed my tongue?
Or is it a sound I remember?

And yet it is coming back,
Having gone, adrift on its spirit,
Down, over and under the river,
And stood in a ring in a meadow
Round a child with a bird gravely dancing.
I hear the king of the owls sing.
I did not awaken that sound,
And yet it is coming back,

In touching every tree upon the hill.
The breath falls out of my voice,
And yet the singing keeps on.
The owls are dancing, fastened by their toes
Upon the pines. Come, son, and find me here,
In love with the sound of my voice.
Come calling the same soft song,
And touching every tree upon the hill.

II. THE OWL KING

I swore to myself I would see
When all but my seeing had failed.
Every light was too feeble to show
My world as I knew it must be.
At the top of the staring night
I sat on the oak in my shape
With my claws growing deep into wood
And my sight going slowly out
Inch by inch, as into a stone,
Disclosing the rabbits running
Beneath my bent, growing throne,
And the foxes lighting their hair,
And the serpent taking the shape
Of the stream of life as it slept.
When I thought of the floating sound
In which my wings would outspread,
I felt the hooked tufts on my head
Enlarge, and dream like a crown,
And my voice unplaceable grow
Like a feathery sigh;
I could not place it myself.

For years I humped on the tree
Whose leaves held the sun and the moon.
At last I opened my eyes
In the sun, and saw nothing there.
That night I parted my lids
Once more, and saw dark burn
Greater than sunlight or moonlight,
For it burned from deep within me.
The still wood glowed like a brain.
I prised up my claws, and spread
My huge, ashen wings from my body,
For I heard what I listened to hear.
Someone spoke to me out of the distance
In a voice like my own, but softer.
I rose like the moon from the branch.

Through trees at his light touch trembling
The blind child drifted to meet me,
His blue eyes shining like mine.
In a ragged clearing he stopped,
And I circled, beating above him,
Then fell to the ground and hopped
Forward, taking his hand in my claw.
Every tree's life lived in his fingers.
Gravely we trod with each other
As beasts at their own wedding, dance.
Through the forest, the questioning voice
Of his father came to us there,
As though the one voice of us both,
Its high, frightened sound becoming
A perfect, irrelevant music
In which we profoundly moved,
I in the innermost shining
Of my blazing, invented eyes,
And he in the total of dark.
Each night, now, high on the oak,
With his father calling like music,
He sits with me here on the bough,
His eyes inch by inch going forward
Through stone dark, burning and picking
The creatures out one by one,

Each waiting alive in its own
Peculiar light to be found:
The mouse in its bundle of terror,
The fox in the flame of its hair,
And the snake in the form of all life.
Each night he returns to his bed,
To the voice of his singing father,
To dream of the owl king sitting
Alone in the crown of my will.
In my ruling passion, he rests.
All dark shall come to light.

III. THE BLIND CHILD'S STORY

I am playing going down
In my weight lightly,
Down, down the hill.
No one calls me
Out of the air.
The heat is falling
On the backs of my hands
And holding coldness.
They say it shines two ways.
The darkness is great
And luminous in my eyes.
Down I am quickly going;
A leaf falls on me,
It must be a leaf I hear it
Be thin against me, and now
The ground is level,
It moves it is not ground,
My feet flow cold
And wet, and water rushes
Past as I climb out.
I am there, on the other side.
I own the entire world.

It closes a little; the sky
Must be cold, must be giving off
Creatures that stand here.
I say they shine one way.

Trees they are trees around me,
Leaves branches and bark;
I can touch them all; I move
From one to another—someone said
I seem to be blessing them.
I am blessing them
Slowly, one after another
Deeper into the wood.

The dark is changing,
Its living is packed in closer
Overhead—more trees and leaves—
Tremendous. It touches
Something touches my hand,
Smelling it, a cold nose
Of breath, an ear of silk
Is gone. It is here I begin
To call to something unearthly.
Something is here, something before
Me sitting above me
In the wood in a crown,
Its eyes newborn in its head
From the death of the sun.
I can hear it rising on wings.
I hear that fluttering
Cease, and become
Pure soundless dancing
Like leaves not leaves;
Now down out of air
It lumbers to meet me,
Stepping oddly on earth,
Awkwardly, royally.
My father is calling

Through the touched trees;
All distance is weeping and singing.
In my hand I feel
A talon, a grandfather's claw
Bone cold and straining
To keep from breaking my skin.
I know this step, I know it,

And we are deep inside.
My father's voice is over
And under us, sighing.
Nothing is strange where we are.
The huge bird bows and returns,
For I, too, have done the same
As he leads me, rustling,
A pile of leaves in my hands;
The dry feathers shuffle like cards
On his dusty shoulders,
Not touching a tree,
Not brushing the side of a leaf
Or a point of grass.

We stop and stand like bushes.
But my father's music comes
In, goes on, comes in,
Into the wood,
Into the ceased dance.
And now the hard beak whispers
Softly, and we climb
Some steps of bark
Living and climbing with us
Into the leaves.
I sit among leaves,
And the whole branch hums
With the owl's full, weightless power
As he closes his feet on the wood.
My own feet dangle
And tingle down;
My head is pointing
Deep into moonlight,
Deep into branches and leaves,
Directing my blackness there,
The personal dark of my sight,
And now it is turning a color.
My eyes are blue at last.

Something within the place
I look is piled and coiled.
It lifts its head from itself.

Its form is lit, and gives back
What my eyes are giving it freely.
I learn from the master of sight
What to do when the sun is dead,
How to make the great darkness work
As it wants of itself to work.
I feel the tree where we sit
Grow under me, and live.
I may have been here for years;
In the coil, the heaped-up creature
May have taken that long to lift
His head, to break his tongue
From his thin lips,
But he is there. I shut my eyes
And my eyes are gold,
As gold as an owl's,
As gold as a king's.
I open them. Farther off,
Beyond the swaying serpent,
A creature is burning itself
In a smoke of hair through the bushes.
The fox moves; a small thing
Being caught, cries out,
And I understand
How beings and sounds go together;
I understand
The voice of my singing father.
I shall be king of the wood.

Our double throne shall grow
Forever, until I see
The self of every substance
As it crouches, hidden and free.
The owl's face runs with tears
As I take him in my arms
In the glow of original light
Of Heaven. I go down
In my weight lightly down
The tree, and now
Through the soul of the wood
I walk in consuming glory

Past the snake, the fox, and the mouse:
I see as the owl king sees,
By going in deeper than darkness.
The wood comes back in a light
It did not know it withheld,
And I can tell
By its breathing glow
Each tree on which I laid
My hands when I was blind.

I cross the cold-footed flowing,
The creek, a religious fire
Streaming my ankles away,
And climb through the slanted meadow.
My father cannot remember
That he ever lived in this house.
To himself he bays like a hound,
Entranced by the endless beauty
Of his grief-stricken singing and calling.
He is singing simply to moonlight,
Like a dog howling,
And it is holy song
Out of his mouth.
Father, I am coming,
I am here on my own;
I move as you sing,
As if it were Heaven.
It is Heaven. I am walking
To you and seeing
Where I walk home.
What I have touched, I see
With the dark of my blue eyes.
Far off, the owl king
Sings like my father, growing
In power. Father, I touch
Your face. I have not seen
My own, but it is yours.
I come, I advance,
I believe everything, I am here.

Between Two Prisoners

I would not wish to sit
In my shape bound together with wire,
Wedged into a child's sprained desk
In the schoolhouse under the palm tree.
Only those who did could have done it.

One bled from a cut on his temple,
And sat with his yellow head bowed,
His wound for him painfully thinking.
A belief in words grew upon them
That the unbound, who walk, cannot know.

The guard at the window leaned close
In a movement he took from the palm tree,
To hear, in a foreign tongue,
All things which cannot be said.
In the splintering clapboard room

They rested the sides of their faces
On the tops of the desks as they talked.
Because of the presence of children
In the deep signs carved in the desk tops,
Signs on the empty blackboard

Began, like a rain, to appear.
In the luminous chalks of all colors,
Green face, yellow breast, white sails
Whose wing feathers made the wall burn
Like a waterfall seen in a fever,

An angel came boldly to light
From his hands casting green, ragged bolts
Each having the shape of a palm leaf.
Also traced upon darkness in chalk
Was the guard at the rear window leaning

Through the red, vital strokes of his tears.
Behind him, men lying with swords
As with women, heard themselves sing,
And woke, then, terribly knowing
That they were a death squad, singing

In its sleep, in the middle of a war.
A wind sprang out of the tree.
The guard awoke by the window,
And found he had talked to himself
All night, in two voices, of Heaven.

He stood in the sunlit playground
Where the quiet boys knelt together
In their bloodletting trusses of wire,
And saw their mussed, severed heads
Make the ground jump up like a dog.

I watched the small guard be hanged
A year later, to the day,
In a closed horse stall in Manila.
No one knows what language he spoke
As his face changed into all colors,

And gave off his red, promised tears,
Or if he learned blindly to read
A child's deep, hacked hieroglyphics
Which can call up an angel from nothing,
Or what was said for an instant, there,

In the tied, scribbled dark, between him
And a figure drawn hugely in chalk,
Speaking words that can never be spoken
Except in a foreign tongue,
In the end, at the end of a war.

Armor

When this is the thing you put on
The world is pieced slowly together
In the power of the crab and the insect.
The make of the eyeball changes
As over your mouth you draw down
A bird's bill made for a man.

As your weight upon earth is redoubled
There is no way of standing alone
More, or no way of being
More with the bound, shining dead.
You have put on what you should wear,
Not into the rattling of battle,

But into a silence where nothing
Threatens but Place itself: the shade
Of the forest, the strange, crowned
Motionless sunlight of Heaven,
With the redbird blinking and shooting
Across the nailed beam of the eyepiece.

In that light, in the wood, in armor,
I look in myself for the being
I was in a life before life
In a glade more silent than breathing,
Where I took off my body of metal
Like a brother whose features I knew

By the feel of their strength on my face
And whose limbs by the shining of mine.
In a vision I fasten him there,
The bright locust shell of my strength
Like a hanged man waiting in Heaven,
And then steal off to my life.

In my home, a night nearer death,
I wake with no shield on my breastbone,
Breathing deep through my sides like an insect,
My closed hand falling and rising
Where it lies like the dead on my heart.
I cannot remember my brother;

Before I was born he went from me
Ablaze with the meaning of typhoid.
In a fever I see him turn slowly
Under the strange, perfect branches
Where somehow I left him to wait
That I might be naked on earth,

His crowned face dazzlingly closed,
His curving limbs giving off
Pure energy into the leaves.
When I give up my hold on my breath
I long to dress deeply at last
In the gold of my waiting brother

Who shall wake and shine on my limbs
As I walk, made whole, into Heaven.
I shall not remember his face
Or my dazed, eternal one
Until I have opened my hand
And touched the grave glow of his breast

To stop the gaunt turning of metal:
Until I have let the still sun
Down into the stare of the eyepiece
And raised its bird's beak to confront
What man is within to live with me
When I begin living forever.

In the Lupanar at Pompeii

There are tracks which belong to wheels
Long since turned to air and time.
Those are the powerful chariots
I follow down cobblestones,
Not being dragged, exactly,
But not of my own will, either,
Going past the flower sellers'
And the cindery produce market
And the rich man's home, and the house
Of the man who kept a dog
Set in mosaic.

As tourist, but mostly as lecher,
I seek out the dwelling of women
Who all expect me, still, because
They expect anybody who comes.
I am ready to pay, and I do,
And then go in among them
Where on the dark walls of their home
They hold their eternal postures,
Doing badly drawn, exacting,
Too-willing, wide-eyed things
With dry-eyed art.

I sit down in one of the rooms
Where it happened again and again.
I could be in prison, or dead,
Cast down for my sins in a cell
Still filled with a terrible motion
Like the heaving and sighing of earth
To be free of the heat it restrains.
I feel in my heart how the heart
Of the mountain broke, and the women
Fled onto the damp of the walls
And shaped their embraces

To include whoever would come here
After the stone-cutting chariots.
I think of the marvel of lust
Which can always, at any moment,
Become more than it believed,
And almost always is less:
I think of its possible passing
Beyond, into tender awareness,
Into helplessness, weeping, and death:
It must be like the first
Soft floating of ash,

When, in the world's frankest hands,
Someone lay with his body shaken
Free of the self: that amazement—
For we who must try to explain
Ourselves in the house of this flesh
Never can tell the quick heat

Of our own from another's breathing,
Nor yet from the floating of feathers
That form in our lungs when the mountain
Settles like odd, warm snow against
Our willing limbs.

We never can really tell
Whether nature condemns us or loves us
As we lie here dying of breath
And the painted, unchanging women,
Believing the desperate dead
Where they stripped to the skin of the soul
And whispered to us, as to
Their panting, observing selves:
"Passion. Before we die
Let us hope for no longer
But truly know it."

Drowning with Others

There are moments a man turns from us
Whom we have all known until now.
Upgathered, we watch him grow,
Unshipping his shoulder bones

Like human, everyday wings
That he has not ever used,
Releasing his hair from his brain,
A kingfisher's crest, confused

By the God-tilted light of Heaven.
His deep, window-watching smile
Comes closely upon us in waves,
And spreads, and now we are

At last within it, dancing.
Slowly we turn and shine
Upon what is holding us,
As under our feet he soars,

Struck dumb as the angel of Eden,
In wide, eye-opening rings.

Yet the hand on my shoulder fears
To feel my own wingblades spring,

To feel me sink slowly away
In my hair turned loose like a thought
Of a fisherbird dying in flight.
If I opened my arms, I could hear

Every shell in the sea find the word
It has tried to put into my mouth.
Broad flight would become of my dancing,
And I would obsess the whole sea,

But I keep rising and singing
With my last breath. Upon my back,
With his hand on my unborn wing,
A man rests easy as sunlight

Who has kept himself free of the forms
Of the deaf, down-soaring dead,
And me laid out and alive
For nothing at all, in his arms.

A View of Fujiyama after the War

Wind, and all the midges in the air,
On wings you cannot see, awake
Where they must have been sleeping in flight.
I breathe, and twenty miles away

Snow streams from the mountain top
And all other mountains are nothing.
The ground of the enemy's country
Shakes; my bones settle back where they stand.

Through the bloom of gnats in the sun,
Shaken less than my heart by the tremor,
The blossom of a cherry tree appears.
The mountain returns my last breath,

And my hair blows, weightless as snow.
When it is still, when it is as still as this,

It could be a country where no one
Ever has died but of love.

I take the snow's breath and I speak it.
What I say has the form of a flame
Going all through the gnats like their spirit,
And for a swarming moment they become,

Almost, my own drunk face in the air
Against the one mountain in Heaven.
It is better to wait here quietly,
Not for my face to take flight,

But for someone to come from the dead
Other side of the war to this place:
Who thinks of this ground as his home,
Who thinks no one else can be here,

And that no one can see him pass
His hand through a visage of insects,
His hand through the cone of the mountain
To pluck the flower. But will he feel

His sobbing be dug like a wellspring
Or a deep water grow from his lids
To light, and break up the mountain
Which sends his last breath from its summit

As it dances together again?
Can he know that to live at the heart
Of his saved, shaken life, is to stand
Overcome by the enemy's peace?

The Island

A light come from my head
Showed how to give birth to the dead
That they might nourish me.
In a wink of the blinding sea
I woke through the eyes, and beheld
No change, but what had been,
And what cannot be seen

Any place but a burnt-out war:
The engines, the wheels, and the gear
That bring good men to their backs
Nailed down into wooden blocks,
With the sun on their faces through sand,
And polyps a-building the land
Around them of senseless stone.
The coral and I understood
That these could come to no good
Without the care I could give,
And that I, by them, must live.
I clasped every thought in my head
That bloomed from the magical dead,
And seizing a shovel and rake,
Went out by the ocean to take
My own sweet time, and start
To set a dead army apart.
I hammered the coffins together
Of patience and hobnails and lumber,
And gave them names, and hacked
Deep holes where they were stacked.
Each wooden body, I took
In my arms, and singingly shook
With its being, which stood for my own
More and more, as I laid it down.
At the grave's crude, dazzling verge
My true self strained to emerge
From all they could not save
And did not know they could give.
I buried them where they lay
In the brass-bound heat of the day,
A whole army lying down
In animal-lifted sand.
And then with rake and spade
I curried each place I had stood
On their chests and on their faces,
And planted the rows of crosses
Inside the blue wind of the shore.
I hauled more wood to that ground
And a white fence put around

The soldiers lying in waves
In my life-giving graves.
And a painless joy came to me
When the troopships took to the sea,
And left the changed stone free
Of all but my image and me:
Of the tonsured and perilous green
With its great, delighted design
Of utter finality,
Whose glowing workman stood
In the intricate, knee-high wood
In the midst of the sea's blind leagues,
Kicked off his old fatigues,
Saluted the graves by their rank,
Paraded, lamented, and sank
Into the intelligent light,
And danced, unimagined and free,
Like the sun taking place on the sea.

Dover: Believing in Kings

As we drove down the ramp from the boat
The sun flashed once
Or through hand-shieldedly twice;
In a silence out of a sound
We watched for channel swimmers dim with grease,
Come, here, to the ale of the shallows.
Within a wind, a wind sprang slowly up.
Birds hovered where they were.
As they were there, the airstream of the cliffs
Overcame, came over them
In the sackcloth and breast-beating gray
The king wears newly, at evening.
In a movement you cannot imagine
Of air, the gulls fall, shaken.

No stronger than the teeth in my head
Or a word laid bare
On chilling glass, the breathed stone over us rode.
From its top, the eye may sail,
Outgrowing the graven nerves
Of the brow's long-thought-out lines,
To France, on its own color.
From a child's tall book, I knew this place
The child must believe, with the king:
Where, doubtless, now, lay lovers
Restrained by a cloud, and the moon
Into force coming justly, above.
In a movement you cannot imagine
Of love, the gulls fall, mating.

We stopped; the birds hung up their arms
Inside the wind
So that they heeled; above, around us,
Their harp-strung feathers made
The sound, quickly mortal, of sighing.
We watched them in pure obsession.
Where they did move, we moved
Along the cliffs, the promenade,
The walls, the pebble beach,
And felt the inmost island turn,
In their cross-cut, wing-walking cries,
To a thing, as weeping, sensitive,
And haunted by the balancement of light
The king wears newly, in singing.

We wandered off from the car
In the light, half-sun,
Half-moon, in a worn-down shine out of stone,
And the taste of an iron ladle on the wind.
In the moon's grimed, thumbprint silver
The anchor spoke through the bell,
Far out, the hour that hung in the sea.
I threw a slow-flying stone; it dropped
Inside the brilliant echo of a light.
In a great, clustered, overdrawn sigh
The gulls went up, on a raiment of wings
The king wears newly, in panic.
In a movement you cannot imagine
Of error, the gulls rise, wholly.

We climbed a wall they had flown.
Each light below
On water, shook like a thing in a lathe.
In the heron crest of a lamp,
Among lights, in their treading motion,
The head of my reflection seemed to sing
A dark, quickened side of the truth.
I touched my wife. I saw my son, unborn,
Left living after me, and my Self,
There, freed of myself,
In a stricken shade dancing together,

As a wave rolled under the water,
Lifted and rode in our shadows
The king wears newly, redoubling.

Where we went in, all power failed the house.
I spooned out light
Upon a candle thread. My wife lay down.
Through the flaming, white-bread nerve
I peered from the eye of the mind.
No child from the windowed dark came forth
To the hand, in its pure-blooded fire,
But the basket glow of the crown.
The glass fetched white to a breath; I understood
How the crown must come from within:
Of water made, and a wheel,
And of the things in the flame that seems to pant.
In a movement you cannot imagine
Of mirrors, the gulls fall, hidden.

I lay in bed. One hand in its sleeve
Lay open, on my breath.
My shadow, laid stilly beneath me,
Rose, through my form. I heard the bell,
In mist, step backwardly onto the waves.
The wind fell off, as candle shade
Unraveled our walls like knitting, and I,
Undone, outstretched through the trampled shining
Of thousands of miles of the moon,
And the fallen king
Breathed like a nosebleed, there,
Two men wear newly, in hiding.
In a movement you cannot imagine
Of bloodshed, the gulls fall, inward.

I listened for the coming of a barge.
In a cat's-cradling motion
Of oars, my father rocked, in the mist. He died;
He was dying. His whisper fell,
As I, beneath the grave. Below the drowned
I breathed, in the pig-iron taste of my beard.
I yelled, as out of a bucket,
Through my fettered mask, before the dawn

When my arms, my big-footed legs would hang
From pothooks, strange and untimely.
The stone beat like a gull; my father's voice
Came to life, in words, in my ear.
In a movement you cannot imagine
Of prison, the gulls turn, calling.

Believing, then, astoundedly, in a son,
I drew from tufted stone
My sword. I slew my murderer, Lightborn, on the stair:
With the flat of steel, I flashed
Him dead, through his eyes high-piled in the hood.
When the tide came in, I rose
And onto the curded dark climbed out.
In the cliffs, where creatures about me swam,
In their thin, slain, time-serving bones,
The heavy page, the animal print of the chalk,
With wounds I glittered, dazzling as a fish.
In my short-horned, wool-gathering crown
I came from the beasts to the kingdoms
The king wears newly, in passing.

The sun fell down, through the moon.
The dead held house.
I hove my father to my back
And climbed from his barrow, there.
Pride helped me pick a queen and get a son.
The heroic drink of the womb
Broke, then, into swanlike song.
One came with scepter, one with cup,
One goatlike back'd, and one with the head of a god.
My mask fell away, and my gyves.
Through my sons I leapt in my ghost
The king wears newly, on fire.
In a movement you cannot imagine
Of birth, the gulls fall, crying.

In the cloudlike, packed, and layered realm
I wept, when I would sing.
I laid my father down where he must lie,
And entered, again, in my passion,
An older, incredible shape

Becoming young, as the cliffs let fall within stone
Their shadow green down from the crest.
I stood on the cliff top, alone.
My father's body in my heart
Like a buried candle danced. I saw it shed on the sea,
On the flats of water, far out:
A rough, selected brightness
Exchanging a flame for a wheel
The king wears slowly, in measure.

Birds drifted in my breath as it was drawn
From the stressing glitter
Of water. Where France becomes
Another blue lid for the eye,
I felt my green eyes turn
Surprisingly blue, of one great look upon distance.
The sword dissolved, in my hands; wings beat.
I watched them rise from my arms, and stood
Excited forever by love. I saw the child's eye shine
From his book, a wave of justified light.
The prison like organs moaned. In a death like life
I sang like a head on a pole.
In a movement you cannot imagine
Of emblems, the gulls fall, silent.

One foot shone to me, from the sun.
I felt the sun's
Mortality increase. In the blown,
Brow-beating light, I woke, and saw the room
Arise like a yeast from the floor,
The window come down like a bee.
In the long-legged, warm-bodied bed
I thought of him who would tell
To himself, gotten-up in his candle-cast bones:
Every man, every man
Not a king. It is I
The king wears newly, in lasting.
In a movement you cannot imagine
Of spells, the gulls fall, listening.

How shall the stranger wake
Who has isssued from dark
With the king? With gulls asleep
In the blue-burning grass? And on the sea,
A blaze that is counting itself,
The white birds holding
Still, on the field of the cloth of gold,
On the self and soul of the air?
Who stands, big-footed with glory, yet,
With the sound falling out of his voice
And his voice halfway to his son
Whose breath Time holds, in a woman?
In a movement you cannot imagine
Of silence, the gulls fall, waiting.

Why not as a prince, who, as
From a distance, wakes?
Who turns from the regular mirror
To watch, at the flawing pane,
Pale fire on a hairspring still burning
In the puddled socket, and the fishing flash
On the shuffled rock of a wave
Overturn, in an inlaid crash
In the window's half-mirror, half-air
As he steps through this room from the sea?
A tossed, green crown on his head,
He combs down the hair of his spirit,
Which is dead, but for the eyes
The king wears newly, at thirty:

Yet who is *he*? Whom does he face, in reflection?
The stained-glass king,
Or the child, grown tall, who cried to earth and air,
To books and water: to sun and father and fire
And nothingness to come and crown him, here?
Or are they, both of them, and neither,
This straw-headed knave, in blue-printed blue jeans appearing:
Who, in exultant tenderness upon a woman's sleep
Onlooks, then leaps out the door, out of that
Up onto the seaside path, and when the sheep track dies,
Two late and idle lovers in the grass

Kicks into love, and goes up the cliffs to be crowned?
In a movement you cannot imagine
Of England, the king smiles, climbing: running.

To His Children in Darkness

You hear my step
Come close, and stop.
I shut the door.
By the two-deck bed
And its breathing sheets
Houselight is killed
From off my breast.
I am unseen,
But sensed, but known,
And now begin

To be what I
Can never be,
But what I am
Within your dream:
A god or beast
Come true at last.
To one, I have
Like leaves grown here,
And furl my wings
As poplars sigh,

And slowly let
On him a breath
Drawn in a cloud,
In which he sees
Angelic hosts
Like blowing trees
Send me to earth
To root among
The secret soil
Of his dark room.

The other hears
A creature shed

Throughout the maze
The same long breath
As he conceives
That he no more
Desires to live
In blazing sun,
Nor shake to death
The animal

Of his own head.
I know what lies
Behind all words,
Like a beast, mismade,
Which finds its brain
Can sing alone
Without a sound
At what he is
And cannot change,
Or like a god

Which slowly breathes
Eternal life
Upon a soul
In deepest sleep.
My heart's one move
Comes now, and now.
A god strikes root
On touching earth.
A beast can hold
The thought of self

Between his horns
Until it shines.
That you may feel
What I must be
And cannot know
By standing here,
My sons, I bring
These beings home
Into your room.
They are. I am.

A Screened Porch in the Country

All of them are sitting
Inside a lamp of coarse wire
And being in all directions
Shed upon darkness,
Their bodies softening to shadow, until
The come to rest out in the yard
In a kind of blurred golden country
In which they more deeply lie
Than if they were being created
Of Heavenly light.

Where they are floating beyond
Themselves, in peace,
Where they have laid down
Their souls and not known it,
The smallest creatures,
As every night they do,
Come to the edge of them
And sing, if they can,
Or, if they can't, simply shine
Their eyes back, sitting on haunches,

Pulsating and thinking of music.
Occasionally, something weightless
Touches the screen
With its body, dies,
Or is unmurmuringly hurt,
But mainly nothing happens
Except that a family continues
To be laid down
In the midst of its nightly creatures,
Not one of which openly comes

Into the golden shadow
Where the people are lying,
Emitted by their own house
So humanly that they become
More than human, and enter the place
Of small, blindly singing things,

Seeming to rejoice
Perpetually, without effort,
Without knowing why
Or how they do it.

The Dream Flood

I ask and receive
The secret of falling unharmed
Forty nights from the darkness of Heaven,
Coming down in sheets and in atoms
Until I descend to the moon

Where it lies on the ground
And finds in my surface the shining
It knew it must have in the end.
No longer increasing, I stand
Taking sunlight transmitted by stone,

And then begin over fields
To expand like a mind seeking truth,
Piling fathoms of brightness in valleys,
Letting no hilltop break through me.
As I rise, the moon rises also

As the reborn look of creation
In the animals' eyes,
In the eyes of horses in stables
Who feel their warm heaviness swarm
Out of their mouths like their souls;

Their bodies in cell blocks of wood
Hang like a dust that has taken
Their shapes without knowing of horses.
When the straight sun strikes them at last
Their grains congeal as they must

And nail their scuffed hoofs to the earth.
I withdraw, in feeling the cloud
Of Heaven call dazzlingly to me
To drop off my horses and forests,
To leave a vague mist in the valleys

And the hilltops steaming.
O grasses and fence wire of glory
That have burned like a coral with depth,
Understand that I have stood shining
About loved and abandoned women:

For acres around their thin beds
Which lifted like mesmerized tables
And danced in mid-air of their rooms
Like the chairs that blind children dance with,
So that each, hanging deep in her morning

Rose-colored bath, shall implore
Those impotent waters, and sunlight
Straining in vain
With her lost, dead weight:
"Lift. I am dreaming. Lift."

The Scratch

Once hid in a fiery twist
Of brier, it binds my wrist.
In this marked place, on a stone,
I watchfully sit down
To lift it wisely, and see
Blood come, as at a play,
Which shall fall outside my life.
It knows neither stone nor leaf,
Nor how it has come from my heart
To find its true color in light.
The glaze of my death is upon it
In the shadowy sun, and yet
A merciful rust shall set in
To kill, not me, but my pain.
My arm opened up by a thorn,
I feel the no-soul of the rock;
I hear, through the trees, the cock
Shout out his long-necked cry.
My patience comes over the wood,

And, caught in the silence of blood,
The wind in the leaves stands still
And delivers its green to my will.
I raise my other-armed sleeve,
And wipe, in a kind of love,
The wellspring of love from its bed,
And, glancing about for the dead,
Look distantly off at my blood
As it forms upon air, as if
It were the first blood of my life,
And the last thing of earth that I owned.
I conjure up sons, all crowned,
Who this drop shall not inherit,
And women who shall not share it,
Who might have borne me that son
To sit on a moss-backed stone
And master the kingdom of silence
Forever: as I do, once.
I feel more alive thereby
Than when the same blood in my eye
Of sleep, brought my real son,
Or my wife, that heavenly one.
I have had no vision but this
Of blood unable to pass
Between father and son,
Yet wedding the brain and the stone,
The cock's cutting cry and the thorn,
And binding me, whole, in a wood,
To a prince of impossible blood.
The rock shall inherit my soul.
The gem at my wrist is dull,
And may or may never fall.
Which will be, I do not know.
I shall dream of a crown till I do.

Hunting Civil War Relics at Nimblewill Creek

As he moves the mine detector
A few inches over the ground,
Making it vitally float
Among the ferns and weeds,
I come into this war
Slowly, with my one brother,
Watching his face grow deep
Between the earphones,
For I can tell
If we enter the buried battle
Of Nimblewill
Only by his expression.

Softly he wanders, parting
The grass with a dreaming hand.
No dead cry yet takes root
In his clapped ears
Or can be seen in his smile.
But underfoot I feel
The dead regroup,
The burst metals all in place,
The battle lines be drawn
Anew to include us
In Nimblewill,
And I carry the shovel and pick

More as if they were
Bright weapons that I bore.
A bird's cry breaks
In two, and into three parts.
We cross the creek; the cry
Shifts into another,
Nearer, bird, and is
Like the shout of a shadow—
Lived-with, appallingly close—
Or the soul, pronouncing

"Nimblewill":
Three tones; your being changes.

We climb the bank;
A faint light glows
On my brother's mouth.
I listen, as two birds fight
For a single voice, but he
Must be hearing the grave,
In pieces, all singing
To his clamped head,
For he smiles as if
He rose from the dead within
Green Nimblewill
And stood in his grandson's shape.

No shot from the buried war
Shall kill me now,
For the dead have waited here
A hundred years to create
Only the look on the face
Of my one brother,
Who stands among them, offering
A metal dish
Afloat in the trembling weeds,
With a long-buried light on his lips
At Nimblewill
And the dead outsinging two birds.

I choke the handle
Of the pick, and fall to my knees
To dig wherever he points,
To bring up mess tin or bullet,
To go underground
Still singing, myself,
Without a sound,
Like a man who renounces war,
Or one who shall lift up the past,
Not breathing "Father,"
At Nimblewill,
But saying, "Fathers! Fathers!"

The Twin Falls

They fall through my life and surround me
Where I stand on a stone held between them,
And help them sing down the lifting

Of leaves in the springtime valley.
If I move my bare arms, the wings
Of water shake and are whiter.

I dance on the unshaken stone
And the rock rises up in my voice
As water the shape of my shoulders

Falls past without passing or moving.
Lifting up the blind spirit of bedrock,
My voice falls in waves on the green

Held up in a storm to receive it,
Where trees with their roots in my standing
Are singing it back to surround me

And telling me how my light body
Falls through the still years of my life
On great, other wings than its own.

The Hospital Window

I have just come down from my father.
Higher and higher he lies
Above me in a blue light
Shed by a tinted window.
I drop through six white floors
And then step out onto pavement.

Still feeling my father ascend,
I start to cross the firm street,
My shoulder blades shining with all
The glass the huge building can raise.
Now I must turn round and face it,
And know his one pane from the others.

Each window possesses the sun
As though it burned there on a wick.
I wave, like a man catching fire.
All the deep-dyed windowpanes flash,
And, behind them, all the white rooms
They turn to the color of Heaven.

Ceremoniously, gravely, and weakly,
Dozens of pale hands are waving
Back, from inside their flames.
Yet one pure pane among these
Is the bright, erased blankness of nothing.
I know that my father is there,

In the shape of his death still living.
The traffic increases around me
Like a madness called down on my head.
The horns blast at me like shotguns,
And drivers lean out, driven crazy—
But now my propped-up father

Lifts his arm out of stillness at last.
The light from the window strikes me
And I turn as blue as a soul,
As the moment when I was born.
I am not afraid for my father—
Look! He is grinning; he is not

Afraid for my life, either,
As the wild engines stand at my knees
Shredding their gears and roaring,
And I hold each car in its place
For miles, inciting its horn
To blow down the walls of the world

That the dying may float without fear
In the bold blue gaze of my father.
Slowly I move to the sidewalk
With my pin-tingling hand half dead
At the end of my bloodless arm.
I carry it off in amazement,

High, still higher, still waving,
My recognized face fully mortal,
Yet not; not at all, in the pale,
Drained, otherworldly, stricken,
Created hue of stained glass.
I have just come down from my father.

PART FOUR

The Magus

It is time for the others to come.
This child is no more than a god.

No cars are moving this night.
The lights in the houses go out.

I put these out with the rest.
From his crib, the child begins

To shine, letting forth one ray
Through the twelve simple bars of his bed

Down into the trees, where two
Long-lost other men shall be drawn

Slowly up to the brink of the house,
Slowly in through the breath on the window.

But how did I get in this room?
Is this my son, or another's?

Where is the woman to tell me
How my face is lit up by his body?

It is time for the others to come.
An event more miraculous yet

Is the thing I am shining to tell you.
This child is no more than a child.

Antipolis

Through the town-making stones I step lightly.
Each thing in the market place looks
Clear through me, not able to help it.
Squid lounging in death in their barrel
See me staring through life down among them.
They deepen the depth of their gaze.
The eyes of the dead hold me brightly.
I take all their looks into mine
And lift them up

Alive, and carry them out through the door
The Greeks made to give on the sea.
The world opens wide and turns blue.
My heart shines in me like sunlight.
I scramble up sill after sill,
Past windows where women are washing
My strange, heavy, foreigner's clothes.
My voice in amazement dwindles
To that of a child,

And with it I call to my son,
Who reads Greek somewhere below me.
He answers: a dead tongue sings.
I leap to the bread-colored rampart,
And stroll there, sweating and staring
Down into the powder-blue ocean
With dozens of dead, round, all-seeing eyes
In my head, which have seen ships sink
Through this water

And gods rise, wearing their sails.
A hundred feet over the ocean,
My hands dead white with the flour
Of the market, knowing and saying
The same timeless thought as the sun,
Which thinks of itself in its glory
As Pericles' head on a coin,
I hear in my voice two children,
My son and my soul,

Sing to each other through ages.
In the windows, men with their women
Among my dark garments burn cleanly.
Because I am drunk on the rampart,
My son reads Homer more deeply,
And the blue sea has caught me alive
In my own glance, the look of some daring,
Unbelieved, believing and dancing
Most loving creature.

The Change

Blue, unstirrable, dreaming.
The hammerhead goes by the boat,
Passing me slowly in looking.

He has singled me out from the others;
He has put his blue gaze in my brain.
The strength of creation sees through me:

The world is yet blind as beginning.
The shark's brutal form never changes.
No millions of years shall yet turn him

From himself to a man in love,
Yet I feel that impossible man
Hover near, emerging from darkness,

Like a creature of light from the ocean.
He is what I would make of myself
In ten millions years, if I could,

And arise from my brute of a body
To a thing the world never thought of
In a place as apparent as Heaven.

I name the blue shark in the water,
And the heart of my brain has spoken
To me, like an unknown brother,

Gently of ends and beginnings,
Gently of sources and outcomes,
Impossible, brighter than sunlight.

Autumn

I see the tree think it will turn
Brown, and tomorrow at dawn
It will change as it thinks it will change,

But faster, bringing in orange,
And smoking and king-killing gold.
The fire of death shall change colors,

But before its rich images die,
Some green will be thought of in glory.
The dead shall withhold it until

The sleep of the world take on
The air of awaiting an angel
To descend into Hell, and to blow

With his once-a-year breath upon grass roots,
And deliver the year from its thinking
To the mindless one color of life.

Snow on a Southern State

Alongside the train I labor
To change wholly into my spirit,
As the place of my birth falls upward

Into the snow,
And my pale, sealed face looks in
From the world where it ripples and sails,
Sliding through culverts,

Plunging through tunnels while flakes
Await my long, streaming return
As they wait for this country to rise

And become something else in mid-air.
With a just-opened clicking, I come
Forth into fresh, buried meadows
Of muffled night light

Where people still sit on their porches
Screened in for eternal summer,
Watching the snow

Like grated shadow sift
Impossibly to them.
Through the window I tell them dumbly
That the snow is like ·

A man, stretched out upon landscape
And a spotless berth,
Who is only passing through

Their country, who means no harm:
Who stars in distrust at his ghost
Also flying, feet first, through the distance.
Numbly, the lips of his spirit

Move, and a fur-bearing steeple looms up
Through the heart of his mirrored breast.
The small town where he was born

Assembles around it,
The neon trying, but obviously unreal,
The parked cars clumsily letting
Pureness, a blinding burden,

Come slowly upon them.
All are still, all are still,
For the breath-holding window and I

Only must move through the silence,
Bearing my huge, prone ghost
Up, out, and now flying over
The vapor-lamp-glowing high school

Into the coming fields
Like a thing we cannot put down.
Yet the glass gives out of my image

And the laid clicking dies, as the land
All around me shines with the power
Of renewing my youth
By changing the place where I lived it.

There is nothing here, now, to watch
The bedclothes whirl into flakes.
What should be warm in these blankets

Has powdered down into its own
Steel-blue and feathery visions
Of weddings opposed by the world:
Is hovering over   ·

A dead cotton field, which awaits
Its touch as awaiting completion:
Is building the pinewoods again

For this one night of their lives:
With the equilibrium
Of bones, is falling, falling,
Falling into the river.

To Landrum Guy, Beginning to Write at Sixty

One man in a house
Consumed by the effort of listening,
Sets down a worried phrase upon a paper.
It is poor, though it has come

From the table as out of a wall,
From his hand as out of his heart.

To sixty years it has come
At the same rate of time as he.
He cannot tell it, ever, what he thinks.
It is time, he says, he must

Be thinking of nothing but singing,
Be singing of nothing but love.

But the right word cannot arrive
Through the dark, light house of one man
With his savage hand on a book,
With a cricket seizing slowly on his ear:

One man in a house cannot hear
His ear, with his hair falling out from the quick.

Even to himself he cannot say
Except with not one word,
How he hears there is no more light
Than this, nor any word

More anywhere: how he is drunk
On hope, and why he calls himself mad.

Weeping is steadily built, and does not fall
From the shadow sitting slowly behind him
On the wall, like an angel who writes him a letter
To tell him his only talent is too late

To tell, to weep, to speak, or to begin
Here, or ever. Here, where he begins.

Facing Africa

These are stone jetties,
And, in the close part of the night,
Connected to my feet by long
Warm, dangling shadows
On the buttressed water,
Boats are at rest.

Beyond, the harbor mouth opens
Much as you might believe
A human mouth would open
To say that all things are a darkness.
I sit believing this
As the boats beneath me dissolve

And shake with a haunted effort
To come into being again,
And my son nods at my side,
Looking out also
Into dark, through the painted
Living shadows of dead-still hulls

Toward where we imagine Africa
To bloom late at night
Like a lamp of sand held up,
A top-heavy hourglass, perhaps,
With its heaped, eternal grains
Falling, falling

Into the lower, green part
Which gives off quick, leafy flashes
Like glimpses of lightning.
We strain to encounter that image
Halfway from its shore to ours:
To understand

The undermined glowing of sand
Lifted at midnight
Somewhere far out above water,
The effortless flicker of trees
Where a rumor of beasts moves slowly
Like wave upon wave.

What life have we entered by this?
Here, where our bodies are,
With a green and gold light on his face,
My staring child's hand is in mine,
And in the stone
Fear like a dancing of peoples.

Inside the River

Dark, deeply. A red.
All levels moving
A given surface.
Break this. Step down.
Follow your right
Foot nakedly in
To another body.
Put on the river
Like a fleeing coat,
A garment of motion,

Tremendous, immortal.
Find a still root

To hold you in it.
Let flowing create
A new, inner being:
As the source in the mountain
Gives water in pulses,
These can be felt at
The heart of the current.
And here it is only
One wandering step
Forth, to the sea.
Your freed hair floating
Out of your brain,

Wait for a coming
And swimming idea.
Live like the dead
In their flying feeling.
Loom as a ghost
When life pours through it.
Crouch in the secret
Released underground
With the earth of the fields
All around you, gone
Into purposeful grains
That stream like dust

In a holy hallway.
Weight more changed
Than that of one
Now being born,
Let go the root.
Move with the world
As the deep dead move,
Opposed to nothing.
Release. Enter the sea
Like a winding wind.
No. Rise. Draw breath.
Sing. See no one.

The Salt Marsh

Once you have let the first blade
Spring back behind you
To the way it has always been,
You no longer know where you are.
All you can see are the tall
Stalks of sawgrass, not sawing,
But each of them holding its tip
Exactly at the level where your hair

Begins to grow from your forehead.
Wherever you come to is
The same as before,
With the same blades of oversized grass,
And wherever you stop, the one
Blade just in front of you leans,
That one only, and touches you
At the place where your hair begins

To grow; at that predestined touch
Your spine tingles crystally, like salt,
And the image of a crane occurs,
Each flap of its wings creating
Its feathers anew, this time whiter,
As the sun destroys all points
Of the compass, refusing to move
From its chosen noon.

Where is the place you have come from
With your buried steps full of new roots?
You cannot leap up to look out,
Yet you do not sink,
But seem to grow, and the sound,
The oldest of sounds, is your breath
Sighing like acres.
If you stand as you are for long,

Green panic may finally give
Way to another sensation,
For when the embodying wind
Rises, the grasses begin to weave

A little, then all together,
Not bending enough for you
To see your way clear of the swaying,
But moving just the same,

And nothing prevents your bending
With them, helping their wave
Upon wave upon wave upon wave
By not opposing,
By willing your supple inclusion
Among fields without promise of harvest,
In their marvelous, spiritual walking
Everywhere, anywhere.

In the Mountain Tent

I am hearing the shape of the rain
Take the shape of the tent and believe it,
Laying down all around where I lie
A profound, unspeakable law.
I obey, and am free-falling slowly

Through the thought-out leaves of the wood
Into the minds of animals.
I am there in the shining of water
Like dark, like light, out of Heaven.

I am there like the dead, or the beast
Itself, which thinks of a poem—
Green, plausible, living, and holy—
And cannot speak, but hears,
Called forth from the waiting of things,

A vast, proper, reinforced crying
With the sifted, harmonious pause,
The sustained intake of all breath
Before the first word of the Bible.

At midnight water dawns
Upon the held skulls of the foxes
And weasels and tousled hares

On the eastern side of the mountain.
Their light is the image I make

As I wait as if recently killed,
Receptive, fragile, half-smiling,
My brow watermarked with the mark
On the wing of a moth

And the tent taking shape on my body
Like ill-fitting, Heavenly clothes.
From holes in the ground comes my voice
In the God-silenced tongue of the beasts.
"I shall rise from the dead," I am saying.

HELMETS

The Dusk of Horses

Right under their noses, the green
Of the field is paling away
Because of something fallen from the sky.

They see this, and put down
Their long heads deeper in grass
That only just escapes reflecting them

As the dream of a millpond would.
The color green flees over the grass
Like an insect, following the red sun over

The next hill. The grass is white.
There is no cloud so dark and white at once;
There is no pool at dawn that deepens

Their faces and thirsts as this does.
Now they are feeding on solid
Cloud, and, one by one,

With nails as silent as stars among the wood
Hewed down years ago and now rotten,
The stalls are put up around them.

Now if they lean, they come
On wood on any side. Not touching it, they sleep.
No beast ever lived who understood

What happened among the sun's fields,
Or cared why the color of grass
Fled over the hill while he stumbled,

Led by the halter to sleep
On his four taxed, worthy legs.
Each thinks he awakens where

The sun is black on the rooftop,
That the green is dancing in the next pasture,
And that the way to sleep

In a cloud, or in a risen lake,
Is to walk as though he were still
In the drained field standing, head down,

To pretend to sleep when led,
And thus to go under the ancient white
Of the meadow, as green goes

And whiteness comes up through his face
Holding stars and rotten rafters,
Quiet, fragrant, and relieved.

Fence Wire

Too tight, it is running over
Too much of this ground to be still
Or to do anything but tremble
And disappear left and right
As far as the eye can see

Over hills, through woods,
Down roads, to arrive at last
Again where it connects,
Coming back from the other side
Of animals, defining their earthly estate

As the grass becomes snow
While they are standing and dreaming
Of grass and snow.
The winter hawk that sits upon its post,
Feeling the airy current of the wires,

Turns into a robin, sees that this is wrong,
Then into a boy, and into a man who holds
His palm on the top tense strand

With the whole farm feeding slowly
And nervously into his hand.

If the wire were cut anywhere
All his blood would fall to the ground
And leave him standing and staring
With a face as white as a Hereford's.
From years of surrounding grain,

Cows, horses, machinery trying to turn
To rust, the humming arrives each second,
A sound that arranges these acres
And holds them highstrung and enthralled.
Because of the light, chilled hand

On the top thread tuned to an E
Like the low string of a guitar,
The dead corn is more
Balanced in death than it was,
The animals more aware

Within the huge human embrace
Held up and borne out of sight
Upon short, unbreakable poles
Wherethrough the ruled land intones
Like a psalm: properly,

With its eyes closed,
Whether on the side of the animals
Or not, whether disappearing
Right, left, through trees or down roads,
Whether outside, around, or in.

At Darien Bridge

The sea here used to look
As if many convicts had built it,

Standing deep in their ankle chains,
Ankle-deep in the water, to smite

The land and break it down to salt.
I was in this bog as a child

When they were all working all day
To drive the pilings down.

I thought I saw the still sun
Strike the side of a hammer in flight

And from it a sea bird be born
To take off over the marshes.

As the gray climbs the side of my head
And cuts my brain off from the world,

I walk and wish mainly for birds,
For the one bird no one has looked for

To spring again from a flash
Of metal, perhaps from the scratched

Wedding band on my ring finger.
Recalling the chains of their feet,

I stand and look out over grasses
At the bridge they built, long abandoned,

Breaking down into water at last,
And long, like them, for freedom

Or death, or to believe again
That they worked on the ocean to give it

The unchanging, hopeless look
Out of which all miracles leap.

Chenille

There are two facing peacocks
      Or a ship flapping
On its own white tufted sail
At roadside, near a mill;

Flamingoes also are hanging
      By their bills on bedspreads
And an occasional mallard.
These you can buy anywhere.
They are made by machine

From a sanctioned, unholy pattern
Rigid with industry.
They hoard the smell of oil

And hum like looms all night
        Into your pores, reweaving
Your body from bobbins.
There is only one quiet

Place—in a scuppernong arbor—
        Where animals as they
Would be, are born into sleep-cloth:
A middle-aged man's grandmother
Sits in the summer green light
Of leaves, gone toothless
For eating grapes better,
And pulls the animals through

With a darning needle:
        Deer, rabbits and birds,
Red whales and unicorns,
Winged elephants, crowned ants:

Beasts that cannot be thought of
        By the wholly sane
Rise up in the rough, blurred
Flowers of fuzzy cloth
In only their timeless outlines
Like the beasts of Heaven:
Those sketched out badly, divinely
By stars not wholly sane.

Love, I have slept in that house.
        There it was winter.
The tattered moonfields crept
Through the trellis, and fell

In vine-tangled shade on my face
        Like thrown-away knitting
Before cloud came and dimmed
Those scars from off me.
My fingernails chilled
To the bone. I called

For another body to be
With me, and warm us both.

A unicorn neighed; I folded
      His neck in my arms
And was safe, as he lay down.
All night, from thickening Heaven,

Someone up there kept throwing
      Bedspreads upon me.
Softly I called, and they came:
The ox and the basilisk,
The griffin, the phoenix, the lion—
Light-bodied, only the essence,
The tufted, creative starfields
Behind the assembling clouds—

The snake from the apple tree came
      To save me from freezing,
And at last the lung-winged ship
On its own sail scented with potash

Fell sighing upon us all.
      The last two nails
Of cold died out in my nostrils
Under the dance-weight of beasts.
I lay, breathing like thread,
An inspired outline of myself,
As rain began greatly to fall,
And closed the door of the Ark.

On the Coosawattee

I. BY CANOE THROUGH THE FIR FOREST

Into the slain tons of needles,
On something like time and dark knowledge
That cannot be told, we are riding
Over white stones forward through fir trees,
To follow whatever the river
Through the clasping of roots follows deeply.

As we go inward, more trunks
Climb from the edge of the water
And turn on the banks and stand growing.
The nerves in the patches of tree-light
On the ripples can feel no death,
But shake like the wings of angels

With light hard-pressed to keep up
Though it is in place on each feather.
Heavy woods in one movement around us
Flow back along either side
Bringing in more essential curves;
Small stones in their thousands turn corners

Under water and bear us on
Through the glittering, surfacing wingbeats
Cast from above. As we pass over,
As we pass through each hover of gold,
We lift up our blades from the water
And the blades of our shoulders,

Our rowing-muscles, our wings,
Are still and tremble, undying,
Drifting deeper into the forest.
Each light comes into our life
Past the man in front's changed hair
Then along the wing-balancing floor

And then onto me and one eye
And into my mouth for an instant.
The stones beneath us grow rounder
As I taste the fretted light fall
Through living needles to be here
Like a word I can feed on forever

Or believe like a vision I have
Or want to conceive out of greenness.
While the world fades, it is *becoming*.
As the trees shut away all seeing,
In my mouth I mix it with sunlight.
Here, in the dark, it is *being*.

Coming into Ellijay on the green
Idling freeway of the broad river
From the hill farms and pine woods,
We saw first the little stores
That backed down the red clay banks,
The blue flash of bottleglass
And the rippled tin heat-haze of sheds

Where country mechanics were frying.
A poultry-processing plant
Smoked in the late morning air;
The bridge we rode under clattered
As we wound back out into fields.
But the water that held us had changed;
The town had slowed it and used it;

The wind had died in the tool sheds.
When we looked overboard, we knew.
Each thing was mistakenly feathered,
Muffled thickly in cast-off whiteness:
Each log was bedraggled in plumage
And accepting more feathers from water;
Each boulder under the green

Was becoming a lewd, setting hen
Moultingly under us brooding
In the sick, buried wind of the river,
Wavering, dying, increasing
From the plucked refuse of the plant,
And beside us uselessly floated—
Following, dipping, returning,

Turning frankly around to eye us,
To eye something else, to eye
Us again—a skinned chicken head,
Its gaze unperturbed and abiding.
All morning we floated on feathers
Among the drawn heads which appeared
Everywhere, from under the logs

Of feathers, from upstream behind us,
Lounging back to us from ahead,

Until we believed ourselves doomed
And the planet corrupted forever,
With stones turned to pullets, not struggling
But into more monstrousness shed,
Our canoe trailing more and more feathers

And the eye of the devil upon us
Closing drunkenly in from all sides,
And could have been on the Styx
In the blaze of noon, till we felt
The quickening pulse of the rapids
And entered upon it like men
Who sense that the world can be cleansed

Among rocks pallid only with water,
And plunged there like the unborn
Who see earthly streams without taint
Flow beneath them, while their wing feathers
Slough off behind them in Heaven
As they dress in the blinding clothes
Of nakedness for their fall.

III. THE INUNDATION

Down there is a stone that holds my deepest sleep
And buries it deeper and deeper
Under the green, skinny lake
That is going back into the Georgia hills
And climbing them day and night
Behind the new dam.

And there is another stone, that boiled with white,
Where Braselton and I clung and fought
With our own canoe
That flung us in the rapids we had ridden
So that it might turn and take on
A ton of mountain water

And swing and bear down through the flying cloud
Of foam upon our violent rock
And pin us there.
With our backs to the wall of that boulder,

We yelled and kept it off us as we could,
Broke both paddles,

Then wedged it with the paddle stumps up over
The rock till the hull split, and it leapt and fell
Into the afterfall.
In life preservers we whirled ourselves away
And floated aimlessly down into calm water,
Turning like objects,

Then crawled upon shore and were found in the afternoon
By Lucas Gentry and his hunting dog, asleep
On a vast, gentle stone.
At a touch we woke, and followed the strange woods boy
Up the bluff, looking down on the roaring river's
Last day in its bed.

And now I cannot sleep at all, until I think
Of the Coosa, out of a clear blue sky
Overswelling its banks,
Its great stones falling through it into dark,
Its creeks becoming inlets, where water
Skiers already poise.

Over me it rises, too, but breathable, like cloud,
A green and silver cloud above which quiet
Lucas Gentry stands.
His dog whines, as the last rock of the wild river
Goes under, its white water lapses green,
And the leaping stone

Where we almost died takes on the settled repose
Of that other where we lay down and met
Our profoundest sleep
Rising from it to us, as the battered sides
Of the canoe gave deeper and deeper shade,
And Lucas Gentry,

Who may have been the accepting spirit of the place
Come to call us to higher ground,
Bent to raise
Us from the sleep of the yet-to-be-drowned,

There, with the black dream of the dead canoe
Over our faces.

Winter Trout

In the concrete cells of the hatchery
He nourished a dream of living
Under the ice, the long preparations
For the strange heat of feeling slowly

Roofs melt to a rhythmic green,
But now, in the first cold of freedom,
Riding motionless under the road
Of ice, shaping the heart

Of the buried stream with his tail,
He knows that his powers come
From the fire and stillness of freezing.
With the small tremors of his form

The banks shift imperceptibly,
Shift back, tremble, settle,
Shift, all within utter stillness.
I keep in my quiver now

An arrow whose head is half-missing.
It is useless, but I will not change
The pulled, broken tooth of its head
For I have walked upon banks

Shaken with the watchfulness of trout
Like walking barefoot in sleep
On the swaying tips of a grainfield,
On the long, just-bending stems,

Almost weightless, able to leap
Great distances, yet not leaping
Because each step on that ground
Gave a new sense of limitless hope.

Under the ice the trout rode,
Trembling, in the mastered heart

Of the creek, with what he could do.
I set myself up as a statue

With a bow, my red woolen back
Climbed slowly by thoughtful brambles
And dead beggar-lice, to shoot
At an angle down through the shadow

Of ice, and spear the trout
With a shot like Ulysses'
Through the ax heads, with the great weapon.
I shot, and the trout did not move

But was gone, and the banks
Went rigid under my feet
As the arrow floated away
Under the paving of ice.

I froze my right hand to retrieve it
As a blessing or warning,
As a sign of the penalties
For breaking into closed worlds

Where the wary controllers lie
At the heart of their power,
A pure void of shadowy purpose
Where the gods live, attuning the world,

Laying plans for the first green
They ever have lived, to melt
The ice from their great crowns.
Their secret enemies break

Like statues, as the king rises slowly,
Keeping only the thinnest film
Of his element—imagination—
Before his eyes as he lifts

Into spring, with the wood upside down
Balanced perfectly in all its leaves
And roots as he deeply has
All winter made provision for,

The surface full of gold flakes
Of the raw undersides of leaves,

And the thing seen right,
For once, that winter bought.

Springer Mountain

Four sweaters are woven upon me,
All black, all sweating and waiting,
And a sheepherder's coat's wool hood,
Buttoned strainingly, holds my eyes
With their sight deepfrozen outside them
From their gaze toward a single tree.
I am here where I never have been,
In the limbs of my warmest clothes,
Waiting for light to crawl, weakly
From leaf to dead leaf onto leaf
Down the western side of the mountain.
Deer sleeping in light far above me

Have already woken, and moved,
In step with the sun moving strangely
Down toward the dark knit of my thicket
Where my breath takes shape on the air
Like a white helmet come from the lungs.
The one tree I hope for goes inward
And reaches the limbs of its gold.
My eyesight hangs partly between
Two twigs on the upslanting ground,
Then steps like a god from the dead
Wet of a half-rotted oak log
Steeply into the full of my brow.
My thighbones groaningly break

Upward, releasing my body
To climb, and to find among humus
New insteps made of snapped sticks.
On my back the faggot of arrows
Rattles and scratches its feathers.

I go up over logs slowly
On my painfully reborn legs,

My ears putting out vast hearing
Among the invisible animals,

Passing under thin branches held still,
Kept formed all night as they were
By the thought of predictable light.
The sun comes openly in
To my mouth, and is blown out white,

But no deer is anywhere near me.
I sit down and wait as in darkness.

The sweat goes dead at the roots

Of my hair: a deer is created
Descending, then standing and looking.
The sun stands and waits for his horns

To move. I may be there, also,
Between them, in head bones uplifted
Like a man in an animal tree
Nailed until light comes:
A dream of the unfeared hunter
Who has formed in his brain in the dark
And rose with light into his horns,
Naked, and I have turned younger

At forty than I ever have been.
I hang my longbow on a branch.
The buck leaps away and then stops,
And I step forward, stepping out

Of my shadow and pulling over
My head one dark heavy sweater
After another, my dungarees falling
Till they can be kicked away,
Boots, socks, all that is on me
Off. The world catches fire.
I put an unbearable light
Into breath skinned alive of its garments:
I think, beginning with laurel,
Like a beast loving
With the whole god bone of his horns:
The green of excess is upon me

Like deer in fir thickets in winter
Stamping and dreaming of men
Who will kneel with them naked to break
The ice from streams with their faces
And drink from the lifespring of beasts.
He is moving. I am with him

Down the shuddering hillside moving
Through trees and around, inside
And out of stumps and groves
Of laurel and slash pine,
Through hip-searing branches and thorn
Brakes, unprotected and sure,
Winding down to the waters of life
Where they stand petrified in a creek bed
Yet melt and flow from the hills
At the touch of an animal visage,

Rejoicing wherever I come to
With the gold of my breast unwrapped,
My crazed laughter pure as good church-cloth,
My brain dazed and pointed with trying
To grow horns, glad that it cannot,
For a few steps deep in the dance
Of what I most am and should be
And can be only once in this life.
He is gone below, and I limp
To look for my clothes in the world,

A middle-aged, softening man
Grinning and shaking his head
In amazement to last him forever.
I put on the warm-bodied wool,
The four sweaters inside out,
The bootlaces dangling and tripping,
Then pick my tense bow off the limb
And turn with the unwinding hooftracks,
In my good, tricked clothes,
To hunt, under Springer Mountain,
Deer for the first and last time.

Cherrylog Road

Off Highway 106
At Cherrylog Road I entered
The '34 Ford without wheels,
Smothered in kudzu,
With a seat pulled out to run
Corn whiskey down from the hills,

And then from the other side
Crept into an Essex
With a rumble seat of red leather
And then out again, aboard
A blue Chevrolet, releasing
The rust from its other color,

Reared up on three building blocks.
None had the same body heat;
I changed with them inward, toward
The weedy heart of the junkyard,
For I knew that Doris Holbrook
Would escape from her father at noon

And would come from the farm
To seek parts owned by the sun
Among the abandoned chassis,
Sitting in each in turn
As I did, leaning forward
As in a wild stock-car race

In the parking lot of the dead.
Time after time, I climbed in

And out the other side, like
An envoy or movie star
Met at the station by crickets.
A radiator cap raised its head,

Become a real toad or a kingsnake
As I neared the hub of the yard,
Passing through many states,
Many lives, to reach
Some grandmother's long Pierce-Arrow
Sending platters of blindness forth

From its nickel hubcaps
And spilling its tender upholstery
On sleepy roaches,
The glass panel in between
Lady and colored driver
Not all the way broken out,

The back-seat phone
Still on its hook.
I got in as though to exclaim,
"Let us go to the orphan asylum,
John; I have some old toys
For children who say their prayers."

I popped with sweat as I thought
I heard Doris Holbrook scrape
Like a mouse in the southern-state sun
That was eating the paint in blisters
From a hundred car tops and hoods.
She was tapping like code,

Loosening the screws,
Carrying off headlights,
Sparkplugs, bumpers,
Cracked mirrors and gear-knobs,
Getting ready, already,
To go back with something to show

Other than her lips' new trembling
I would hold to me soon, soon,
Where I sat in the ripped back seat

Talking over the interphone,
Praying for Doris Holbrook
To come from her father's farm

And to get back there
With no trace of me on her face
To be seen by her red-haired father
Who would change, in the squalling barn,
Her back's pale skin with a strop,
Then lay for me

In a bootlegger's roasting car
With a string-triggered 12-gauge shotgun
To blast the breath from the air.
Not cut by the jagged windshields,
Through the acres of wrecks she came
With a wrench in her hand,

Through dust where the blacksnake dies
Of boredom, and the beetle knows
The compost has no more life.
Someone outside would have seen
The oldest car's door inexplicably
Close from within:

I held her and held her and held her,
Convoyed at terrific speed
By the stalled, dreaming traffic around us,
So the blacksnake, stiff
With inaction, curved back
Into life, and hunted the mouse

With deadly overexcitement,
The beetles reclaimed their field
As we clung, glued together,
With the hooks of the seat springs
Working through to catch us red-handed
Amidst the gray, breathless batting

That burst from the seat at our backs.
We left by separate doors
Into the changed, other bodies
Of cars, she down Cherrylog Road

And I to my motorcycle
Parked like the soul of the junkyard

Restored, a bicycle fleshed
With power, and tore off
Up Highway 106, continually
Drunk on the wind in my mouth,
Wringing the handlebar for speed,
Wild to be wreckage forever.

The Scarred Girl

All glass may yet be whole
She thinks, it may be put together
From the deep inner flashing of her face.
One moment the windshield held

The countryside, the green
Level fields and the animals,
And these must be restored
To what they were when her brow

Broke into them for nothing, and began
Its sparkling under the gauze.
Though the still, small war for her beauty
Is stitched out of sight and lost,

It is not this field that she thinks of.
It is that her face, buried
And held up inside the slow scars,
Knows how the bright, fractured world

Burns and pulls and weeps
To come together again.
The green meadow lying in fragments
Under the splintered sunlight,

The cattle broken in pieces
By her useless, painful intrusion
Know that her visage contains
The process and hurt of their healing,

The hidden wounds that can
Restore anything, bringing the glass
Of the world together once more,
All as it was when she struck,

All except her. The shattered field
Where they dragged the telescoped car
Off to be pounded to scrap
Waits for her to get up,

For her calm, unimagined face
To emerge from the yards of its wrapping,
Red, raw, mixed-looking but entire,
A new face, an old life,

To confront the pale glass it has dreamed
Made whole and backed with wise silver,
Held in other hands brittle with dread,
A doctor's, a lip-biting nurse's,

Who do not see what she sees
Behind her odd face in the mirror:
The pastures of earth and of heaven
Restored and undamaged, the cattle

Risen out of their jagged graves
To walk in the seamless sunlight
And a newborn countenance
Put upon everything,

Her beauty gone, but to hover
Near for the rest of her life,
And good no nearer, but plainly
In sight, and the only way.

Kudzu

Japan invades. Far Eastern vines
Run from the clay banks they are

Supposed to keep from eroding,
Up telephone poles,
Which rear, half out of leafage,

As though they would shriek,
Like things smothered by their own
Green, mindless, unkillable ghosts.
In Georgia, the legend says
That you must close your windows

At night to keep it out of the house.
The glass is tinged with green, even so,

As the tendrils crawl over the fields.
The night the kudzu has
Your pasture, you sleep like the dead.
Silence has grown Oriental
And you cannot step upon ground:
Your leg plunges somewhere
It should not, it never should be,
Disappears, and waits to be struck

Anywhere between sole and kneecap:
For when the kudzu comes,

The snakes do, and weave themselves
Among its lengthening vines,
Their spade heads resting on leaves,
Growing also, in earthly power
And the huge circumstance of concealment.
One by one the cows stumble in,
Drooling a hot green froth,
And die, seeing the wood of their stalls

Strain to break into leaf.
In your closed house, with the vine

Tapping your window like lightning,
You remember what tactics to use.
In the wrong yellow fog-light of dawn
You herd them in, the hogs,
Head down in their hairy fat,
The meaty troops, to the pasture.
The leaves of the kudzu quake
With the serpents' fear, inside

The meadow ringed with men
Holding sticks, on the country roads.

The hogs disappear in the leaves.
The sound is intense, subhuman,
Nearly human with purposive rage.
There is no terror
Sound from the snakes.
No one can see the desperate, futile
Striking under the leaf heads.
Now and then, the flash of a long

Living vine, a cold belly,
Leaps up, torn apart, then falls
Under the tussling surface.
You have won, and wait for frost,
When, at the merest touch
Of cold, the kudzu turns
Black, withers inward and dies,
Leaving a mass of brown strings
Like the wires of a gigantic switchboard.
You open your windows,

With the lightning restored to the sky
And no leaves rising to bury

You alive inside your frail house,
And you think, in the opened cold,
Of the surface of things and its terrors,
And of the mistaken, mortal
Arrogance of the snakes
As the vines, growing insanely, sent
Great powers into their bodies
And the freedom to strike without warning:

From them, though they killed
Your cattle, such energy also flowed

To you from the knee-high meadow
(It was as though you had
A green sword twined among
The veins of your growing right arm—
Such strength as you would not believe
If you stood alone in a proper
Shaved field among your safe cows—):
Came in through your closed

Leafy windows and almighty sleep
And prospered, till rooted out.

The Beholders

Far away under us, they are mowing on the green steps
Of the valley, taking long, unending swings
Among the ripe wheat.
It is something about them growing,
Growing smaller, that makes us look up and see
That what has come over them is a storm.

It is a blue-black storm the shape of this valley,
And includes, perhaps, in its darkness,
Three men in the air
Taking long, limber swings, cutting water.
Swaths start to fall and, on earth,
The men come closer together as they mow.

Now in the last stand of wheat they bend.
From above, we watch over them like gods,
Our chins on our hands,
Our great eyes staring, our throats dry
And aching to cry down on their heads
Some curse or blessing,

Some word we have never known, but we feel
That when the right time arrives, and more stillness,
Lightning will leap
From our mouths in reasonless justice
As they arc their scythes more slowly, taking care
Not to look up.

As darkness increases there comes
A dancing into each of their swings,
A dancing like men in a cloud.
We two are coming together
Also, along the wall.
No lightning yet falls from us

Where their long hooks catch on the last of the sun
And the color of the wheat passes upward,

Drawn off like standing water
Into the cloud, turning green;
The field becomes whiter and darker,
And fire in us gathers and gathers

Not to call down death to touch brightly
The only metal for miles
In the hands of judged, innocent men,
But for our use only, who in the first sheaves of rain
Sit thunderstruck, having now the power to speak
With deadly intent of love.

The Poisoned Man

When the rattlesnake bit, I lay
In a dream of the country, and dreamed
Day after day of the river,

Where I sat with a jackknife and quickly
Opened my sole to the water.
Blood shed for the sake of one's life

Takes on the hid shape of the channel,
Disappearing under logs and through boulders.
The freezing river poured on

And, as it took hold of my blood,
Leapt up round the rocks and boiled over.
I felt that my heart's blood could flow

Unendingly out of the mountain,
Splitting bedrock apart upon redness,
And the current of life at my instep

Give deathlessly as a spring.
Some leaves fell from trees and whirled under.
I saw my struck bloodstream assume,

Inside the cold path of the river,
The inmost routes of a serpent
Through grass, through branches and leaves.

When I rose, the live oaks were ashen
And the wild grass was dead without flame.
Through the blasted cornfield I hobbled,

My foot tied up in my shirt,
And met my old wife in the garden,
Where she reached for a withering apple.

I lay in the country and dreamed
Of the substance and course of the river
While the different colors of fever

Like quilt patches flickered upon me.
At last I arose, with the poison
Gone out of the seam of the scar,

And brought my wife eastward and weeping,
Through the copper fields springing alive
With the promise of harvest for no one.

In the Marble Quarry

    Beginning to dangle beneath
The wind that blows from the undermined wood,
    I feel the great pulley grind,

    The thread I cling to lengthen
And let me soaring and spinning down into marble,
    Hooked and weightlessly happy

    Where the squared sun shines
Back equally from all four sides, out of stone
    And years of dazzling labor,

    To land at last among men
Who cut with power saws a Parian whiteness
    And, chewing slow tobacco,

    Their eyebrows like frost,
Shunt house-sized blocks and lash them to cables
    And send them heavenward

    Into small-town banks,

Into the columns and statues of government buildings,
But mostly graves.

I mount my monument and rise
Slowly and spinningly from the white-gloved men
Toward the hewn sky

Out of the basement of light,
Sadly, lifted through time's blinding layers
On perhaps my tombstone

In which the original shape
Michelangelo believed was in every rock upon earth
Is heavily stirring,

Surprised to be an angel,
To be waked in North Georgia by the ponderous play
Of men with ten-ton blocks

But no more surprised than I
To feel sadness fall off as though I myself
Were rising from stone

Held by a thread in midair,
Badly cut, local-looking, and totally uninspired,
Not a masterwork

Or even worth seeing at all
But the spirit of this place just the same,
Felt here as joy.

A Folk Singer of the Thirties

On a bed of gravel moving
Over the other gravel
Roadbed between the rails, I lay
As in my apartment now.
I felt the engine enter
A tunnel a half-mile away
And settled deeper
Into the stones of my sleep
Drifting through North Dakota.
I pulled them over me

For warmth, though it was summer,
And in the dark we pulled

Into the freight yards of Bismarck.
In the gravel car buried
To my nose in sledge-hammered stones,
My guitar beside me straining
Its breast beneath the rock,
I lay in the buzzing yards
And crimson hands swinging lights
Saw my closed eyes burn
Open and shine in their lanterns.
The yard bulls pulled me out,
Raining a rockslide of pebbles.
Bashed in the head, I lay

On the ground
As in my apartment now.
I spat out my teeth
Like corn, as they jerked me upright
To be an example for
The boys who would ride the freights
Looking for work, or for
Their American lives.
Four held me stretching against
The chalked red boards,
Spreading my hands and feet,
And nailed me to the boxcar
With twenty-penny nails.
I hung there open-mouthed
As though I had no more weight
Or voice. The train moved out.

Through the landscape I edged
And drifted, my head on my breast
As in my clean sheets now,
And went flying sideways through
The country, the rivers falling
Away beneath my safe
Immovable feet,
Close to me as they fell
Down under the boiling trestles,

And the fields and woods
Unfolded. Sometimes, behind me,
Going into the curves,
Cattle cried in unison,
Singing of stockyards
Where their tilted blood
Would be calmed and spilled.
I heard them until I sailed
Into the dark of the woods,
Flying always into the moonlight
And out again into rain
That filled my mouth
With a great life-giving word,
And into the many lights
The towns hung up for Christmas
Sales, the berries and tinsel,
And then out again
Into the countryside.
Everyone I passed

Could never believe what they saw,
But gave me one look
They would never forget, as I stood
In my overalls, stretched on the nails,
And went by, or stood
In the steaming night yards,
Waiting to couple on,
Overhanging the cattle coming
Into the cars from the night-lights.
The worst pain was when
We shuddered away from the platforms.
I lifted my head and croaked
Like a crow, and the nails
Vibrated with something like music
Endlessly clicking with movement
And the powerful, simple curves.
I learned where the oil lay
Under the fields,
Where the water ran
With the most industrial power,
Where the best corn would grow

And what manure to use
On any field that I saw.
If riches were there,
Whatever it was would light up
Like a bonfire seen through an eyelid
And begin to be words
That would go with the sound of the rails.
Ghostly bridges sprang up across rivers,
Mills towered where they would be,
Slums tottered, and buildings longed
To bear up their offices.
I hung for years
And in the end knew it all
Through pain: the land,
The future of profits and commerce
And also humility
Without which none of it mattered.
In the stockyards east of Chicago

One evening, the orphans assembled
Like choir boys
And drew the nails from my hands
And from my accustomed feet.
I stumbled with them to their homes
In Hooverville

And began to speak
In a chapel of galvanized tin
Of what one wishes for
When streaming alone into woods
And out into sunlight and moonlight
And when having a station lamp bulb
In one eye and not the other
And under the bites
Of snowflakes and clouds of flies
And the squandered dust of the prairies
That will not settle back
Beneath the crops.
In my head the farms
And industrial sites were burning
To produce.

One night, I addressed the A.A.,
Almost singing,
And in the fiery,
Unconsummated desire

For drink that rose around me
From those mild-mannered men,
I mentioned a place for a shoe store
That I had seen near the yards
As a blackened hulk with potential.
A man rose up,
Took a drink from a secret bottle,
And hurried out of the room.
A year later to the day
He knelt at my feet
In a silver suit of raw silk.
I sang to industrial groups
With a pearl-inlaid guitar

And plucked the breast-straining strings
With a nail that had stood through my hand.
I could not keep silent
About the powers of water,
Or where the coal beds lay quaking,
Or where electrical force
Should stalk in its roofless halls
Alone through the night wood,
Where the bridges should leap,
Striving with all their might
To connect with the other shore
To carry the salesmen.
I gave all I knew
To the owners, and they went to work.
I waked, not buried in pebbles

Behind the tank car,
But in the glimmering steeple
That sprang as I said it would
And lifted the young married couples,
Clutching their credit cards,
Boldly into and out of
Their American lives.

I said to myself that the poor
Would always be poor until
The towers I knew of should rise
And the oil be tapped:
That I had literally sung
My sick country up from its deathbed,
But nothing would do,
No logical right holds the truth.
In the sealed rooms I think of this,
Recording the nursery songs
In a checkered and tailored shirt,
As a guest on TV shows
And in my apartment now:
This is all a thing I began
To believe, to change, and to sell
When I opened my mouth to the rich.

The Being

I

It is there, above him, beyond, behind,

Distant, and near where he lies in his sleep
Bound down as for warranted torture.
Through his eyelids he sees it

Drop off its wings or its clothes.
He groans, and breaks almost from

Or into another sleep.
Something fills the bed he has been
Able only to half-fill.

He turns and buries his head.

I I

Moving down his back,
Back up his back,
Is an infinite, unworldly frankness,
Showing him what an entire

Possession nakedness is.
Something over him

Is praying.
        It reaches down under
His eyelids and gently lifts them.
He expects to look straight into eyes
And to see thereby through the roof.

Darkness. The windowpane stirs.
His lids close again, and the room

Begins to breathe on him
As through the eyeholes of a mask.

The praying of prayer
Is not in the words but the breath.

It sees him and touches him
All over, from everywhere.
It lifts him from the mattress
To be able to flow around him

In the heat from a coal bed burning
Far under the earth.
He enters—enters with . . .

What? His tongue? A word?
His own breath? Some part of his body?
All.
       None.

He lies laughing silently
In the dark of utter delight.

IV

It glides, glides
Lightly over him, over his chest and legs.
All breath is called suddenly back

Out of laughter and weeping at once.
His face liquifies and freezes

Like a mask. He goes rigid
And breaks into sweat from his heart
All over his body

In something's hands.

V

He sleeps, and the windowpane
Ceases to flutter.

Frost crawls down off it
And backs into only
The bottom two corners of glass.

VI

He stirs, with the sun held at him
Out of late-winter dawn, and blazing
Levelly into his face.
He blazes back with his eyes closed,
Given, also, renewed

Fertility, to raise
Dead plants and half-dead beasts

Out of their thawing holes,

And children up,
From mortal women or angels,
As true to themselves as he

Is only in visited darkness
For one night out of the year,

And as he is now, seeing straight
Through the roof   wide   wider

Wide awake.

Breath

Breath is on my face when the cloudy sun
     Is on my neck.
By it, the dangers of water are carefully
     Kept; kept back:

This is done with your father again
     In memory, it says.
Let me kneel on the boards of the rowboat,
     Father, where it sways

Among the fins and shovel heads
     Of surfaced sharks

And remember how I saw come shaping up
    Through lightening darks

    Of the bay another thing that rose
      From the depths on air
And opened the green of its skull to breathe
    What we breathed there.

    A porpoise circled around where I
      Lay in your hands
And felt my fear apportioned to the sharks,
    Which fell to sands

    Two hundred feet down within cold.
      Looking over the side,
I saw that beak rise up beneath my face
    And a hole in the head

    Open greenly, and then show living pink,
      And breath come out
In a mild, unhurried, unfathomable sigh
    That raised the boat

    And left us all but singing in midair.
      Have you not seen,
Father, in Heaven, the eye of earthly things
    Open and breathe green,

    Bestowing comfort on the mortal soul
      In deadly doubt,
Sustaining the spirit moving on the waters
    In hopeless light?

    We arched and plunged with that beast to land.
      Amazing, that unsealed lung
Come up from the dark; that breath, controlled,
    Greater than song,

    That huge body raised from the sea
      Secretly smiling
And shaped by the air it had carried
    Through the stark sailing

    And changeless ignorance of brutes,
      So that a dream

Began in my closed head, of the curves and rolling
      Powers of seraphim,

   That lift the good man's coffin on their breath
      And bear it up,
A rowboat, from the sons' depleting grief
      That will not stop:

   Those that hide within time till the time
      Is wholly right,
Then come to us slowly, out of nowhere and anywhere risen,
      Breathlessly bright.

The Ice Skin

All things that go deep enough
Into rain and cold
Take on, before they break down,
A shining in every part.
The necks of slender trees
Reel under it, too much crowned,
Like princes dressing as kings,

And the redwoods let sink their branches
Like arms that try to hold buckets
Filling slowly with diamonds

Until a cannon goes off
Somewhere inside the still trunk
And a limb breaks, just before midnight,
Plunging houses into the darkness
And hands into cupboards, all seeking
Candles, and finding each other.
There is this skin

Always waiting in cold-enough air.
I have seen aircraft, in war,
Squatting on runways,

Dazed with their own enclosed,
Coming-forth, intensified color
As though seen by a child in a poem.

I have felt growing over
Me in the heated death rooms
Of uncles, the ice
Skin, that which the dying

Lose, and we others,
In their thawing presence, take on.
I have felt the heroic glaze

Also, in hospital waiting
Rooms: that masterly shining
And the slow weight that makes you sit
Like an emperor, fallen, becoming
His monument, with the stiff thorns
Of fear upside down on the brow,
An overturned kingdom:

Through the window of ice
I have stared at my son in his cage,
Just born, just born.

I touched the frost of my eyebrows
To the cold he turned to
Blindly, but sensing a thing.
Neither glass nor the jagged
Helm on my forehead would melt.
My son now stands with his head
At my shoulder. I

Stand, stooping more, but the same,
Not knowing whether
I will break before I can feel,

Before I can give up my powers,
Or whether the ice light
In my eyes will ever snap off
Before I die. I am still,
And my son, doing what he was taught,
Listening hard for a buried cannon,
Stands also, calm as glass.

Bums, on Waking

Bums, on waking,
Do not always find themselves
In gutters with water running over their legs
And the pillow of the curbstone
Turning hard as sleep drains from it.
Mostly, they do not know

But hope for where they shall come to.
The opening of the eye is precious,

And the shape of the body also,
Lying as it has fallen,
Disdainfully crumpling earthward
Out of alcohol.
Drunken under their eyelids
Like children sleeping toward Christmas,

They wait for the light to shine
Wherever it may decide.

Often it brings them staring
Through glass in the rich part of town,
Where the forms of humanized wax
Are arrested in midstride
With their heads turned, and dressed
By force. This is ordinary, and has come

To be disappointing.
They expect and hope for

Something totally other:
That while they staggered last night
For hours, they got clear,
Somehow, of the city; that they
Have burst through a hedge, and are lying
In a trampled rose garden,

Pillowed on a bulldog's side,
A watchdog's, whose breathing

Is like the earth's, unforced—
Or that they may, once a year

(Any dawn now), awaken
In church, not on the coffin boards
Of a back pew, or on furnace-room rags,
But on the steps of the altar

Where candles are opening their eyes
With all-seeing light

And the green stained glass of the windows
Falls on them like sanctified leaves.
Who else has quite the same
Commitment to not being sure
What he shall behold, come from sleep—
A child, a policeman, an effigy?

Who else has died and thus risen?
Never knowing how they have got there,

They might just as well have walked
On water, through walls, out of graves,
Through potter's fields and through barns,
Through slums where their stony pillows
Refused to harden, because of
Their hope for this morning's first light,

With water moving over their legs
More like living cover than it is.

Goodbye to Serpents

Through rain falling on us no faster
Than it runs down the wall we go through,
My son and I shed Paris like a skin
And slip into a cage to say goodbye.
Through a hole in the wall
of the Jardin des Plantes
We come to go round

The animals for the last time;
Tomorrow we set out for home.
For some reason it is the snakes
To which we seem to owe

The longest farewell of our lives.
These have no bars, but drift
On an island held still by a moat,

Unobstructedly gazing out.
My son will not move from watching
Them through the dust of cold water,
And neither will I, when I realize
That this is my farewell
To Europe also. I begin to look
More intently than I ever have.

In the moat one is easily swimming
Like the essence of swimming itself,
Pure line and confident curve
Requiring no arms or legs.
In a tree, a bush, there is one
Whose body is living there motionless,
Emotionless, with drops running down,

His slack tail holding a small
Growing gem that will not fall.
I can see one's eyes in the brush,
As fixed as a portrait's,
Gazing into, discovering, forgetting
The heart of all rainfall and sorrow.
He licks at the air,

Tasting the carded water
Changed by the leaves of his home.
The rain stops in midair before him
Mesmerized as a bird—
A harmony of drops in which I see
Towers and churches, domes,
Capitals, streets like the shining

Paths of the Jardin des Plantes,
All old, all cold with my gaze
In glittering, unearthly fascination.
I say, "Yes! So I have seen them!
But I have brought also the human,
The presence of self and of love."
Yet it is not so. My son shifts

Uneasily back and away, bored now,
A tourist to the bitter end,
And I know I have not been moved
Enough by the things I have moved through,
And I have seen what I have seen

Unchanged, hypnotized, and perceptive:
The jewelled branches,
The chandeliers, the windows
Made for looking through only when weeping,
The continent hazy with grief,
The water in the air without support
Sustained in the serpent's eye.

In the Child's Night

On distant sides of the bed
We lie together in the winter house
Trying to go away.

Something thinks, "You must be made for it,
And tune your quiet body like a fish
To the stars of the Milky Way

To pass into the star-sea, into sleep,
By means of the heart of the current,
The holy secret of flowing."

Yet levels of depth are wrestling
And rising from us; we are still.
The quilt pattern—a child's pink whale—

Has surfaced through ice at midnight
And now is dancing upon
The dead cold and middle of the air

On my son's feet:
His short legs are trampling the bedclothes
Into the darkness above us

Where the chill of consciousness broods
Like a thing of absolute evil.
I rise to do freezing battle

With my bare hands.
I enter the faraway other
Side of the struggling bed

And turn him to face me.
The stitched beast falls, and we
Are sewn warmly into a sea-shroud

It begins to haul through the dark.
Holding my son's
Best kicking foot in my hand,

I begin to move with the moon
As it must have felt when it went
From the sea to dwell in the sky,

As we near the vast beginning,
The unborn stars of the wellhead,
The secret of the game.

Approaching Prayer

A moment tries to come in
Through the windows, when one must go
Beyond what there is in the room,

But it must come straight down.
Lord, it is time,

And I must get up and start
To circle through my father's empty house
Looking for things to put on
Or to strip myself of
So that I can fall to my knees
And produce a word I can't say
Until all my reason is slain.

Here is the gray sweater
My father wore in the cold,
The snapped threads growing all over it
Like his gray body hair.
The spurs of his gamecocks glimmer
Also, in my light, dry hand.

And here is the head of a boar
I once helped to kill with two arrows:

Two things of my father's
Wild, Bible-reading life
And my own best and stillest moment
In a hog's head waiting for glory.

All these I set up in the attic,
The boar's head, gaffs, and the sweater
On a chair, and gaze in the dark
Up into the boar's painted gullet.

Nothing. Perhaps I should feel more foolish,
Even, than this.
I put on the ravelled nerves

And gray hairs of my tall father
In the dry grave growing like fleece,
Strap his bird spurs to my heels
And kneel down under the skylight.
I put on the hollow hog's head
Gazing straight up
With star points in the glass eyes
That would blind anything that looked in

And cause it to utter words.
The night sky fills with a light

Of hunting: with leaves
And sweat and the panting of dogs

Where one tries hard to draw breath,
A single breath, and hold it.
I draw the breath of life
For the dead hog:
I catch it from the still air,
Hold it in the boar's rigid mouth,
And see

> *A young aging man with a bow*
> *And a green arrow pulled to his cheek*
> *Standing deep in a mountain creek bed,*

Stiller than trees or stones,
Waiting and staring

Beasts, angels,
I am nearly that motionless now

There is a frantic leaping at my sides
Of dogs coming out of the water

The moon and the stars do not move

I bare my teeth, and my mouth
Opens, a foot long, popping with tushes

A word goes through my closed lips

I gore a dog, he falls, falls back
Still snapping, turns away and dies
While swimming. I feel each hair on my back
Stand up through the eye of a needle

Where the hair was
On my head stands up
As if it were there

The man is still; he is stiller: still

Yes.

Something comes out of him
Like a shaft of sunlight or starlight.
I go forward toward him

(Beasts, angels)

With light standing through me,
Covered with dogs, but the water
Tilts to the sound of the bowstring

The planets attune all their orbits

The sound from his fingers,
Like a plucked word, quickly pierces
Me again, the trees try to dance
Clumsily out of the wood

I have said something else

> *And underneath, underwater,*
> *In the creek bed are dancing*
> *The sleepy pebbles*

The universe is creaking like boards
Thumping with heartbeats
And bonebeats

> *And every image of death*
> *In my head turns red with blood.*
> *The man of blood does not move*

My father is pale on my body

> *The dogs of blood*
> *Hang to my ears,*
> *The shadowy bones of the limbs*
> *The sun lays on the water*
> *Mass darkly together*

Moonlight, moonlight

> *The sun mounts my hackles*
> *And I fall; I roll*
> *In the water;*
> *My tongue spills blood*
> *Bound for the ocean;*
> *It moves away, and I see*
> *The trees strain and part, see him*
> *Look upward*

Inside the hair helmet
I look upward out of the total
Stillness of killing with arrows.
I have seen the hog see me kill him
And I was as still as I hoped.
I am that still now, and now.
My father's sweater
Swarms over me in the dark.
I see nothing, but for a second

Something goes through me
Like an accident, a negligent glance,
Like the explosion of a star

Six billion light years off
Whose light gives out

Just as it goes straight through me.
The boar's blood is sailing through rivers
Bearing the living image
Of my most murderous stillness.
It picks up speed
And my heart pounds.
The chicken-blood rust at my heels
Freshens, as though near a death wound
Or flight. I nearly lift
From the floor, from my father's grave
Crawling over my chest,

And then get up
In the way I usually do.
I take off the head of the hog
And the gaffs and the panting sweater
And go down the dusty stairs
And never come back.

I don't know quite what has happened
Or that anything has,

Hoping only that
The irrelevancies one thinks of
When trying to pray
Are the prayer,

And that I have got by my own
Means to the hovering place
Where I can say with any
Other than the desert fathers—
Those who saw angels come,
Their body glow shining on bushes
And sheep's wool and animal eyes,
To answer what questions men asked
In Heaven's tongue,
Using images of earth
Almightily:

PROPHECIES, FIRE IN THE SINFUL TOWERS,
WASTE AND FRUITION IN THE LAND,
CORN, LOCUSTS AND ASHES,
THE LION'S SKULL PULSING WITH HONEY,
THE BLOOD OF THE FIRST-BORN,
A GIRL MADE PREGNANT WITH A GLANCE
LIKE AN EXPLODING STAR
AND A CHILD BORN OF UTTER LIGHT—

Where I can say only, and truly,
That my stillness was violent enough,
That my brain had blood enough,
That my right hand was steady enough,
That the warmth of my father's wool grave
Imparted love enough
And the keen heels of feathery slaughter
Provided lift enough,
That reason was dead enough
For something important to be:

That, if not heard,
It may have been somehow said.

The Driver

At the end of the war I arose
From my bed in the tent and walked
Where the island fell through white stones
Until it became the green sea.
Into light that dazzled my brain
Like the new thought of peace, I walked
Until I was swimming and singing.

Over the foundered landing craft
That took the island, I floated,
And then like a thistle came
On the deep wind of water to rest
Far out, my long legs of shadow down-
pointing to ground where my soul
Could take root and spring as it must.

Below me a rusted halftrack
Moved in the depths with the movement
One sees a thing take through tears
Of joy, or terrible sorrow,
A thing which in quietness lies
Beyond both. Slowly I sank
And slid into the driver's shattered seat.

Driving through the country of the drowned
On a sealed, secret-keeping breath,
Ten feet under water, I sat still,
Getting used to the burning stare
Of the wide-eyed dead after battle.
I saw, through the sensitive roof—

The uneasy, lyrical skin that lies

Between death and life, trembling always—
An airplane come over, perfectly
Soundless, but could not tell
Why I lived, or why I was sitting,
With my lungs being shaped like two bells,
At the wheel of a craft in a wave
Of attack that broke upon coral.

"I become pure spirit," I tried
To say, in a bright smoke of bubbles,
But I was becoming no more
Than haunted, for to be so
Is to sink out of sight, and to lose
The power of speech in the presence
Of the dead, with the eyes turning green,

And to leap at last for the sky
Very nearly too late, where another
Leapt and could not break into
His breath, where it lay, in battle
As in peace, available, secret,
Dazzling and huge, filled with sunlight,
For thousands of miles on the water.

Horses and Prisoners

In the war where many men fell
Wind blew in a ring, and was grass.
Many horses fell also to rifles
On a track in the Philippine Islands
And divided their still, wiry meat
To be eaten by prisoners.
I sat at the finish line
At the end of the war

Knowing that I would live.
Long grass went around me, half wind,
Where I rode the rail of the infield
And the dead horses travelled in waves

On past the finishing post.
Dead wind lay down in live grass,
The flowers, pounding like hooves,
Stood up in the sun and were still,

And my mind, like a fence on fire,
Went around those unknown men:
Those who tore from the red, light bones
The intensified meat of hunger
And then lay down open-eyed
In a raw, straining dream of new life.
Joy entered the truth and flowed over
As the wind rose out of the grass

Leaping with red and white flowers:
Joy in the bone-strewn infield
Where clouds of barbed wire contained
Men who ran in a vision of greenness,
Sustained by the death of beasts,
On the tips of the sensitive grass blades,
Each footstep putting forth petals,
Their bones light and strong as the wind.

From the fence I dropped off and waded
Knee-deep in the billowing homestretch
And picked up the red of one flower.
It beat in my hand like my heart,
Filled with the pulse of the air,
And I felt my long thighbones yearn
To leap with the trained, racing dead.
When beasts are fallen in wars

For food, men seeking a reason to live
Stand mired in the on-going grass
And sway there, sweating and thinking,
With fire coming out of their brains
Like the thought of food and life
Of prisoners. When death moves close
In the night, I think I can kill it:
Let a man let his mind burn and change him

To one who was prisoner here
As he sings in his sleep in his home,
His mane streaming over the pillows,
The white threads of time
Mixed with the hair of his temples,
His grave-grass risen without him:
Now, in the green of that sleep,
Let him start the air of the island

From the tangled gate of jute string
That hangs from the battered grandstand
Where hope comes from animal blood
And the hooves of ghosts become flowers
That a captive may run as in Heaven:
Let him strip the dead shirt from his chest
And, sighing like all saved men,
Take his nude child in his arms.

Drinking from a Helmet

I

I climbed out, tired of waiting
For my foxhole to turn in the earth
On its side or its back for a grave,
And got in line
Somewhere in the roaring of dust.
Every tree on the island was nowhere,
Blasted away.

II

In the middle of combat, a graveyard
Was advancing after the troops
With laths and balls of string;
Grass already tinged it with order.
Between the new graves and the foxholes
A green water-truck stalled out.
I moved up on it, behind
The hill that cut off the firing.

III

My turn, and I shoved forward
A helmet I picked from the ground,
Not daring to take mine off
Where somebody else may have come
Loose from the steel of his head.

IV

Keeping the foxhole doubled
In my body and begging
For water, safety, and air,
I drew water out of the truckside
As if dreaming the helmet full.
In my hands, the sun
Came on in a feathery light.

V

In midair, water trimming
To my skinny dog-faced look
Showed my life's first all-out beard
Growing wildly, escaping from childhood,
Like the beards of the dead, all now
Underfoot beginning to grow.
Selected ripples wove through it,
Knocked loose with a touch from all sides
Of a brain killed early that morning,
Most likely, and now
In its absence holding
My sealed, sunny image from harm,
Weighing down my hands,
Shipping at the edges,
Too heavy on one side, then the other.

VI

I drank, with the timing of rust.
A vast military wedding
Somewhere advanced one step.

VII

All around, equipment drifting in light,
Men drinking like cattle and bushes,
Cans, leather, canvas and rifles,
Grass pouring down from the sun
And up from the ground.
Grass: and the summer advances
Invisibly into the tropics.
Wind, and the summer shivers
Through many men standing or lying
In the GI gardener's hand
Spreading and turning green
All over the hill.

VIII

At the middle of water
Bright circles dawned inward and outward
Like oak rings surviving the tree
As its soul, or like
The concentric gold spirit of time.
I kept trembling forward through something
Just born of me.

IX

My nearly dead power to pray
Like an army increased and assembled,
As when, in a harvest of sparks,
The helmet leapt from the furnace
And clamped itself
On the heads of a billion men.
Some words directed to Heaven
Went through all the strings of the graveyard
Like a message that someone sneaked in,
Tapping a telegraph key
At dead of night, then running
For his life.

X

I swayed, as if kissed in the brain.
Above the shelled palm-stumps I saw
How the tops of huge trees might be moved
In a place in my own country
I never had seen in my life.
In the closed dazzle of my mouth
I fought with a word in the water
To call on the dead to strain
Their muscles to get up and go there.
I felt the difference between
Sweat and tears when they rise,
Both trying to melt the brow down.

XI

On even the first day of death
The dead cannot rise up,
But their last thought hovers somewhere
For whoever finds it.
My uninjured face floated strangely
In the rings of a bodiless tree.
Among them, also, a final
Idea lived, waiting
As in Ariel's limbed, growing jail.

XII

I stood as though I possessed
A cool, trembling man
Exactly my size, swallowed whole.
Leather swung at his waist,
Web-cord, buckles, and metal,
Crouching over the dead
Where they waited for all their hands
To be connected like grass-roots.

XIII

In the brown half-life of my beard
The hair stood up
Like the awed hair lifting the back

Of a dog that has eaten a swan.
Now light like this
Staring into my face
Was the first thing around me at birth.
Be no more killed, it said.

XIV

The wind in the grass
Moved gently in secret flocks,
Then spread to be
Nothing, just where they were.
In delight's
Whole shining condition and risk,
I could see how my body might come
To be imagined by something
That thought of it only for joy.

XV

Fresh sweat and unbearable tears
Drawn up by my feet from the field
Between my eyebrows became
One thing at last.
And I could cry without hiding.
The world dissolved into gold;
I could have stepped up into air.
I drank and finished
Like tasting of Heaven,
Which is simply of,
At seventeen years,
Not dying wherever you are.

XVI

Enough
Shining, I picked up my carbine and said.
I threw my old helmet down
And put the wet one on.
Warmed water ran over my face.
My last thought changed, and I knew
I inherited one of the dead.

XVII

I saw tremendous trees
That would grow on the sun if they could,
Towering. I saw a fence
And two boys facing each other,
Quietly talking,
Looking in at the gigantic redwoods,
The rings in the trunks turning slowly
To raise up stupendous green.
They went away, one turning
The wheels of a blue bicycle,
The smaller one curled catercornered
In the handlebar basket.

XVIII

I would survive and go there,
Stepping off the train in a helmet
That held a man's last thought,
Which showed him his older brother
Showing him trees.
I would ride through all
California upon two wheels
Until I came to the white
Dirt road where they had been,
Hoping to meet his blond brother,
And to walk with him into the wood
Until we were lost,
Then take off the helmet
And tell him where I had stood,
What poured, what spilled, what swallowed:

XIX

And tell him I was the man.

BUCKDANCER'S
CHOICE

PART ONE

The Firebombing

Denke daran, dass nach den grossen Zerstörungen
Jedermann beweisen wird, dass er unschuldig war. *—Günter Eich*

Or hast thou an arm like God? —The Book of Job

Homeowners unite.

All families lie together, though some are burned alive.
The others try to feel
For them. Some can, it is often said.

Starve and take off

Twenty years in the suburbs, and the palm trees willingly leap
Into the flashlights,
And there is beneath them also
A booted crackling of snailshells and coral sticks.
There are cowl flaps and the tilt cross of propellers,
The shovel-marked clouds' far sides against the moon,
The enemy filling up the hills
With ceremonial graves. At my somewhere among these,

Snap, a bulb is tricked on in the cockpit

And some technical-minded stranger with my hands
Is sitting in a glass treasure-hole of blue light,
Having potential fire under the undeodorized arms
Of his wings, on thin bomb-shackles,
The "tear-drop-shaped" 300-gallon drop-tanks
Filled with napalm and gasoline.

Thinking forward ten minutes
From that, there is also the burst straight out

Of the overcast into the moon; there is now
The moon-metal-shine of propellers, the quarter-
moonstone, aimed at the waves,
Stopped on the cumulus.

There is then this re-entry
Into cloud, for the engines to ponder their sound.
In white dark the aircraft shrinks; Japan

Dilates around it like a thought.
Coming out, the one who is here is over
Land, passing over the all-night grainfields,
In dark paint over
The woods with one silver side,
Rice-water calm at all levels
Of the terraced hill.
                                        Enemy rivers and trees
Sliding off me like snakeskin,
Strips of vapor spooled from the wingtips
Going   invisible   passing   over   on
Over   bridges   roads for nightwalkers
Sunday night in the enemy's country   absolute
Calm   the moon's face   coming   slowly
About
              the inland sea
Slants   is woven with wire thread
Levels out   holds together like a quilt
Off the starboard wing   cloud flickers
At my glassed-off forehead   the moon's now and again
Uninterrupted face going forward
Over the waves in a glide-path
Lost into land.

Going: going with it

Combat booze by my side in a cratered canteen,
Bourbon frighteningly mixed
With GI pineapple juice,
Dogs trembling under me for hundreds of miles, on many
Islands, sleep-smelling that ungodly mixture
Of napalm and high-octane fuel,
Good bourbon and GI juice.

Rivers circling behind me around
Come to the fore, and bring
A town with everyone darkened.
Five thousand people are sleeping off
An all-day American drone.
Twenty years in the suburbs have not shown me
Which ones were hit and which not.

Haul on the wheel   racking slowly
The aircraft blackly around
In a dark dream   that   this is
That is like flying inside someone's head

Think of this   think of this

I did not think of my house
But think of my house now

Where the lawn mower rests on its laurels
Where the diet exists
For my own good   where I try to drop
Twenty years, eating figs in the pantry
Blinded by each and all
Of the eye-catching cans that gladly have caught my wife's eye
Until I cannot say
Where the screwdriver is   where the children
Get off the bus   where the fly
Hones his front legs   where the hammock folds
Its erotic daydreams   where the Sunday
School text for the day has been put   where the fire
Wood is   where the payments
For everything under the sun
Pile peacefully up,

But in this half-paid-for pantry
Among the red lids that screw off
With an easy half-twist to the left
And the long drawers crammed with dim spoons,
I still have charge—secret charge—
Of the fire developed to cling
To everything: to golf carts and fingernail
Scissors as yet unborn   tennis shoes
Grocery baskets   toy fire engines

New Buicks stalled by the half-moon
Shining at midnight on crossroads   green paint
Of jolly garden tools   red Christmas ribbons:

Not atoms, these, but glue inspired
By love of country to burn,
The apotheosis of gelatin.

Behind me having risen the Southern Cross
Set up by chaplains in the Ryukyus—
Orion, Scorpio, the immortal silver
Like the myths of king-
insects at swarming time—
One mosquito, dead drunk
On altitude, drones on, far under the engines,
And bites between
The oxygen mask and the eye.
The enemy-colored skin of families
Determines to hold its color
In sleep, as my hand turns whiter
Than ever, clutching the toggle—
The ship shakes   bucks
Fire hangs   not yet fire
In the air above Beppu
For I am fulfilling

And "anti-morale" raid upon it.
All leashes of dogs
Break under the first bomb, around those
In bed, or late in the public baths: around those
Who inch forward on their hands
Into medicinal waters.
Their heads come up with a roar
Of Chicago fire:
Come up with the carp pond showing
The bathhouse upside down,
Standing stiller to show it more
As I sail artistically over
The resort town followed by farms,
Singing and twisting
All the handles in heaven   kicking
The small cattle off their feet

In a red costly blast
Flinging jelly over the walls
As in a chemical war-
fare field demonstration.
With fire of mine like a cat

Holding onto another man's walls,
My hat should crawl on my head
In streetcars, thinking of it,
The fat on my body should pale.

Gun down
The engines, the eight blades sighing
For the moment when the roofs will connect
Their flames, and make a town burning with all
American fire.
                    Reflections of houses catch;
Fire shuttles from pond to pond
In every direction, till hundreds flash with one death.
With this in the dark of the mind,
Death will not be what it should;
Will not, even now, even when
My exhaled face in the mirror
Of bars, dilates in a cloud like Japan.
The death of children is ponds
Shutter-flashing; responding mirrors; it climbs
The terraces of hills
Smaller and smaller, a mote of red dust
At a hundred feet; at a hundred and one it goes out.
That is what should have got in
To my eye

And shown the insides of houses, the low tables
Catch fire from the floor mats,
Blaze up in gas around their heads
Like a dream of suddenly growing
Too intense for war. Ah, under one's dark arms
Something strange-scented falls—when those on earth
Die, there is not even sound;
One is cool and enthralled in the cockpit,
Turned blue by the power of beauty,
In a pale treasure-hole of soft light

Deep in aesthetic contemplation,
Seeing the ponds catch fire
And cast it through ring after ring
Of land: O death in the middle
Of acres of inch-deep water!   Useless

Firing   small arms
Speckles   from the river
Bank   one ninety-millimeter
Misses   far down   wrong petals   gone

It is this detachment,
The honored aesthetic evil,
The greatest sense of power in one's life,
That must be shed in bars, or by whatever
Means, by starvation
Visions in well-stocked pantries:
The moment when the moon sails in between
The tail-booms   the rudders nod   I swing
Over   directly over the heart
The *heart* of the fire. A mosquito burns out on my cheek
With the cold of my face   there are the eyes
In blue light   bar light
All masked but them   the moon
Crossing from left to right   in the streams below
Oriental fish form quickly
In the chemical shine,
In their eyes one tiny seed
Of deranged, Old Testament light.

Letting go   letting go
The plane rises gently   dark forms
Glide off me   long water   pales
In safe zones   a new cry enters
The voice box of chained family dogs

We buck   leap over something
Not there   settle back
Leave it   leave it clinging and crying
It consumes them in a hot
Body-flash, old age or menopause
Of children, clings and burns

                   eating through
And when a reed mat catches fire
From me, it explodes through field after field
Bearing its sleeper   another

Bomb finds a home
And clings to it like a child. And so

Goodbye to the grassy mountains
To cloud streaming from the night engines
Flags   pennons   curved silks
Of air   myself streaming also
My body covered
With flags, the air of flags
Between the engines.
Forever I do sleep in that position,
Forever in a turn
For home that breaks out streaming banners
From my wingtips,
Wholly in position to admire.

O then I knock it off
And turn for home over the black complex thread worked through
The silver night-sea,
Following the huge, moon-washed steppingstones
Of the Ryukyus south,
The nightgrass of mountains billowing softly
In my rising heat.
                   Turn and tread down
The yellow stones of the islands
To where Okinawa burns,
Pure gold, on the radar screen,
Beholding, beneath, the actual island form
In the vast water-silver poured just above solid ground,
An inch of water extending for thousands of miles
Above flat ploughland. Say "down," and it is done.

All this, and I am still hungry,
Still twenty years overweight, still unable
To get down there or see
What really happened.
                 But it may be that I could not,

If I tried, say to any
Who lived there, deep in my flames: say, in cold
Grinning sweat, as to another
Of these homeowners who are always curving
Near me down the different-grassed street: say
As though to the neighbor
I borrowed the hedge-clippers from
On the darker-grassed side of the two,
Come in, my house is yours, come in
If you can, if you
Can pass this unfired door. It is that I can imagine
At the threshold nothing
With its ears crackling off
Like powdery leaves,
Nothing with children of ashes, nothing not
Amiable, gentle, well-meaning,
A little nervous for no
Reason   a little worried   a little too loud
Or too easygoing   nothing I haven't lived with
For twenty years, still nothing not as
American as I am, and proud of it.

Absolution? Sentence? No matter;
The thing itself is in that.

Buckdancer's Choice

So I would hear out those lungs,
The air split into nine levels,
Some gift of tongues of the whistler

In the invalid's bed: my mother,
Warbling all day to herself
The thousand variations of one song;

It is called Buckdancer's Choice.
For years, they have all been dying
Out, the classic buck-and-wing men

Of traveling minstrel shows;
With them also an old woman
Was dying of breathless angina,

Yet still found breath enough
To whistle up in my head
A sight like a one-man band,

Freed black, with cymbals at heel,
An ex-slave who thrivingly danced
To the ring of his own clashing light

Through the thousand variations of one song
All day to my mother's prone music,
The invalid's warbler's note,

While I crept close to the wall
Sock-footed, to hear the sounds alter,
Her tongue like a mockingbird's break

Through stratum after stratum of a tone
Proclaiming what choices there are
For the last dancers of their kind,

For ill women and for all slaves
Of death, and children enchanted at walls
With a brass-beating glow underfoot,

Not dancing but nearly risen
Through barnlike, theatrelike houses
On the wings of the buck and wing.

Faces Seen Once

Faces seen once are seen

To fade from around one feature,
Leaving a chin, a scar, an expression

Forever in the air beneath a streetlight,
Glancing in boredom from the window
Of a bus in a country town,
Showing teeth for a moment only,
All of which die out of mind, except
One silver one.

Who had the dog-bitten ear?
The granulated lids? The birthmark?

Faces seen once change always

Into and out of each other:
An eye you saw in Toulon
Is gazing at you down a tin drainpipe
You played with as a dull child
In Robertstown, Georgia.
There it is April; the one eye

Concentrates, the rusty pipe

Is trembling; behind the eye
Is a pine tree blurring with tears:

You and someone's blue eye
Transforming your boyhood are weeping
For an only son drowned in warm water
With the French fleet off Senegal.
Soon after, the cancer-clamped face
Of your great-grandfather relaxes,

Smiles again with the lips of a newsboy.
Faces seen once make up

One face being organized

And changed and known less all the time,
Unsexed, amorphous, growing in necessity
As you deepen in age.
The brow wrinkles, a blind, all-knowing
Questioning look comes over it,
And every face in the street begins

To partake of the look in the eyes,

Every nose is part of that nose
And changes the nose; every innocence and every

Unspoken-of guilt goes into it,
Into the face of the one
Encountered, unknowable person who waits
For you all over the world,
In coffee shops, filling stations, bars,
In mills and orphan asylums,

In hospitals, prisons, at parties,
Yearning to be one thing.

At your death, they—it is there,

And the features congeal,
Having taken the last visage in,
Over you, pretesting its smile,
The skin the indwelling no
Color of all colors mingled,
The eyes asking all there is.

Composed, your own face trembles near

Joining that other, knowing
That finally something must break

Or speak. A silver tooth gleams;
You mumble, whispering "You
Are human, are what I have witnessed.
You are all faces seen once."
Through the bent, staring, unstable dark
Of a drainpipe, Unity hears you—

A God-roar of hearing—say only
"You are an angel's too-realized

Unbearable memoryless face."

The Common Grave

I

Some sit and stare
In an unknown direction, through most lie still,
Knowing that every season
Must be wintered.

II

The mover of mists and streams
Is usually in the weeds
By twilight, taking slowly
A dark dedicated field-shape.

III

Of all those who are under,
Many are looking over
Their shoulder, although it is only one leap
To beyond-reason gold, only one
Breath to the sun's great city.
All ages of mankind unite
Where it is dark enough.

IV

The midstrides of out-of-shape runners,
The discarded strokes of bad swimmers,
Open-mouthed at the wrong time—
All these are hooked wrongly together.
A rumor runs through them like roots:
They must try even harder
To bring into their vast,
Indiscriminate embrace
All of humanity.

V

In someone's hand an acorn
Pulses, thinking
It is only one leap,
Only one.

VI

In the field by twilight are
The faller in leaves through October,
The white-headed flyer in thistles
Finding out secret currents of air,
The raiser of mists from the creekbed,
A fish extending his body
Through all the curves of the river,
The incredible moon in the voice box
Of dogs on All Souls' Night.

VII

All creatures tumbled together
Get back in their wildest arms
No single thing but each other,
Hear only sounds like train sounds,
Cattle sounds, earth-shakers.

VIII

The mover of all things struggles
In the green-crowded, green-crowned nightmare

Of a great king packed in an acorn.
A train bends round a curve
Like a fish. An oak tree breaks
Out and shoves for the moonlight,
Bearing leaves which shall murmur for years,
Dumfoundedly, like mouths opened all at once
At just the wrong time to be heard,
    Others, others.

Reincarnation

Still, passed through the spokes of an old wheel, on and around
The hub's furry rust in the weeds and shadows of the riverbank,
This one is feeling his life as a man move slowly away.
Fallen from that estate, he has gone down on his knees
And beyond, disappearing into the egg buried under the sand

And wakened to the low world being born, consisting now
Of the wheel on its side not turning, but leaning to rot away
In the sun a few feet farther off than it is for any man.
The roots bulge quietly under the earth beneath him;
With his tongue he can hear them in their concerted effort

To raise something, anything, out of the dark of the ground.
He has come by gliding, by inserting the head between stems.
Everything follows that as naturally as the creation
Of the world, leaving behind arms and legs, leaving behind
The intervals between tracks, leaving one long wavering step

In sand and none in grass: he moves through, moving nothing,
And the grass stands as never entered. It is in the new
Life of resurrection that one can come in one's own time
To a place like a rotting wheel, the white paint flaking from it,
Rust slowly emerging, and coil halfway through it, stopped

By a just administration of light and dark over the diamonds
Of the body. Here, also naturally growing, is a flat leaf
To rest the new head upon. The stem bends but knows the weight
And does not touch the ground, holding the snub, patterned face
Swaying with the roots of things. Inside the jaws, saliva

Has turned ice cold, drawn from bird eggs and thunderstruck rodents,
Dusty pine needles, blunt stones, horse dung, leaf mold,
But mainly, now, from waiting—all the time a symbol of evil—
Not for food, but for the first man to walk by the gentle river:
Minute by minute the head becomes more poisonous and poised.

Here in the wheel is the place to wait, with the eyes unclosable,
Unanswerable, the tongue occasionally listening, this time
No place in the body desiring to burn the tail away or to warn,
But only to pass on, handless, what yet may be transferred
In a sudden giving-withdrawing move, like a county judge striking a
      match.

Them, Crying

In the well-fed cage-sound of diesels,
Here, in the cab's boxed wind,
He is called to by something beyond
His life. In the sun's long haul
Of light, each week at this place,
He sings to the truck's eight wheels

But at night it is worse than useless:
The great building shoots and holds

Its rays, and he hears, through the engine,
Through the killed words of his own song,
Them: them crying. Unmarried, unchildlike,
Half-bearded and foul-mouthed, he feels
His hands lean away to the right
And bear the truck spiraling down

To the four streets going around
And around and around the hospital.

He sits, and the voices are louder,
An awakening, part-song sound
Calling anyone out of the life
He thought he led: a sound less than twelve
Years old, which wakes to the less-than-nothing
Of a bent glass straw in a glass

With small sleepless bubbles stuck to it:
Which feels a new mouth sewn shut

In a small body's back or its side
And would free some angelic voice
From the black crimped thread,
The snipped cat-whiskers of a wound—
A sound that can find no way
To attack the huge, orderly flowers.

At one-thirty he is drawn in,
Drawn in, drawn in and in,

Listening, through dozens of Bakelite floors
And walls, brogan-stepping along
Through green-tiled nightlighted rooms
Where implements bake in glass cases,
Through halls full of cloudy test tubes,
Up and down self-service elevators

That open both sides at once,
Through closets of lubricants,

Through a black beehive of typed labels,
Through intimate theatres
Scrubbed down with Lysol and salt,
Through a sordid district of pails,
Until, on the third floor rear
Of the donated Southeast Wing,

He comes on a man holding wrongly
A doll with feigning-closed eyes,

And a fat woman, hat in her lap,
Has crashed through a chairback to sleep.
Unbelonging, he circles their circle;
Then, as though a stitch broke
In his stomach, he wheels and goes through
The double-frosted warning-marked door.

Twelve parents at bay intone
In the brain waves that wash around heroes:

> *Come, stripped to your T-shirt sleeves,*
> *Your coveralls, blue jeans, or chains,*

Your helmets or thickening haircuts,
Your white coats, your rock-pounding foreheads,
For our children lie there beyond us
In the still, foreign city of pain

Singing backward into the world
To those never seen before,

Old cool-handed doctors and young ones,
Capped girls bearing vessels of glucose,
Ginger ward boys, pan handlers, technicians,
Thieves, nightwalkers, truckers, and drunkards
Who must hear, not listening, them:
Them, crying: for they rise only unto

Those few who transcend themselves,
The superhuman tenderness of strangers.

The Celebration

All wheels; a man breathed fire,
Exhaling like a blowtorch down the road
And burnt the stripper's gown
Above her moving-barely feet.
A condemned train climbed from the earth
Up stilted nightlights zooming in a track.
I ambled along in that crowd

Between the gambling wheels
At carnival time with the others
Where the dodgem cars shuddered, sparking
On grillwire, each in his vehicle half
In control, half helplessly power-mad
As he was in the traffic that brought him.
No one blazed at me; then I saw

My mother and my father, he leaning
On a dog-chewed cane, she wrapped to the nose
In the fur of exhausted weasels.
I believed them buried miles back
In the country, in the faint sleep

Of the old, and had not thought to be
On this of all nights compelled

To follow where they led, not losing
Sight, with my heart enlarging whenever
I saw his crippled Stetson bob, saw her
With the teddy bear won on the waning
Whip of his right arm. They laughed;
She clung to him; then suddenly
The Wheel of wheels was turning

The colored night around.
They climbed aboard. My God, they rose
Above me, stopped themselves and swayed
Fifty feet up; he pointed
With his toothed cane, and took in
The whole Midway till they dropped,
Came down, went from me, came and went

Faster and faster, going up backward,
Cresting, out-topping, falling roundly.
From the crowd I watched them,
Their gold teeth flashing,
Until my eyes blurred with their riding
Lights, and I turned from the standing
To the moving mob, and went on:

Stepped upon sparking shocks
Of recognition when I saw my feet
Among the others, knowing them given,
Understanding the whirling impulse
From which I had been born,
The great gift of shaken lights,
The being wholly lifted with another,

All this having all and nothing
To do with me. Believers, I have seen
The wheel in the middle of the air
Where old age rises and laughs,
And on Lakewood Midway became
In five strides a kind of loving,
A mortal, a dutiful son.

The Escape

From my great-grandmother on,
My family lies at Fairmount
In a small rigid house of Tate marble.
A Civil War general, a small one,
Rises into the air,
Always fifty feet away,
And there are always flowers
Surrounding him as he lifts
His sword and calls back over his shoulder
To his troops, none of which lie
Under the decent plots and polished stones
Of the civilian dead. Once I saw,
Or said I did, a lily wrapped
Around his tense hand and sword hilt.
An enormous glass-fronted hospital
Rises across the street, the traffic
Roars equally from all four sides,
And often, from a textile mill,
A teen-age girl wanders by,
Her head in a singing cloth
Still humming with bobbins and looms.
In summer, the hospital orderlies eat
Their lunches on the lawn
From wet-spotted brown paper bags,
While behind them the portioned glass
Of the hospital blindingly fits
The noon sun together:
A tremendous vertical blaze
From which one piece—off-center, northwest—
Is gone, where a window is open.
I have escaped from Fairmount
Through that square hole in the light,
Having found where that piece of the sun's
Stupendous puzzle resides. It is
Lying in the woods, in a small, unfenced
County graveyard in Alabama.
It is on an open book
Of cardboard and paper, a simulated Bible,

All white, like a giant bride's,
The only real pages the ones
The book opens to; light
From the trees is falling squarely
On the few large, hand-written words.
On a hunting trip I walked through
That place, far from all relatives .
And wars, from bobbins and lilies and trucks.
Because of what I had seen,

I walked through the evergreen gates
Of the forest ranger's station,
And out to my car, and drove
To the county seat, and bought
My own secret grave-plot there
For thirty-seven dollars and a half.
A young deer, a spike buck, stood
Among the graves, slowly puzzling out
The not-quite-edible words
Of the book lying under
A panel of the sun forever
Missing from the noonlight of Fairmount.
I remember that, and sleep
Easier, seeing the animal head
Nuzzling the fragment of Scripture,
Browsing, before the first blotting rain
On the fragile book
Of the new dead, on words I take care,
Even in sleep, not to read,
Hoping for Genesis.

The Shark's Parlor

Memory: I can take my head and strike it on a wall   on Cumberland Island
Where the night tide came crawling under the stairs   came up the first
Two or three steps   and the cottage stood on poles all night
With the sea sprawled under it   as we dreamed of the great fin circling
Under the bedroom floor. In daylight there was my first brassy taste of beer

And Payton Ford and I came back from the Glynn County slaughterhouse
With a bucket of entrails and blood. We tied one end of a hawser
To a spindling porch pillar and rowed straight out of the house
Three hundred yards into the vast front yard of windless blue water
The rope outslithering its coil   the two-gallon jug stoppered and sealed
With wax   and a ten-foot chain leader   a drop-forged shark hook nestling.
We cast our blood on the waters   the land blood easily passing
For sea blood   and we sat in it for a moment with the stain spreading
Out from the boat   sat in a new radiance   in the pond of blood in the sea
Waiting for fins   waiting to spill our guts also in the glowing water.
We dumped the bucket, and baited the hook with a run-over collie pup. The jug
Bobbed, trying to shake off the sun as a dog would shake off the sea.
We rowed to the house   feeling the same water lift the boat a new way,
All the time seeing where we lived rise and dip with the oars.
We tied up and sat down in rocking chairs, one eye or the other responding
To the blue-eye wink of the jug. Payton got us a beer and we sat

All morning sat there with blood on our minds   the red mark out
In the harbor slowly failing us   then   the house groaned   the rope
Sprang out of the water   splinters flew   we leapt from our chairs
And grabbed the rope   hauled   did nothing   the house coming subtly
Apart   all around us   underfoot   boards beginning to sparkle like sand
With the glinting of the bright hidden parts of ten-year-old nails
Pulling out   the tarred poles we slept propped-up on   leaning to sea
As in land wind   crabs scuttling from under the floor   as we took turns about
Two more porch pillars   and looked out and saw   something, a fish-flash
An almighty fin in trouble   a moiling of secret forces   a false start
Of water   a round wave growing: in the whole of Cumberland Sound the one ripple.
Payton took off without a word   I could not hold him either

But clung to the rope anyway: it was the whole house bending
Its nails that held whatever it was   coming in a little and like a fool
I took up the slack on my wrist. The rope drew gently   jerked   I lifted
Clean off the porch and hit the water   the same water it was in
I felt in blue blazing terror at the bottom of the stairs and scrambled
Back up looking desperately into the human house as deeply as I could
Stopping my gaze before it went out the wire screen of the back door
Stopped it on the thistled rattan   the rugs I lay on and read
On my mother's sewing basket with next winter's socks spilling from it
The flimsy vacation furniture   a bucktoothed picture of myself.

Payton came back with three men from a filling station   and glanced at me
Dripping water   inexplicable   then we all grabbed hold like a tug-of-war.

We were gaining a little   from us a cry went up   from everywhere
People came running. Behind us the house filled with men and boys.
On the third step from the sea I took my place   looking down the rope
Going into the ocean, humming and shaking off drops. A houseful
Of people put their backs into it   going up the steps from me
Into the living room   through the kitchen   down the back stairs
Up and over a hill of sand   across the dust road   and onto a raised field
Of dunes   we were gaining   the rope in my hands began to be wet
With deeper water   all other haulers retreated through the house
But Payton and I on the stairs   drawing hand over hand on our blood
Drawing into existence by the nose   a huge body   becoming
A hammerhead   rolling in beery shallows   and I began to let up
But the rope still strained behind me   the town had gone
Pulling-mad in our house: far away in a field of sand they struggled
They had turned their backs on the sea   bent double   some on their knees
The rope over their shoulders like a bag of gold   they strove for the ideal
Esso station across the scorched meadow   with the distant fish coming up
The front stairs   the sagging boards   still coming in   up   taking
Another step   toward the empty house   where the rope stood straining
By itself through the rooms   in the middle of the air. "Pass the word,"
Payton said, and I screamed it: "Let up, good God, let up!"   to no one there.
The shark flopped on the porch, grating with salt-sand   driving back in
The nails he had pulled out   coughing chunks of his formless blood.
The screen door banged and tore off   he scrambled on his tail   slid
Curved   did a thing from another world   and was out of his element and in
Our vacation paradise   cutting all four legs from under the dinner table
With one deep-water move   he unwove the rugs in a moment, throwing pints
Of blood over everything we owned   knocked the buck teeth out of my picture
His odd head full of crushed jelly-glass splinters and radio tubes   thrashing
Among the pages of fan magazines   all the movie stars drenched in sea-blood.
Each time we thought he was dead   he struggled back and smashed
One more thing   in all coming back to die   three or four more times after death
At last we got him out   log-rolling him   greasing his sandpaper skin
With lard to slide him   pulling on his chained lips as the tide came
Tumbled him down the steps as the first night wave went under the floor.
He drifted off   head back   belly white as the moon. What could I do but buy
That house   for the one black mark still there   against death   a forehead-

toucher in the room he circles beneath   and has been invited to wreck?
Blood hard as iron on the wall   black with time   still bloodlike
Can be touched whenever the brow is drunk enough: all changes: Memory:
Something like three-dimensional dancing in the limbs   with age
Feeling more in two worlds than one   in all worlds the growing encounters.

Pursuit from Under

Often, in these blue meadows,
I hear what passes for the bark of seals

And on August week ends the cold of a personal ice age
Comes up through my bare feet
Which are trying to walk like a boy's again
So that nothing on earth can have changed
On the ground where I was raised.

The dark grass here is like
The pads of mukluks going on and on

Because I once burned kerosene to read
Myself near the North Pole
In the journal of Arctic explorers
Found, years after death, preserved
In a tent, part of whose canvas they had eaten

Before the last entry.
All over my father's land

The seal holes sigh like an organ,
And one entry carries more terror
Than the blank page that signified death
In 1912, on the icecap.
It says that, under the ice,

The killer whale darts and distorts,
Cut down by the flawing glass

To a weasel's shadow,
And when, through his ceiling, he sees

Anything darker than snow
He falls away
To gather more and more force

From the iron depths of cold water,
His shadow dwindling

Almost to nothing at all, then charges
Straight up, looms up at the ice and smashes
Into it with his forehead
To splinter the roof, to isolate seal or man
On a drifting piece of the floe

Which he can overturn.
If you run, he will follow you

Under the frozen pane,
Turning as you do, zigzagging,
And at the most uncertain of your ground
Will shatter through, and lean,
And breathe frankly in your face

An enormous breath smelling of fish.
With the stale lungs staining your air

You know the unsaid recognition
Of which the explorers died:
They had been given an image
Of how the downed dead pursue us.
They knew, as they starved to death,

That not only in the snow
But in the family field

The small shadow moves,
And under bare feet in the summer:
That somewhere the turf will heave,
And the outraged breath of the dead,
So long held, will form

Unbreathably around the living.
The cows low oddly here

As I pass, a small bidden shape
Going with me, trembling like foxfire

Under my heels and their hooves.
I shall write this by kerosene,
Pitch a tent in the pasture, and starve.

Fox Blood

Blood blister over my thumb-moon
Rising, under clear still plastic
Still rising strongly, on the rise
Of unleashed dog-sounds: sound broke,
Log opened. Moon rose

Clear bright. Dark homeland
Peeled backward, scrambling its vines.
Stream showed, scent paled
In the spray of mountain-cold water.
The smell dogs followed

In the bush-thorns hung like a scarf,
The silver sharp creek
Cut; off yonder, fox feet
Went printing into the dark: *there,*
In the other wood,

The uncornered animal's, running
Is half floating off
Upon instinct. Sails spread, fox wings
Lift him alive over gullies,
Hair tips all over him lightly

Touched with the moon's red silver,
Back-hearing around
The stream of his body the tongue of hounds
Feather him. In his own animal sun
Made of human moonlight,

He flies like a bolt running home,
Whose passage kills the current in the river,
Whose track through the cornfield shakes
The symmetry from the rows.
Once shot, he dives through a bush

And disappears into air.
That is the bush my hand
Went deeply through as I followed.
Like a wild hammer blazed my right thumb
In the flashlight and moonlight

And dried to one drop
Of fox blood I nail-polished in,
That lopsided animal sun
Over the nearly buried
Or rising human half-moon,

My glassed skin halfmooning wrongly.
Between them, the logging road, the stopped
Stream, the disappearance into
The one bush's common, foreseen
Superhuman door:

All this where I nailed it,
With my wife's nailbrush, on my finger,
To keep, not under, but over
My thumb, a hammering day-and-night sign
Of that country.

Fathers and Sons

I. THE SECOND SLEEP

Curled, too much curled, he was sleeping

In a chair too small for him, a restless chair
That held no place for his arms.

In his sleep he grew legs to replace them

As his father liftingly strained
And carried him to the next room.

All the time he settled away

A gentle man looked upon him
And then walked out of the house

And started his evergreen car.

Terrific impact, none his,
Killed him three blocks to the north.

In his second sleep the boy heard

The reared-up tearing of metal
Where a glassed-in face leapt and broke,

But to him it was something else,

An animal clash, a shock of resolving antlers,
And slept on, deeper and deeper

Into the mating season.

The next room filled with women; his nostrils
Flared, his eyes grew wide

And shot with blood under eyelids.

Brow lowered in strife, he stamped
In the laurel thicket, a herd of does

Trembling around him. Into the rhododendron

His rival faded like rain.
He stared around wildly, head down.

In the undying green, they woke him.

II. THE AURA

He used to wake to him
With a sense of music coming
Along with a body in movement.
It swayed with the motion of a hip
Rolling into the bathroom,
And, lying in bed in the winter dark

Of fathers, he heard rock-and-roll
Closed off while water ran through it,
Then the door opening, music
Opening, strolling down the hall,
Bad music moving all over
The house, electric guitars that followed

Some body around. It was his son,
With his portable radio always

At his belt, leaning over, adjusting the dial
For disc jockeys. That would be
The Skimmers, and that the Last
Survivors, moaning afar in the kitchen,

Who moved when the living moved.
He could hear him coming
From far away, every dawn,
And now the sound still coming
From everywhere is grief,
Unstoppable. At the beginning

Of his teens, his last year
Of bicycles, the wild
Music, traveling through the suburbs
From junior high, was broken on the road.
But it leapt everywhere
Into odd places: from every angle

It does not cease to be heard, the aura
Surrounding his son. He cannot hear it early
In the morning, unless he turns on his radio
By the bed, or leaves it on all night,
But in supermarkets it comes
Forth from the walls; it glances

From plate glass in department stores,
And he moves within his boy's
Chosen sounds: in cars, theatres,
In filling stations, in beer joints
Where he sits as though in the next phase
His son would have lived, hearing voices

Giving prizes for naming of tunes, those stations
Never off the air. He sits still
Wherever he is, as though caught
With music on him, or as if he were
About to be given it somewhere
In the region of the stomach:

That sound is the same, and yet not—
There is too much steadiness in it: none
Is carried rightly, none wavers

With the motion of adolescent walking, none
Lumbers as it should. Still, it is there
In trios of girls, in fake folk singers

From Brooklyn, and he enters, anywhere,
His son's life without the waking-
to-it, the irreplaceable motion
Of a body. Bongoes. Steel
Guitars. A precious cheapness
He would have grown out of. Something. Music.

Sled Burial, Dream Ceremony

While the south rains, the north
Is snowing, and the dead southerner
Is taken there. He lies with the top of his casket
Open, his hair combed, the particles in the air
Changing to other things. The train stops

In a small furry village, and men in flap-eared caps
And others with women's scarves tied around their heads
And business hats over those, unload him,
And one of them reaches inside the coffin and places
The southerner's hand at the center

Of his dead breast. They load him onto a sled,
An old-fashioned sled with high-curled runners,
Drawn by horses with bells, and begin
To walk out of town, past dull red barns
Inching closer to the road as it snows

Harder, past an army of gunny-sacked bushes,
Past horses with flakes in the hollows of their sway-backs,
Past round faces drawn by children
On kitchen windows, all shedding basic-shaped tears.
The coffin top still is wide open;

His dead eyes stare through his lids,
Not fooled that the snow is cotton. The woods fall
Slowly off all of them, until they are walking
Between rigid little houses of ice-fishers
On a plain which is a great plain of water

Until the last rabbit track fails, and they are
At the center. They take axes, shovels, mattocks,
Dig the snow away, and saw the ice in the form
Of his coffin, lifting the slab like a door
Without hinges. The snow creaks under the sled

As they unload him like hay, holding his weight by ropes.
Sensing an unwanted freedom, a fish
Slides by, under the hole leading up through the snow
To nothing, and is gone. The coffin's shadow
Is white, and they stand there, gunny-sacked bushes,

Summoned from village sleep into someone else's dream
Of death, and let him down, still seeing the flakes in the air
At the place they are born of pure shadow
Like his dead eyelids, rocking for a moment like a boat
On utter foreignness, before he fills and sails down.

Gamecock

Fear, jealousy and murder are the same
When they put on their long reddish feathers,
Their shawl neck and moccasin head
In a tree bearing levels of women.
There is yet no thread

Of light, and his scabbed feet tighten,
Holding sleep as though it were lockjaw,
His feathers damp, his eyes crazed
And cracked like the eyes
Of a chicken head cut off or wrung-necked

While he waits for the sun's only cry
All night building up in his throat
To leap out and turn the day red,
To tumble his hens from the pine tree,
And then will go down, his hackles

Up, looking everywhere for the other
Cock who could not be there,
Head ruffed and sullenly stepping

As upon his best human-curved steel:
He is like any fierce

Old man in a terminal ward:
There is the same look of waiting
That the sun prepares itself for;
The enraged, surviving-
another-day blood,

And from him at dawn comes the same
Cry that the world cannot stop.
In all the great building's blue windows
The sun gains strength; on all floors, women
Awaken—wives, nurses, sisters and daughters—

And he lies back, his eyes filmed, unappeased,
As all of them, clucking, pillow-patting,
Come to help his best savagery blaze, doomed, dead-
game, demanding, unreasonably
Battling to the death for what is his.

The Night Pool

There is this other element that shines
At night near human dwellings, glows like wool
From the sides of itself, far down:

From the deep end of heated water
I am moving toward her, first swimming,
Then touching my light feet to the floor,

Rising like steam from the surface
To take her in my arms, beneath the one window
Still giving off unsleeping light.

There is this other element, it being late
Enough, and in it I lift her, and can carry
Her over any threshold in the world,

Into any of these houses, apartments,
Her shoulders streaming, or above them
Into the mythical palaces. Her body lies

In my arms like a child's, not drowned,
Not drowned, and I float with her off
My feet. We are here; we move differently,

Sustained, closer together, not weighing
On ourselves or on each other, not near fish
Or anything but light, the one human light

From above that we lie in, breathing
Its precious abandoned gold. We rise out
Into our frozen land-bodies, and her lips

Turn blue, sealed against me. What I can do
In the unforgivable cold, in the least
Sustaining of all brute worlds, is to say

Nothing, not ask forgiveness, but only
Give her all that in my condition
I own, wrap her in many towels.

The War Wound

    It wounded well—one time and
A half: once with instant blood and again
Reinfecting blackly, years later. Now all
    Is calm at the heel of my hand

    Where I grabbed, in a bellied-
in airplane, and caught the dark glass
Offered once in a lifetime by
    The brittle tachometer.

    Moons by the thousands
Have risen in all that time; I hold
The healed half-moon of that night.
    I tell it to shine as still

    As it can in the temperate flesh
That never since has balled into a fist,
To hover on nylon guitar strings
    Like the folk-moon itself;

I tell it to burn like a poison
When my two children threaten themselves,
Wall-walking, or off the deep end
　　Of a county swimming pool,

And with thousands of moons
Coming over me year after year,
I lie with it well under cover,
　　The war of the millions,

　　Through glass ground under
Heel twenty-one years ago
Concentrating its light on my hand,
　　Small, but with world-fury.

Mangham

Somewhere between bells the right angles staggered
And Mangham poised, sensing thunder,
Something crooked in the straight lines of his brain.
Chalk dust rose from his shoulders, lost more
Weight, settled upward. The blackboard altered
Its screech, and the teeth of the children were set
On edge.

Above our doped heads the ceiling whitened
As the part in Mr. Mangham's hair
Lost its way; a gray lock fell;
Behind him as he turned, the Law
Of Cosines. He pressed the middle of his brow
With a handkerchief, looking at all of us
As he stepped

Quickly out of the room. In the center
Of the high school a sound arose from us,
A hive sound, amazing, increasing. I tore up my note
To Serena Hill, and leaned and spoke
Boldly to her in person. At the threshold
Mr. Mangham appeared with a handkerchief
Full of lumps;

He had raided the lunchroom icebox, and held
A knotted cloth full of soupy cubes
Dripping down his gray face: held it
Left-handed, lifted his good
Right arm. The signs appeared again,
The blackboard filled
With crazy proofs,

Lines wavering on the powdery blackness,
The dark night of the adolescent mind,
Conceiving drunken constellations,
Equilateral triangles, others of thirty-
sixty-ninety degrees, traced by a seismograph,
All figures melting from the ice-
colors of his chalk.

It should be in a tent in the desert
That I remember Mangham's last day
In that class, for his cracked voice was speaking
Of perfection, sphere-music,
Through the stroke that blazed in his mind
As our hive toned down
And Pythagoras howled

For more ice: it should be in contemplative sand
Or in a corner that I ought to sit
On a high stool, Mangham's age now,
On my head a conical hat, a dunce cap
Covered with moons and stars and jagged bands
Of brain-lightning, the ceiling above me
White with the chalk motes

Of stars from my shoulders, the night blazoned
With the angles of galaxies forming
To a silent music's accords,
Proving once and for all that I have no head
For figures, but knowing that that did not stop
Mangham for one freezing minute
Of his death

From explaining for my own good, from the good
Side of his face, while the other
Mixed unfelt sweat and ice water, what I never

Could get to save my soul: those things that, once
Established, cannot be changed by angels,
Devils, lightning, ice or indifference:
Identities! Identities!

Angina

That one who is the dreamer lies mostly in her left arm,
Where the pain shows first,
Tuned in on the inmost heart,
Never escaping. On the blue, bodied mound of chenille,
That limb lies still.
Death in the heart must be calm,

Must not look suddenly, but catch the windowframed squirrel
In a mild blue corner
Of an eye staring straight at the ceiling
And hold him there.
Cornered also, the oak tree moves
All the ruffled green way toward itself

Around the squirrel thinking of the sun
As small boys and girls tiptoe in
Overawed by their own existence,
For courtly doctors long dead
Have told her that to bear children
Was to die, and they are the healthy issue

Of four of those. Oh, beside that room the oak leaves
Burn out their green in an instant, renew it all
From the roots when the wind stops.
All afternoon she dreams of letters
To disc jockeys, requesting the "old songs,"
The songs of the nineties, when she married, and caught

With her first child rheumatic fever.
Existence is family: sometime,
Inadequate ghosts round the bed,
But mostly voices, low voices of serious drunkards
Coming in with the night light on
And the pink radio turned down;

She hears them ruin themselves
On the rain-weeping wires, the bearing-everything poles,
Then dozes, not knowing sleeping from dying—
It is day. Limbs stiffen when the heart beats
Wrongly. Her left arm tingles,
The squirrel's eye blazes up, the telephone rings,

Her children and her children's children fail
In school, marriage, abstinence, business.
But when I think of love
With the best of myself—that odd power—
I think of riding, by chairlift,
Up a staircase burning with dust

In the afternoon sun slanted also
Like stairs without steps
To a room where an old woman lies
Who can stand on her own two feet
Only six strange hours every month:
Where such a still one lies smiling

And takes her appalling risks
In absolute calm, helped only by the most
Helplessly bad music in the world, where death,
A chastened, respectful presence
Forced by years of excessive quiet
To be stiller than wallpaper roses,

Waits, twined in the roses, saying slowly
To itself, as sprier and sprier
Generations of disc jockeys chatter,
I must be still and not worry,
Not worry, not worry, to hold
My peace, my poor place, my own.

Dust

Lying at home
Anywhere   it can change not only the color
But the shape of the finger that runs along it   leaving a trail
That disappears from the earth; nothing can follow

Where that hand has walked and withdrawn.
And I have lain in bed at home and watched

Through a haze
Of afternoon liquor   the sun come down through it
Dropping off at the window sill from which the dust has risen
With no voice   the voices of children   to spin
In a stunned silence   the individual motes
All with a shape apiece   wool fragments

Small segments
Of rope tricks   spirochetes boring into the very
Body of light   and if you move your hand through their air
They dip   weave   then assume in the altered brightness
The places they have had, and all
Their wandering. Wherever it is,

It rises;
The place stands up and whirls   as in valleys
Of Arizona   where the world-armies of dust gather in sleeping
Hordes. I have seen them walking
Nearly out of the world   on a crazed foot
Spinning the ground beneath them

Into chaos.
These are dust devils, and in that sunny room
With the shape of their motes unmassed   not given a desert
I have closed my eyes and changed them into forms
Of fire   the dying's vision
Of incandescent worms:

For moment
After moment have lain as though whirling
Toward myself from the grains of the earth   in a cone
Of sunlight   massing my forces
To live in time   drawn into a shape
Of dust   and in that place

A woman
Came from my spinning side. There we lay
And stared at the ceiling of our house   at the extra motes
That danced about the raising of our hands

Unable to get in-
to a human form at this time

But ready
For children we might raise and call our own,
Teach to sing   to sweep the sills   to lift their hands
And make the dust dance in the air
Like bodies: ready:
Ready, always, for the next.

The Fiend

He has only to pass by a tree   moodily walking   head down
A worried accountant   not with it   and he is swarming
He is gliding up the underside light of leaves   upfloating
In a seersucker suit   passing window after window of her building.
He finds her at last, chewing gum   talking on the telephone.
The wind sways him softly   comfortably sighing   she must bathe
Or sleep.   She gets up, and he follows her along the branch
Into another room.   She stands there for a moment   and the teddy bear
On the bed feels its guts spin as she takes it by the leg and tosses
It off.   She touches one button at her throat, and rigor mortis
Slithers into his pockets, making everything there—keys, pen
and secret love—stand up.   He brings from those depths the knife
And flicks it open   it glints on the moon one time   carries
Through the dead walls   making a wormy static on the TV screen.
He parts the swarm of gnats that live excitedly at this perilous level
Parts the rarified light high windows give out into inhabited trees
Opens his lower body to the moon. This night the apartments are sinking

To ground level   burying their sleepers in the soil   burying all floors
But the one where a sullen shopgirl gets ready to take a shower,
Her hair in rigid curlers, and the rest.   When she gives up
Her aqua terry-cloth robe the wind quits in mid-tree   the birds
Freeze to their perches round his head   a purely human light
Comes out of a one-man oak   around her an energy field   she stands
Rooted   not turning to anything else   then begins to move like a saint
Her stressed nipples rising like things about to crawl off her   as he gets
A hold on himself.   With that clasp she changes   senses   something

Some breath through the fragile walls   some all-seeing eye
Of God   some touch that enfolds her body   some hand come up out of roots
That carries her as she moves   swaying   at this rare height. She wraps
The curtain around her and streams.   The room fades.   Then coming
Forth magnificently   the window blurred from within   she moves in a cloud
Chamber   the tree in the oak currents sailing   in clear air keeping pace
With her white breathless closet—he sees her mistily part her lips
As if singing to him   come up from river-fog   almost hears her as if
She sang alone in a cloud   its warmed light streaming into his branches
Out through the gauze glass of the window.   She takes off her bathing cap
The tree with him ascending   himself and the birds all moving
In darkness together   sleep crumbling the bark in their claws.
By this time he holds in his awkward, subtle limbs the limbs

Of a hundred understanding trees.   He has learned what a plant is like
When it moves near a human habitation   moving closer the later it is
Unfurling its leaves near bedrooms   still keeping its wilderness life
Twigs covering his body with only one way out   for his eyes into inner light
Of a chosen window   living with them night after night   watching
Watching with them at times their favorite TV shows   learning—
Though now and then he hears a faint sound: gunshot, bombing,
Building-fall—how to read lips: the lips of laconic cowboys
Bank robbers   old and young doctors tense-faced   gesturing savagely
In wards and corridors   like reading the lips of the dead

The lips of men interrupting the program at the wrong time
To sell you a good used car on the Night Owl Show   men silently reporting
The news out the window.   But the living as well, three-dimensioned,
Silent as the small gray dead, must sleep at last   must save their lives
By taking off their clothes. It is his beholding that saves them:
God help the dweller in windowless basements   the one obsessed
With drawing curtains this night. At three o'clock in the morning
He descends   a medium-sized shadow   while that one sleeps and turns
In her high bed in loss   as he goes limb by limb   quietly down
The trunk with one lighted side. Ground upon which he could not explain
His presence he walks with toes uncurled from branches, his bird-movements
Dying hard. At the sidewalk he changes   gains weight   a solid citizen

Once more.   At apartments there is less danger from dogs, but he has
For those a super-quiet hand   a hand to calm sparrows and rivers,
And watchdogs in half-tended bushes lie with him watching their women
Undress   the dog's honest eyes and the man's the same pure beast's

Comprehending the same essentials. Not one of these beheld would ever give
Him a second look   but he gives them all a first look that goes
On and on   conferring immortality while it lasts   while the suburb's leaves
Hold still enough   while whatever dog he has with him holds its breath
Yet seems to thick-pant   impatient as he with the indifferent men
Drifting in and out of the rooms   or staying on, too tired to move
Reading the sports page   dozing   plainly unworthy   for what women want
Dwells in bushes and trees: what they want is to look outward,

To look with the light streaming into the April limbs   to stand straighter
While their husbands' lips dry out   feeling that something is there
That could dwell in no earthly house: that in poplar trees or beneath
The warped roundabout of the clothesline   in the sordid disorder
Of communal backyards   some being is there in the shrubs
Sitting comfortably on a child's striped rubber ball filled with rainwater
Muffling his glasses with a small studious hand against a sudden
Flash of houselight from within   or flash from himself   a needle's eye
Uncontrollable   blaze of uncompromised being. Ah, the lingerie
Hung in the bathroom! The domestic motions of single girls living together
A plump girl girding her loins against her moon-summoned blood:
In that moon he stands   the only male lit by it, covered with leaf-shapes.
He coughs, and the smallest root responds   and in his lust he is set
By the wind in motion. That movement can restore the green eyes
Of middle age   looking   renewed   through the qualified light
Not quite reaching him where he stands again on the usual branch
Of his oldest love   his tie not loosened   a plastic shield
In his breast pocket full of pencils and ballpoint pens given him by salesmen
His hat correctly placed to shade his eyes   a natural gambler's tilt
And in summer wears an eyeshade   a straw hat Caribbean style.
In some guise or other he is near them when they are weeping without sound
When the teen-age son has quit school   when the girl has broken up
With the basketball star   when the banker walks out on his wife.
He sees mothers counsel desperately with pulsing girls face down
On beds full of overstuffed beasts   sees men dress as women
In ante-bellum costumes with bonnets   sees doctors come, looking oddly
Like himself   though inside the houses   worming a medical arm
Up under the cringing covers   sees children put angrily to bed
Sees one told an invisible fairy story   with lips moving silently as his
Are also moving   the book's few pages bright. It will take years
But at last he will shed his leaves   burn his roots   give up
Invisibility   will step out   will make himself known to the one

He cannot see loosen her blouse   take off luxuriously   with lips
Compressed against her mouth-stain   her dress   her stockings
Her magic underwear.   To that one he will come   up frustrated pines
Down alleys   through window blinds   blind windows   kitchen doors
On summer evenings. It will be something small that sets him off:
Perhaps a pair of lace pants on a clothesline   gradually losing
Water to the sun   filling out in the warm light with a well-rounded
Feminine wind as he watches   having spent so many sleepless nights
Because of her   because of her hand on a shade always coming down
In his face   not leaving even a shadow stripped naked upon the brown paper
Waiting for her now in a green outdated car with a final declaration
Of love   pretending to read   and when she comes and takes down
Her pants, he will casually follow her in   like a door-to-door salesman
The godlike movement of trees stiffening with him   the light
Of a hundred favored windows   gone wrong somewhere in his glasses
Where his knocked-off panama hat was   in his painfully vanishing hair.

Slave Quarters

In the great place the great house is gone from   in the sun
Room, near the kitchen of air   I look across at low walls
Of slave quarters, and feel my imagining loins

Rise with the madness of Owners
To take off the Master's white clothes
And slide all the way into moonlight
Two hundred years old with this moon.
Let me go,

Ablaze with my old me-
scent, in moonlight made by the mind
From the dusk sun, in the yard where my dogs would smell
For once what I totally am,
Flaming up in their brains as the Master
They but dimly had sensed through my clothes:
Let me stand as though moving

At midnight, now at the instant of sundown
When the wind turns

From sea wind to land, and the marsh grass
Hovers, changing direction:
                    there was this house
That fell before I got out. I can pull
It over me where I stand, up from the earth,
Back out of the shells
Of the sea:
            become with the change of this air
A coastal islander, proud of his grounds,

His dogs, his spinet
From Savannah, his pale daughters,
His war with the sawgrass, pushed back into
The sea it crawled from. Nearer dark, unseen,
I can begin to dance
Inside my gabardine suit
As though I had left my silk nightshirt

In the hall of mahogany, and crept
To slave quarters to live out
The secret legend of Owners. Ah, stand up,
Blond loins, another
Love is possible! My thin wife would be sleeping
Or would not mention my absence:

                           the moonlight

On these rocks can be picked like cotton
By a crazed Owner dancing-mad
With the secret repossession of his body

Phosphorescent and mindless, shedding
Blond-headed shadow on the sand,
Hounds pressing in their sleep
Around him, smelling his footblood
On the strange ground that lies between skins
With the roof blowing off slave quarters
To let the moon in burning
The years away
In just that corner where crabgrass proves it lives
Outside of time.
Who seeks the other color of his body,
His loins giving off a frail light
On the dark lively shipwreck of grass   sees
Water live where
The half-moon touches,
The moon made whole in one wave
Very far from the silent piano   the copy of Walter Scott
Closed on its thin-papered battles
Where his daughter practiced, decorum preventing the one
Bead of sweat in all that lace   collected at her throat
From breaking and humanly running

Over Mozart's unmortal keys—

                          I come past
A sand crab pacing sideways   his eyes out
On stalks   the bug-eyed vision of fiddler
Crabs sneaking a light on the run
From the split moon   holding in it a white man stepping
Down the road of clamshells and cotton   his eyes out
On stems   the tops of the sugar
Cane soaring   the sawgrass walking:
                          I come past
The stale pools left
Over from high tide—where the crab in the night sand
Is basting himself with his claws   moving ripples outward
Feasting on brightness
                 and above
A gull also crabs slowly,
Tacks, jibes   then turning the corner
Of wind, receives himself like a brother
As he glides down upon his reflection:

My body has a color not yet freed:
In that ruined house let me throw
Obsessive gentility off;
Let Africa rise upon me like a man
Whose instincts are delivered from their chains
Where they lay close-packed and wide-eyed
In muslin sheets
As though in the miserly holding
Of too many breaths by one ship.   Now

Worked in silver   their work lies all
Around me   the fields dissolving
Into the sea   and   not on a horse
I stoop to the soil   working
Gathering   moving to the rhythm of a music
That has crossed the ocean in chains

In the grass the great singing void of slave

Labor about me   the moonlight bringing
Sweat out of my back as though   the sun
Changed skins upon me   some other

Man moving near me on horseback   whom I look in the eyes
Once a day:
                        there in that corner

Her bed turned to grass. Unsheltered by these walls
The outside fields form slowly
Anew, in a kind of barrelling blowing,
Bend in all the right places   as faintly Michael rows
The boat ashore   his spiritual lungs
Entirely filling the sail.   How take on the guilt

Of slavers? How shudder like one who made
Money from buying a people
To work as ghosts
In this blowing solitude?
I only stand here upon shells   dressed poorly
For nakedness   poorly
For the dark wrecked hovel of rebirth

Picking my way in thought
To the black room
Where starlight blows off the roof
And the great beasts that died with the minds
Of the first slaves, stand at the door, asking
For death, asking to be
Forgotten: the sadness of elephants
The visionary pain in the heads
Of incredibly poisonous snakes
Lion   wildebeest   giraffe   all purchased also
When one wished only
Labor
            those beasts becoming
For the white man the animals of Eden
Emblems of sexual treasure   all beasts attending
Me now   my dreamed dogs snarling at the shades
Of eland and cheetah
On the dispossessed ground where I dance
In my clothes beyond movement:

In nine months she would lie
With a knife between her teeth to cut the pain
Of bearing

A child who belongs in no world   my hair in that boy
Turned black   my skin
Darkened by half   his, lightened
By that half exactly   the beasts of Africa reduced
To cave shadows flickering on his brow
As I think of him: a child would rise from that place
With half my skin.   He could for an instant
Of every day   when the wind turns   look
Me in the eyes.   What do you feel when passing

Your blood beyond death
To another in secret: into
Another who takes your features   and adds
A misplaced Africa to them,
Changing them forever
As they must live? What happens
To you, when such a one bears
You after your death into rings
Of battling light   a heavyweight champion
Through the swirling glass of four doors,
In epauletted coats   into places
Where you learn to wait
On tables   into sitting in all-night cages
Of parking lots   into raising
A sun-sided spade in a gang
Of men on a tar road working
Until the crickets give up?
What happens when the sun goes down

And the white man's loins still stir
In a house of air   still draw him toward
Slave quarters? When Michael's voice is heard
Bending the sail like grass,
The real moon begins to come
Apart on the water
And two hundred years are turned back
On with the headlights of a car?
When you learn that there is no hatred
Like love in the eyes
Of a wholly owned face? When you think of what
It would be like   what it has been

What it is to look once a day
Into an only
Son's brown, waiting, wholly possessed
Amazing eyes, and not
Acknowledge, but own?

FALLING, MAY DAY SERMON, AND OTHER POEMS

Falling

A 29-year-old stewardess fell . . . to her death tonight when
she was swept through an emergency door that suddenly
sprang open. . . . The body . . . was found . . . three hours
after the accident. —*New York Times*

The states when they black and out and lie there rolling   when they turn
To something transcontinental   move by   drawing moonlight out of the great
One-sided stone hung off the starboard wingtip   some sleeper next to
An engine is groaning for coffee   and there is faintly coming in
Somewhere the vast beast-whistle of space. In the galley with its racks
Of trays   she rummages for a blanket   and moves in her slim tailored
Uniform to pin it over the cry at the top of the door. As though she blew

The door down with a silent blast from her lungs   frozen   she is black
Out finding herself   with the plane nowhere and her body taking by the throat
The undying cry of the void   falling   living   beginning to be something
That no one has ever been and lived through   screaming without enough air
Still neat   lipsticked   stockinged   girdled by regulation   her hat
Still on   her arms and legs in no world   and yet spaced also strangely
With utter placid rightness on thin air   taking her time   she holds it
In many places   and now, still thousands of feet from her death she seems
To slow   she develops interest   she turns in her maneuverable body

To watch it. She is hung high up in the overwhelming middle of things in her
Self   in low body-whistling wrapped intensely   in all her dark dance-weight
Coming down from a marvellous leap   with the delaying, dumfounding ease
Of a dream of being drawn   like endless moonlight to the harvest soil
Of a central state of one's country   with a great gradual warmth coming
Over her   floating   finding more and more breath in what she has been using
For breath   as the levels become more human   seeing clouds placed honestly

Below her left and right   riding slowly toward them   she clasps it all
To her and can hang her hands and feet in it in peculiar ways   and
Her eyes opened wide by wind, can open her mouth as wide   wider and suck
All the heat from the cornfields   can go down on her back with a feeling
Of stupendous pillows stacked under her   and can turn   turn as to someone
In bed   smile, understood in darkness   can go away   slant   slide
Off tumbling   into the emblem of a bird with its wings half-spread
Or whirl madly on herself   in endless gymnastics in the growing warmth
Of wheatfields rising toward the harvest moon.   There is time to live
In superhuman health   seeing mortal unreachable lights far down seeing
An ultimate highway with one late priceless car probing it   arriving
In a square town   and off her starboard arm the glitter of water catches
The moon by its one shaken side   scaled, roaming silver   My God it is good
And evil   lying in one after another of all the positions for love
Making   dancing   sleeping   and now cloud wisps at her no
Raincoat   no matter   all small towns brokenly brighter from inside
Cloud   she walks over them like rain   bursts out to behold a Greyhound
Bus shooting light through its sides   it is the signal to go straight
Down like a glorious diver   then feet first   her skirt stripped beautifully
Up   her face in fear-scented cloths   her legs deliriously bare   then
Arms out   she slow-rolls over   steadies out   waits for something great
To take control of her   trembles near feathers   planes head-down
The quick movements of bird-necks turning her head   gold eyes   the insight-
eyesight of owls blazing into hencoops   a taste for chicken overwhelming
Her   the long-range vision of hawks enlarging all human lights of cars
Freight trains   looped bridges   enlarging the moon racing slowly
Through all the curves of a river   all the darks of the midwest blazing
From above. A rabbit in a bush turns white   the smothering chickens
Huddle   for over them there is still time for something to live
With the streaming half-idea of a long stoop   a hurtling   a fall
That is controlled   that plummets as it wills   turns gravity
Into a new condition, showing its other side like a moon   shining
New Powers   there is still time to live on a breath made of nothing
But the whole night   time for her to remember to arrange her skirt
Like a diagram of a bat   tightly it guides her   she has this flying-skin
Made of garments   and there are also those sky-divers on TV   sailing
In sunlight   smiling under their goggles   swapping batons back and forth
And He who jumped without a chute and was handed one by a diving
Buddy. She looks for her grinning companion   white teeth   nowhere
She is screaming   singing hymns   her thin human wings spread out

From her neat shoulders   the air beast-crooning to her   warbling
And she can no longer behold the huge partial form of the world   now
She is watching her country lose its evoked master shape   watching it lose
And gain   get back its houses and people   watching it bring up
Its local lights   single homes   lamps on barn roofs   if she fell
Into water she might live   like a diver   cleaving   perfect   plunge

Into another   heavy silver   unbreathable   slowing   saving
Element: there is water   there is time to perfect all the fine
Points of diving   feet together   toes pointed   hands shaped right
To insert her into water like a needle   to come out healthily dripping
And be handed a Coca-Cola   there they are   there are the waters
Of life   the moon packed and coiled in a reservoir   so let me begin
To plane across the night air of Kansas   opening my eyes superhumanly
Bright   to the dammed moon   opening the natural wings of my jacket
By Don Loper   moving like a hunting owl toward the glitter of water
One cannot just *fall   just tumble screaming all that time   one must use*
It   she is now through with all   through all   clouds   damp   hair
Straightened   the last wisp of fog pulled apart on her face like wool revealing
New darks   new progressions of headlights along dirt roads   from chaos

And night   a gradual warming   a new-made, inevitable world of one's own
Country   a great stone of light in its waiting waters   hold   hold out
For water: who knows when what correct young woman must take up her body
And fly   and head for the moon-crazed inner eye of midwest imprisoned
Water   stored up for her for years   the arms of her jacket slipping
Air up her sleeves to go   all over her? What final things can be said
Of one who starts out sheerly in her body in the high middle of night
Air   to track down water like a rabbit where it lies like life itself
Off to the right in Kansas? She goes toward   the blazing-bare lake
Her skirts neat   her hands and face warmed more and more by the air
Rising from pastures of beans   and under her   under chenille bedspreads
The farm girls are feeling the goddess in them struggle and rise brooding
On the scratch-shining posts of the bed   dreaming of female signs
Of the moon   male blood like iron   of what is really said by the moan
Of airliners passing over them at dead of midwest midnight   passing
Over brush fires   burning out in silence on little hills   and will wake
To see the woman they should be   struggling on the rooftree to become
Stars: for her the ground is closer   water is nearer   she passes
It   then banks   turns   her sleeves fluttering differently as she rolls
Out to face the east, where the sun shall come up from wheatfields she must

Do something with water   fly to it   fall in it   drink it   rise
From it   but there is none left upon earth   the clouds have drunk it back
The plants have sucked it down   there are standing toward her only
The common fields of death   she comes back from flying to falling
Returns to a powerful cry   the silent scream with which she blew down
The coupled door of the airliner   nearly   nearly losing hold
Of what she has done   remembers   remembers the shape at the heart
Of cloud   fashionably swirling   remembers she still has time to die
Beyond explanation. Let her now take off her hat in summer air the contour
Of cornfields   and have enough time to kick off her one remaining
Shoe with the toes   of the other foot   to unhook her stockings
With calm fingers, noting how fatally easy it is to undress in midair
Near death   when the body will assume without effort any position
Except the one that will sustain it   enable it to rise   live ·
Not die   nine farms hover close   widen   eight of them separate, leaving
One in the middle   then the fields of that farm do the same   there is no
Way to back off   from her chosen ground   but she sheds the jacket
With its silver sad impotent wings   sheds the bat's guiding tailpiece
Of her skirt   the lightning-charged clinging of her blouse   the intimate
Inner flying-garment of her slip in which she rides like the holy ghost
Of a virgin   sheds the long windsocks of her stockings   absurd
Brassiere   then feels the girdle required by regulations squirming
Off her: no longer monobuttocked   she feels the girdle flutter   shake
In her hand   and float   upward   her clothes rising off her ascending
Into cloud   and fights away from her head the last sharp dangerous shoe
Like a dumb bird   and now will drop in   SOON   now will drop

In like this   the greatest thing that ever came to Kansas   down from all
Heights   all levels of American breath   layered in the lungs from the frail
Chill of space to the loam where extinction slumbers in corn tassels thickly
And breathes like rich farmers counting: will come among them after
Her last superhuman act   the last slow careful passing of her hands
All over her unharmed body   desired by every sleeper in his dream:
Boys finding for the first time their loins filled with heart's blood
Widowed farmers whose hands float under light covers to find themselves
Arisen at sunrise   the splendid position of blood unearthly drawn
Toward clouds   all feel something   pass over them as she passes
Her palms over *her* long legs   *her* small breasts   and deeply between
Her thighs   her hair shot loose from all pins   streaming in the wind
Of her body   let her come openly   trying at the last second to land
On her back   This is it   THIS

　　　　　　　　　　　　　　All those who find her impressed
In the soft loam　gone down　driven well into the image of her body
The furrows for miles flowing in upon her where she lies very deep
In her mortal outline　in the earth as it is in cloud　can tell nothing
But that she is there　inexplicable　unquestionable　and remember
That something broke in them as well　and began to live and die more
When they walked for no reason into their fields to where the whole earth
Caught her　interrupted her maiden flight　told her how to lie　she cannot
Turn　go away　cannot move　cannot slide off it and assume another
Position　no sky-diver with any grin could save her　hold her in his arms
Plummet with her　unfold above her his wedding silks　she can no longer
Mark the rain with whirling women that take the place of a dead wife
Or the goddess in Norwegian farm girls　or all the back-breaking whores
Of Wichita. All the known air above her is not giving up quite one
Breath　it is all gone　and yet not dead　not anywhere else
Quite　lying still in the field on her back　sensing the smells
Of incessant growth try to lift her　a little sight left in the corner
Of one eye　fading　seeing something wave　lies believing
That she could have made it　at the best part of her brief goddess
State　to water　gone in headfirst　come out smiling　invulnerable
Girl in a bathing-suit ad　but she is lying like a sunbather at the last
Of moonlight　half-buried in her impact on the earth　not far
From a railroad trestle　a water tank　she could see if she could
Raise her head from her modest hole　with her clothes beginning
To come down all over Kansas　into bushes　on the dewy sixth green
Of a golf course　one shoe　her girdle coming down fantastically
On a clothesline, where it belongs　her blouse on a lighting rod:

Lies in the fields　in *this* field　on her broken back as though on
A cloud she cannot drop through　while farmers sleepwalk without
Their women from houses　a walk like falling toward the far waters
Of life　in moonlight　toward the dreamed eternal meaning of their farms
Toward the flowering of the harvest in their hands　that tragic cost
Feels herself go　go toward　go outward　breathes at last fully
Not　and tries　less　once　tries　tries　AH, GOD—

The Sheep Child

Farm boys wild to couple
With anything   with soft-wooded trees
With mounds of earth   mounds
Of pinestraw   will keep themselves off
Animals by legends of their own:
In the hay-tunnel dark
And dung of barns, they will
Say   I have heard tell

That in a museum in Atlanta
Way back in a corner somewhere
There's this thing that's only half
Sheep   like a woolly baby
Pickled in alcohol   because
Those things can't live   his eyes
Are open   but you can't stand to look
I heard from somebody who . . .

But this is now almost all
Gone. The boys have taken
Their own true wives in the city,
The sheep are safe in the west hill
Pasture   but we who were born there
Still are not sure. Are we,
Because we remember, remembered
In the terrible dust of museums?

Merely with his eyes, the sheep-child may

Be saying   saying

I am here, in my father's house.
I who am half of your world, came deeply
To my mother in the long grass
Of the west pasture, where she stood like moonlight
Listening for foxes. It was something like love
From another world that seized her
From behind, and she gave, not lifting her head
Out of dew, without ever looking, her best
Self to that great need. Turned loose, she dipped her face
Farther into the chill of the earth, and in a sound
Of sobbing   of something stumbling
Away, began, as she must do,
To carry me. I woke, dying,

In the summer sun of the hillside, with my eyes
Far more than human. I saw for a blazing moment
The great grassy world from both sides,
Man and beast in the round of their need,
And the hill wind stirred in my wool,
My hoof and my hand clasped each other,
I ate my one meal
Of milk, and died
Staring. From dark grass I came straight

To my father's house, whose dust
Whirls up in the halls for no reason
When no one comes   piling deep in a hellish mild corner,
And, through my immortal waters
I meet the sun's grains eye
To eye, and they fail at my closet of glass.
Dead, I am most surely living
In the minds of farm boys: I am he who drives
Them like wolves from the hound bitch and calf
And from the chaste ewe in the wind.
They go into woods   into bean fields   they go
Deep into their known right hands. Dreaming of me,
They groan   they wait   they suffer
Themselves, they marry, they raise their kind.

Reincarnation (II)

> —the white thing was so white, its
>   wings
> so wide, and in those for ever exiled
>   waters —*Melville*

> As apparitional as sails that cross
> Some page of figures to be filed
>   away —*Hart Crane*

One can do   one begins to   one can only

Circle   eyes wide with fearing the spirit

Of weight   as though to be born   to awaken to what one is
Were to be carried   passed out
With enormous cushions of air under the arms
Straight up   the head growing stranger
And released between wings near an iceberg

It is too much to ask   to ask
For   under the white mild sun
On that huge frozen point to move

As one is so easily doing

Boring into it with one's new
born excessive eye   after a long
Half-sleeping self-doubting voyage   until
The unbased mountain falters
Turns over like a whale   one screams for the first time

With a wordless voice   swings over
The berg's last treasured bubble
Straightens   wings trembling   RIDING!
Rises into a new South

Sensitive current   checks each wing
It is living there
                    and starts out.

There is then this night
Crawling slowly in under one wing
This night of all nights
Aloft   a night five thousand feet up
Where he soars among the as-yet-unnamed

The billion unmentionable stars
Each in its right relation
To his course   he shivers   changes his heading
Slightly   feels the heavenly bodies
Shake   alter   line up in the right conjunction
For mating   for the plunge
Toward the egg   he soars   borne toward his offspring

By the Dragon balanced exactly
Again the Lion   the sense of the galaxies
Right from moment to moment
Drawing slowly for him a Great
Circle   all the stars in the sky
Embued with the miracle of
The single human Christmas one
Conjoining to stand now over
A rocky island ten thousand
Miles of water away.
                              With a cold new heart
With celestial feathered crutches
A "new start" like a Freudian dream
Of a new start   he hurtles as if motionless
All the air in the upper world
Splitting apart on his lips.

Sleep   *wingless*—NO!
The stars appear, rimmed with red
Space under his breastbone maintains
Itself   he sighs like a man
Between his cambered wings
Letting down now   curving around
Into the wind   slowly toward
Any wave   that—
That one.   He folds his wings and moves
With the mid-Pacific
Carried for miles in no particular direction
On a single wave   a wandering hill
Surging softly along in a powerful
Long-lost phosphorous seethe   folded in those wings
Those ultimate wings   home is like   home is
A folding of wings   Mother

Something whispers   one eye opens   a star shifts
Does not fall   from the eye of the Swan   he dreams

He sees the Southern Cross
Painfully over the horizon   drawing itself
Together   inching
Higher each night of the world   thorn
Points   tilted   he watches   not to be taken in
By the False Cross   as in   in
Another life   not taken

Knowing the true south rises
In a better make of cross   smaller   compact
And where its lights must appear.
Just after midnight he rises
And goes for it   joy with him
Springing out of the water
Disguised as wind   he checks each feather
As the stars burn out   waiting
Taking his course on faith until
The east begins
To pulse with unstoppable light.
Now darkness and dawn melt exactly
Together on one indifferent rill
Which sinks and is
Another   he lives

In renewed light, utterly alone!
In five days there is one ship
Dragging its small chewed off-white
Of ship-water   one candle in a too-human cabin
One vessel moving embedded
In its blue endurable country

Water warms   thereafter it is not
That the sea begins to tinge
Like a vast, laid smoke
But that he closes his eyes and feels himself
Turning whiter and whiter   upheld

At his whitest it is

Midnight   the equator   the center of the world
He sneaks across   afire
With himself   the stars change all their figures
Reach toward him   closer
And now begin to flow
Into his cracked-open mouth   down his throat
A string of lights   emblems   patterns of fire   all
Directions   myths   Hydras
Centaurs   Wolves   Virgins
Eating them all   eating
The void   possessing
Music   order   repose
Hovering   moving on his armbones   crawling
On warm air   covering the whole ocean   the sea deadens
He dulls   new constellations pale off
Him   unmapped roads open out of his breast
Beyond the sick feeling
Of those whose arms drag at treasures   it is like

Roosting   like holding one's arms out
In a clean nightshirt   a good dream   it is all
Instinct   he thinks   I have been born
This way.
                    Goes on
His small head holding
It all   the continents firmly fixed
By his gaze   five new ships turned
Rusty by his rich shadow.
His seamless shoulders of dawn-gold
Open   he opens
Them wider   an inch wider and he would

Trees   voices   white garments   meadows
Fail   under him again are
Mullet believing their freedom
Is to go anywhere they like in their collected shape
The form of an unthrown net
With no net anywhere near them.
Of these he eats.
                    Taking off again
He rocks forward three more days

Twenty-four hours a day
Balancing without thinking—
In doubt, he opens his bill
And vastness adjusts him
He trims his shoulders and planes   up

Up   stalls

In midocean   falls off
Comes down in a long, unbeheld
Curve that draws him deep into
                                    evening

Incredible pasture.

The Cross is up.   Looking in through its four panes
He sees something   a clean desk-top
Papers shuffled   hears
Something   a bird word
A too-human word   a word
That should have been somewhere spoken
That now can be frankly said
With long stiff lips into
The center of the Southern Cross
A word enabling one to fly

Out the window of office buildings
Lifts up on wings of its own
To say itself over and over   sails on
Under the unowned stars   sails as if walking
Out the window
That is what I said
That is what I should   that is

Dawn.   Panic   one moment of thinking
Himself in the hell of thumbs   once more   a man
Disguised in these wings   alone   No   again
He thinks   I am here   I have been born
This way   raised up from   raised up in
Myself   my soul
Undivided at last   thrown slowly forward
Toward an unmanned island.

Day overcomes   night comes over
Day with day already

Coming behind it   the sun halved in the east
The moon pressing feathers together.
Who thinks his bones are light
Enough, should try it   it is for everyone
He thinks   the world is for everything born—
I always had
These wings   buried deep in my back:
There is a wing-growing motion
Half-alive in every creature.

Comes down   skims for fifty miles
All afternoon lies skimming
His white shadow burning his breast
The flying-fish darting before him
In and out of the ash-film glaze

Or "because it is there"   into almighty cloud

In rain crying hoarsely
No place to go except
Forward into water in the eyes
Tons of water falling on the back
For hours   no sight   no insight
Beating up   trying
To rise above it   not knowing which way
Is up   no stars   crying
Home   fire   windows   for God
Sake   beating down   up   up-down
No help   streaming   another
Death   vertigo   falling
Upward   mother   God   country
Then seizing one grain of water in his mouth
Glides forward   heavy with cloud
Enveloped   gigantic   blazing with St. Elmo's
Fire   alone at the heart
Of rain   pure bird   heaving up   going

Up from that
                    and from that

Finally breaking

Out   where the sun is violently shining

On the useless enormous ploughland
Of cloud   then up
From just above it   up
Reducing the clouds more and more
To the color of their own defeat
The beauty of history   forgotten bird-
kingdoms packed in batting
The soft country   the endless fields
Raining away beneath him   to be dead
In one life is to enter
Another   to break out   to rise above   the clouds
Fail   pull back their rain

Dissolve.   All the basic blue beneath
Comes back, tattering through. He cries out
As at sight of home   a last human face
In a mirror dazzles   he reaches
Glides off on one wing   stretching himself wider
Floats into night   dark follows
At his pace
                    the stars' threads all connect
On him   and, each in its place, the islands
Rise   small form of beaches

Treeless   tons of guano   eggshells
Of generations
                    down
                              circling

Mistrusting

The land   coming in
Wings ultra-sensitive
To solids   the ground not reflecting his breast
Feet tentatively out
Creaking   close   closer
Earth blurring   tilt back and brace
Against the wind   closest   touch

Sprawl.   In ridiculous wings, he flounders,
He waddles   he goes to sleep
In a stillness of body not otherwhere to be found
Upheld for one night
With his wings closed   the stiff land failing to rock him.

Here mating   the new life
Shall not be lost   wings tangle
Over the beaches   over the pale
Sketches of coral reefs   treading the air
The father moving almost
At once out the vast blue door
He feels it swing open
The island fall off him   the sun

Rise in the shape of an egg   enormous
Over the islands
                            passing out
Over the cliffs   scudding
Fifteen feet from the poor skinned sod
Dazing with purity the eyes of turtles
Lizards   then feeling the world at once
Sheerly restore the sea   the island not
Glanced back at   where the egg
Fills with almighty feathers
The dead rise, wrapped in their wings
The last thread of white
Is drawn from the foot of the cliffs
As the great sea takes itself back
From around the island

And he sails out   heads north
His eyes already on icebergs
Ten thousand miles off   already feeling
The shiver of the equator as it crosses
His body at its absolute
Midnight whiteness
                            and death also
Stands waiting   years away
In midair   beats
Balanced on starpoints

Latitude and longitude correct
Oriented by instinct   by stars
By the sun in one eye the moon
In the other   bird-death

Hovers for years on its wings
With a time-sense that cannot fail
Waits to change
Him again   circles   abides   no feather
Falling   conceived by stars and the void
Is born perpetually
In midair   where it shall be
Where it is.

Sun

O Lord, it was all night
Consuming me   skin crawling tighter than any
Skin of my teeth. Bleary with ointments, dazzling
Through the dark house   man red as iron   glowing
Blazing up anew with each bad
Breath from the bellowing curtains

I had held the sun longer
Than it could stay   and in the dark it turned
My face on, infra-red: there were cracks circling
My eyes where I had squinted
Up from stone-blind sand, and seen
Eternal fire   coronas   huge

Vertical banners of flame
Leap scrollingly from the sun and tatter
To nothing in blue-veined space
On the smoked-crimson glass of my lids.
When the sun fell, I slit my eyeskins
In the dazed ruddy muddle of twilight

And in the mirror saw whiteness
Run from my eyes like tears   going upward
And sideways   slanting   as well as falling,

All in straight lines like rays
Shining   and behind me, careful not
To touch without giving me a chance

To brace myself   a smeared
Suffering woman came merging her flame-shaken
Body halo with mine   her nose still clownish
With oxides: walked to me sweating
Blood, and turned around. I peeled off
Her bathing suit like her skin   her colors

Wincing   she silently biting
Her tongue off   her back crisscrossed with stripes
Where winter had caught her and whipped her.
We stumbled together, and in the double heat
The last of my blond hair blazed up,
Burned off me forever   as we dived

For the cool of the bed
In agony even at holding hands   the blisters
On our shoulders shifting   crackling
Releasing boiling water on the sheets. *O Lord*
Who can turn out the sun, turn out that neighbor's
One bulb on his badminton court

For we are dying
Of light   searing each other   not able
To stop   to get away   she screaming O Lord
Apollo or *Water, Water*   as the moonlight drove
Us down on the tangled grid
Where in the end we lay

Suffering equally   in the sun
Backlashed from the moon's brutal stone
And meeting itself where we had stored it up
All afternoon in pain   in the gentlest touch
As we lay, O Lord,
In Hell, in love.

Power and Light

. . . only connect . . . —*E. M. Forster*

I may even be
A man, I tell my wife: all day I climb myself
Bowlegged up those damned poles   rooster-heeled in all
Kinds of weather   and what is there when I get
Home? Yes, woman trailing ground-oil
Like a snail, home is where I climb down,
And this is the house I pass through on my way

To power and light.
Going into the basement is slow, but the built-on smell of home
Beneath home gets better with age   the ground fermenting
And spilling through the barrel-cracks of plaster   the dark
Lying on the floor, ready for use   as I crack
The seal on the bottle   like I tell you it takes
A man to pour whiskey in the dark   and CLOSE THE DOOR between

The children and me.
The heads of nails drift deeper through their boards
And disappear. Years in the family dark have made me good
At this   nothing else is so good   pure fires of the Self
Rise crooning in lively blackness   and the silence around them,
Like the silence inside a mouth, squirms with colors,
The marvellous worms of the eye float out into the real

World   sunspots
Dancing as though existence were
One huge closed eye   and I feel the wires running
Like the life-force along the limed rafters   and all connections
With poles   with the tarred naked belly-buckled black
Trees I hook to my heels   with the shrill phone calls leaping
Long distance   long distances through my hands   all connections

Even the one
With my wife, turn good   turn better than good   turn good
Not quite, but in the deep sway of underground   among the roots
That bend like branches   all things connect   and stream
Toward light and speech   tingle   rock like a powerline in wind,
Like a man working, drunk on pine-moves   the sun in the socket
Of his shoulder   and on his neck dancing like dice-dots,

And I laugh
Like my own fate watching over me night and day   at home
Underground   or flung up on towers walking
Over mountains   my charged hair standing on end   crossing
The sickled, slaughtered alleys of timber
Where the lines loop and crackle on their gallows.
Far under the grass of my grave, I drink like a man

The night before
Resurrection Day. My watch glows with the time to rise
And shine. Never think I don't know my profession
Will lift me: why, all over hell the lights burn in your eyes,
People are calling each other   weeping with a hundred thousand
Volts   making deals   pleading   laughing like fate,
Far off, invulnerable   or with the right word pierced

To the heart
By wires I held, shooting off their ghostly mouths,
In my gloves. The house spins   I strap crampons to my shoes
To climb the basement stairs, sinking my heels in the tree-
life of the boards. Thorns! Thorns! I am bursting
Into the kitchen, into the sad way-station
Of my home, holding a double handful of wires

Spitting like sparklers
On the Fourth of July. Woman, I know the secret of sitting
In light   of eating a limp piece of bread   under
The red-veined eyeball of a bulb. It is all in how you are
Grounded. To bread I can see, I say, as it disappears and agrees
With me   the dark is drunk   and I am a man
Who turns on. I am a man.

The Flash

Something far off   buried deep and free
In the country   can always strike you dead
Center of the brain. There is never anything

It could be   but you go dazzled
Dazzled   and all the air in that
Direction swarms   waits

For that day-lightning,
For hoe blade   buckle   bifocal
To reach you. Whatever it does

Again is worth waiting for
Worth stopping the car   worth standing alone
For   and arranging the body

For light to score off you
In its own way, and send
Across the wheat   the broad silent

Blue valley, your long-awaited,
Blinding, blood-brotherly
Beyond-speech answer.

Adultery

We have all been in rooms
We cannot die in, and they are odd places, and sad.
Often Indians are standing eagle-armed on hills

In the sunrise   open wide to the Great Spirit
Or gliding in canoes   or cattle are browsing on the walls
Far away   gazing down with the eyes of our children

Not far away   or there are men driving
The last railspike, which has turned
Gold in their hands. Gigantic forepleasure lives

Among such scenes, and we are alone with it
At last. There is always some weeping
Between us   and someone is always checking

A wrist watch by the bed to see how much
Longer we have left. Nothing can come
Of this   nothing can come

Of us: of me with my grim techniques
Or you who have sealed your womb
With a ring of convulsive rubber:

Although we come together,
Nothing will come of us. But we would not give
It up, for death is beaten

By praying Indians   by distant cows   historical
Hammers   by hazardous meetings that bridge
A continent. One could never die here

Never die   never die
While crying. My lover, my dear one
I will see you next week

When I'm in town. I will call you
If I can. Please get hold of   please don't
Oh God, Please don't any more I can't bear . . . Listen:

We have done it again   we are
Still living. Sit up and smile,
God bless you. Guilt is magical.

Hedge Life

At morning we all look out
As our dwelling lightens; we have been somewhere.
With dew our porous home
Is dense, wound up like a spring,

Which is solid as motherlode
At night. Those who live in these apartments
Exist for the feeling of growth
As thick as it can get, but filled with

Concealment. When lightning
Strikes us, we are safe; there is nothing to strike, no bole
For all-fire's shattered right arm.
We are small creatures, surviving

On the one breath that grows
In our lungs in the complex green, reassured in the dawn-
silver heavy as wool. We wait
With crowded excitement

For our house to spring
Slowly out of night-wet to the sun; beneath us,
The moon hacked to pieces on the ground.
None but we are curled

Here, rising another inch,
Knowing that what held us solid in the moon is still
With us, where the outside flowers flash
In bits, creatures travel

Beyond us, like rain,
The great sun floats in a fringed bag, all stones quiver
With the wind that moves us.
We trade laughters silently

Back and forth, and feel,
As we dreamed we did last night, our noses safe in our fur,
That what is happening to us in our dwelling
Is true: That on either side

As we sleep, as we wake, as we rise
Like springs, the house is winding away across the fields,
Stopped only momentarily by roads,
King-walking hill after hill.

Snakebite

I am the one

And there is no way not
To be me   not to have been flagged

Down from underneath where back
Drop ten deadly and
Dead pine logs   here and where
They have fallen. Now come

To surprise:

Surprise at the dosage   at the shot
In the foot   at the ground

Where I walk   at what
It can do and the ways

Of giving: at dry fish scales
That can float away

In a long dusty arm

Now getting itself   frankly lost
Swimming against the current

Of pinestraw   winging under a stump
And a stone. Here is where
I am the one chosen:
Something has licked my heel

Like a surgeon

And I have a problem with
My right foot and my life.

It is hard to think of dying
But not of killing: hold the good
Foot ready to put on his head
Except that it leaves me only

On a stage of pine logs

Something like an actor   so
Let me sit down and draw

My tiny sword   unfold it
Where the dead sharpen needles
By the million. It is the role
I have been cast in;

It calls for blood.

Act it out before the wind
Blows: unspilt blood

Will kill you. Open
The new-footed tingling. Cut.
Cut deep, as a brother would.
Cut to save it. Me.

Bread

Old boys, the cracked boards spread before
You, bread and spam   fruit cocktail   powder
Of eggs. I who had not risen, but just come down
From the night sky   knew always this was nothing
Like home   for under the table I was cut deep
    In the shoes

To make them like sandals no stateside store
Ever sold   and my shirtsleeves were ragged as
Though chopped off by propellers in the dark.
It was all our squadron, old boys: it was thus
I sat with you on your first morning
    On the earth,

Old boys newly risen from a B-25 sinking slowly
Into the swamps of Ceram. Patrick said
We got out   we got out on the wings
And lived there   we spread our weight
Thin as we could   arms and legs spread, we lay
    Down night and day,

We lived on the wings. When one of us got to one
Knee to spear a frog   to catch a snake
To eat, we lost another inch. O that water,
He said. O that water. Old boys, when you first
Rose, I sat with you in the mess-tent
    On solid ground,

At the unsinkable feast, and looked at the bread
Given to lizard-eaters. They set it down
And it glowed from under   your tongues
Fluttered   you reached   the scales fell
From your eyes   all of us weightless from living
    On wings so long

No one could escape   no one could sink or swim
Or fly. I looked at your yellow eyeballs
Come up   evolved   drawn out of the world's slime
Amphibious eyes   and Patrick said Bread

Is good   I sat with you in my own last war
        Poem   I closed my eyes

I ate the food I ne'er had eat.

Sustainment

Here at the level of leaves supposedly for good
Stopped dead on the ground,
From the safety of picturesque height she was suddenly
Falling into the creek, the path
That held her become a flight of dirt. She
And the horse screamed all together, and went down.

Not knowing her, but knowing who she was
Before the creek bank gave
Way and the hooves broke through into creek-shaped air,
I come walking past all the remaining leaves
At the edge, knowing the snow of dirt
Down the bank has long since stopped,

Seeing the gap in the ledge above the stream
Still hold the print
Of a horse's head-down side, aware that I can stoop
With my love, who is with me, and feel
The earth of that blurred impression
Where it is cold with time and many unmeaningful rains.

Love, this wood can support our passion, though leaves
Are not enough death
To balance what we must act out. Let me double down
My autumn raincoat near the summer pit
Where the unknowable woman was riding proudly
The high crest of June, her pink shirt open-throated,

Her four hooves knocking deeply on the earth, the water
Unconsciously holding
Its flow in the pressure of sunlight, a snail
Glinting like a molar at the brink,
And felt it all give way in one clear scream
Lifted out the horse through her lipsticked mouth,

And then, ripping the path clean out of the woods,
Landslid down fifty feet,
Snapping high-grade leather, past any help in the world
As the horse turned over her, in a long changed shape
Loomed once, crossed the sun and the upper trees
Like a myth with a hold on her feet, and fell on her

With all his intended mass. Know, love, that we
Shall rise from here
Where she did not, lying now where we have come
Beneath the scrambling animal weight
Of lust, but that we may sense also
What it involves to change in one half-breath

From a thing half-beast—that huge-striding joy
Between the thighs—
To the wholly human in time
To die, here at this height
Near the vague body-print of a being that struggled
Up, all animal, leaving the human clothes

In their sodden bundle, and wandered the lane of water
Upstream and home,
His bridle dragging, his saddle
Maniacally wrenched, stopping often to drink
Entirely, his eyes receiving bright pebbles,
His head in his own image where it flowed.

A Letter

Looking out of the dark of the town
At midnight, looking down
Into water under the lighthouse:
Abstractedly, timelessly looking
For something beneath the jetty,
Waiting for the dazed, silent flash,

Like the painless explosion that kills one,
To come from above and slide over
And empty the surface for miles—
The useless, imperial sweep

Of utter light—you see
A thicket of little fish

Below the squared stone of your window,
Catching, as it passes,
The blue afterthought of the blaze.
Shone almost into full being,
Inlaid in frail gold in their floor,
Their collected vision sways

Like dust among them;
You can see the essential spark
Of sight, of intuition,
Travel from eye to eye.
The next leg of light that comes round
Shows nothing where they have been,

But words light up in the head
To take their deep place in the darkness,
Arcing quickly from image to image
Like mica catching the sun:
The words of a love letter,
Of a letter to a long-dead father,

To an unborn son, to a woman
Long another man's wife, to her children,
To anyone out of reach, not born,
Or dead, who lives again,
Is born, is young, is the same:
Anyone who can wait no longer

Beneath the huge blackness of time
Which lies concealing, concealing
What must gleam forth in the end,
Glimpsed, unchanging, and gone
When memory stands without sleep
And gets its strange spark from the world.

The Head-Aim

Sick of your arms,
You must follow an endless track

Into the world that crawls,
That gets up on four legs
When the moon rises from a bed of grass,
The night one vast and vivid
Tangle of scents.

You must throw your arms
Like broken sticks into the alder creek

And learn to aim the head.
There is nothing you can pick up
With fingers any more, nothing
But the new head choked with long teeth,
The jaws, on fire with rabies,

Lifting out of the weeds.
This is the whole secret of being

Inhuman: to aim the head as you should,
And to hold back in the body
What the mouth might otherwise speak:
Immortal poems—those matters of life and death—
When the lips curl back

And the eyes prepare to sink
Also, in the jerking fur of the other.

Fox, marten, weasel,
No one can give you hands.
Let the eyes see death say it all
Straight into your oncoming face, the head
Not fail, not tell.

Dark Ones

We in all lights are coming
Home   transfixed and carried away
From where we work:

                              when the sun moves down
The railroad tracks, and dies a little way
Off in the weeds, lights we have made come on
And carry us: this is how
We are coming, O all
Our dark ones, our darlings.

Now we float down from aircraft

From trains   now at our car
Lights the doors
                    of our home
Garage spring open   we enter and fall
Down in our souls to pray for light
To fail: fail pleasantly with gin,
With problems of children   but fail   fade
Back into our tinted walls:

Let the airports carry it all night

Let the highways support it on their poles
Shining on beer cans
                           rolling drunk in the weeds
After their one fearful bounce:
Lord, let those lights give up
On us: office lights, cast like shade
On fire, from their banks of blue sticks:
A light like the mange, on papers,

On the heads emerging from scratch pads,

Those crammed, volcanic faces
Dreadful to see.
                    All those are creatures
Of light. Let them leave me   let all
Human switches be finally snapped
Off at once   let me go with my dark
Darling, into myself: O let there be
Someone in it with me:

Let us move everything

Off us, and lie touching
With all we have.

O creature
Of darkness, let us lie stretched out
Without shadow or weight.
Fasten your hand where my heart
Would burst, if I moved
From your side. You are

Who holds. Hold then   hold my heart

Down from bursting
Into light: hold it still and at rest
In the center of walls
That cannot get their colors
Back without light: O Glory, there is nothing
Yet at the sill   no grain or thread
Of sun   no light as the heart

Beats, feeding from your hand.

Encounter in the Cage Country

What I was would not work
For them all, for I had not caught
The lion's eye. I was walking down

The cellblock in green glasses   and came
At last to the place where someone was hiding
His spots in his black hide.

Unchangeably they were there,
Driven in as by eyes
Like mine, his darkness ablaze

In the stinking sun of the beast house.
Among the crowd, he found me
Out   and dropped his bloody snack

And came to the perilous edge
Of the cage, where the great bars tremble
Like wire. All Sunday ambling stopped,

The curved cells tightened around
Us all   as we saw he was watching only

Me. I knew the stage was set, and I began

To perform   first saunt'ring   then stalking
Back and forth like a sentry   faked
As if to run   and at one brilliant move

I made as though drawing a gun from my hip-
bone, the bite-sized children broke
Up   changing their concept of laughter,

But none of this changed his eyes, or changed
My green glasses. Alert, attentive,
He waited for what I could give him:

My moves   my throat   my wildest love,
The eyes behind my eyes. Instead, I left
Him, though he followed me right to the end

Of concrete. I wiped my face, and lifted off
My glasses. Light blasted the world of shade
Back under every park bush   the crowd

Quailed from me   I was inside and out
Of myself   and something was given a life-
mission to say to me hungrily over

And over and over   *your moves are exactly right*
For a few things in this world: we know you
When you come, Green Eyes, Green Eyes.

For the Last Wolverine

They will soon be down

To one, but he still will be
For a little while   still will be stopping

The flakes in the air with a look,
Surrounding himself with the silence
Of whitening snarls. Let him eat
The last red meal of the condemned

To extinction, tearing the guts

From an elk. Yet that is not enough
For me. I would have him eat

The heart, and, from it, have an idea
Stream into his gnawing head
That he no longer has a thing
To lose, and so can walk

Out into the open, in the full

Pale of the sub-Arctic sun
Where a single spruce tree is dying

Higher and higher. Let him climb it
With all his meanness and strength.
Lord, we have come to the end
Of this kind of vision of heaven,

As the sky breaks open

Its fans around him and shimmers
And into its northern gates he rises

Snarling   complete   in the joy of a weasel
With an elk's horned heart in his stomach
Looking straight into the eternal
Blue, where he hauls his kind. I would have it all

My way: at the top of that tree I place

The New World's last eagle
Hunched in mangy feathers   giving

Up on the theory of flight.
Dear God of the wildness of poetry, let them mate
To the death in the rotten branches,
Let the tree sway and burst into flame

And mingle them, crackling with feathers,

In crownfire. Let something come
Of it   something gigantic   legendary

Rise beyond reason over hills
Of ice   SCREAMING   that it cannot die,
That it has come back, this time
On wings, and will spare no earthly thing:

That it will hover, made purely of northern

Lights, at dusk   and fall
On men building roads: will perch

On the moose's horn like a falcon
Riding into battle   into holy war against
Screaming railroad crews: will pull
Whole traplines like fibres from the snow

In the long-jawed night of fur trappers.

But, small, filthy, unwinged,
You will soon be crouching

Alone, with maybe some dim racial notion
Of being the last, but none of how much
Your unnoticed going will mean:
How much the timid poem needs

The mindless explosion of your rage,

The glutton's internal fire   the elk's
Heart in the belly, sprouting wings,

The pact of the "blind swallowing
Thing," with himself, to eat
The world, and not to be driven off it
Until it is gone, even if it takes

Forever. I take you as you are

And make of you what I will,
Skunk-bear, carcajou, bloodthirsty

Non-survivor.
                    Lord, let me die   but not die
Out.

The Bee

To the football coaches of Clemson College, 1942

One dot
Grainily shifting   we at roadside and

The smallest wings coming   along the rail fence out
Of the woods   one dot   of all that green. It now
Becomes flesh-crawling   then the quite still
Of stinging. I must live faster for my terrified
Small son   it is on him. Has come. Clings.

Old wingback, come
To life. If your knee action is high
Enough, the fat may fall in time   God damn
You, Dickey, *dig*   this is your last time to cut
And run   but you must give it everything you have
Left, for screaming near your screaming child is the sheer
Murder of California traffic: some bee hangs driving

Your child
Blindly onto the highway. Get there however
Is still possible. Long live what I badly did
At Clemson   and all of my clumsiest drives
For the ball   all of my trying to turn
The corner downfield   and my spindling explosions
Through the five-hole over tackle. O backfield

Coach Shag Norton,
Tell me as you never yet have told me
To get the lead out   scream whatever will get
The slow-motion of middle age off me   I cannot
Make it this way   I will have to leave
My feet   they are gone   I have him where
He lives   and down we go singing with screams into

The dirt,
Son-screams of fathers   screams of dead coaches turning
To approval   and from between us the bee rises screaming
With flight   grainily shifting   riding the rail fence
Back into the woods   traffic blasting past us
Unchanged, nothing heard through the air-
conditioning glass   we lying at roadside full

Of the forearm prints
Of roadrocks   strawberries on our elbows as from
Scrimmage with the varsity   now we can get
Up   stand   turn away from the highway   look straight
Into trees. See, there is nothing coming out   no

Smallest wing   no shift of a flight-grain   nothing
Nothing. Let us go in, son, and listen

For some tobacco-
mumbling voice in the branches   to say "That's
a little better,"   to our lives still hanging
By a hair. There is nothing to stop us   we can go
Deep   deeper   into elms, and listen to traffic die
Roaring, like a football crowd from which we have
Vanished. Dead coaches live in the air, son   live

In the ear
Like fathers, and *urge*   and *urge*. They want you better
Than you are. When needed, they rise and curse you   they scream
When something must be saved. Here, under this tree,
We can sit down. You can sleep, and I can try
To give back what I have earned by keeping us
Alive, and safe from bees: the smile of some kind

Of savior—
Of touchdowns, of fumbles, battles,
Lives. Let me sit here with you, son
As on the bench, while the first string takes back
Over, far away   and say with my silentest tongue, with the man-
creating bruises of my arms   with a live leaf a quick
Dead hand on my shoulder, "Coach Norton, I am your boy."

Mary Sheffield

Forever at war news   I am
thinking there   nearly naked
low green of water   hard overflowed forms

water sits running   quietly carving
red rocks forcing white from the current

parts of midstream   join
I sit with one hand   joining
the other hand shyly   fine sand under

still feet   and Mary Sheffield
singing   passed-through

sustained in the   poured forms of live oaks
taking root   in the last tracks
of left and right foot   river flowing

into my mind   nearly naked
the last day but one   before world war.

When the slight wind dies
each leaf still has   two places
such music   touched alive

guitar strings   sounds   join
In the stone's shoal   of swimming

the best twigs I have   the best
sailing leaves   in memory
pass   threading through

all things spread sail   sounds gather
on blunt stone   streaming white

E minor   gently running
I sit with one hand   in the strange life
of the other   watching water throng

on one stone   loving Mary Sheffield
for her chord changes   river always

before war   I sit down and
anywhere   water flows   the breastplate of time
rusts off me   sounds   green forms   low voice

new music   long   long
past.

Deer Among Cattle

Here and there in the searing beam
Of my hand going through the night meadow
They all are grazing

With pins of human light in their eyes.
A wild one also is eating
The human grass,

Slender, graceful, domesticated
By darkness, among the bred-
for-slaughter,

Having bounded their paralyzed fence
And inclined his branched forehead onto
Their green frosted table,

The only live thing in this flashlight
Who can leave whenever he wishes,
Turn grass into forest,

Foreclose inhuman brightness from his eyes
But stands here still, unperturbed,
In their wide-open country,

The sparks from my hand in his pupils
Unmatched anywhere among cattle,

Grazing with them the night of the hammer
As one of their own who shall rise.

The Leap

The only thing I have of Jane MacNaughton
Is one instant of a dancing-class dance.
She was the fastest runner in the seventh grade,
My scrapbook says, even when boys were beginning
To be as big as the girls,
But I do not have her running in my mind,
Though Frances Lane is there, Agnes Fraser,
Fat Betty Lou Black in the boys-against-girls
Relays we ran at recess: she must have run

Like the other girls, with her skirts tucked up
So they would be like bloomers,
But I cannot tell; that part of her is gone.
What I do have is when she came,
With the hem of her skirt where it should be
For a young lady, into the annual dance
Of the dancing class we all hated, and with a light

Grave leap, jumped up and touched the end
Of one of the paper-ring decorations

To see if she could reach it. She could,
And reached me now as well, hanging in my mind
From a brown chain of brittle paper, thin
And muscular, wide-mouthed, eager to prove
Whatever it proves when you leap
In a new dress, a new womanhood, among the boys
Whom you easily left in the dust
Of the passionless playground. If I said I saw
In the paper where Jane MacNaughton Hill,

Mother of four, leapt to her death from a window
Of a downtown hotel, and that her body crushed-in
The top of a parked taxi, and that I held
Without trembling a picture of her lying cradled
In that papery steel as though lying in the grass,
One shoe idly off, arms folded across her breast,
I would not believe myself. I would say
The convenient thing, that it was a bad dream
Of maturity, to see that eternal process

Most obsessively wrong with the world
Come out of her light, earth-spurning feet
Grown heavy: would say that in the dusty heels
Of the playground some boy who did not depend
On speed of foot, caught and betrayed her.
Jane, stay where you are in my first mind:
It was odd in that school, at that dance.
I and the other slow-footed yokels sat in corners
Cutting rings out of drawing paper

Before you leapt in your new dress
And touched the end of something I began,
Above the couples struggling on the floor,
New men and women clutching at each other
And prancing foolishly as bears: hold on
To that ring I made for you, Jane—
My feet are nailed to the ground
By dust I swallowed thirty years ago—
While I examine my hands.

Coming Back to America

We descended the first night from Europe   riding the ship's sling
Into the basement.   Forty floors of home weighed on us.   We broke through
To a room, and fell to drinking madly with all those boozing, reading
The Gideon Bible in a dazzle of homecoming scripture   Assyrian armies
The scythes of chariots blazing like the windows of the city   all cast
Into our eyes in all-night squinting barbaric rays of violent unavoidable glory.
There were a "million dollars in ice cubes" outside our metal door;
The dead water clattered down hour after hour as we fought with salesmen
For the little blocks that would make whole our long savage drinks.
I took a swaying shower, and we packed the whole bathroom of towels into
Our dusty luggage, battling paid-for opulence with whatever weapon
Came to hand.   We slept; I woke up early, knowing that I was suffering
But not why. My breath would not stir, nor the room's.   I sweated
Ice in the closeness   my head hurt with the Sleep of a Thousand Lights
That the green baize drapes could not darken.   I got up, bearing
Everything   found my sharp Roman shoes   went out   following signs
That said SWIMMING POOL.   Flashing bulbs on a red-eyed panel, I passed
Through ceiling after ceiling of sleeping salesmen and whores, and came out
On the roof.   The pool water trembled with the few in their rooms
Still making love.   This was air.   A skinny girl lifeguard worked
At her nails; the dawn shone on her right leg in a healthy, twisted flame.
It made me squint   slick and lacquered with scars   with the wild smoky city
Around it   the great breath to be drawn above sleepers   the hazy
Morning towers.   We sat and talked   she said a five-car wreck
Of taxis in Bensonhurst had knocked her out and taken her kneecap
But nothing else.   I pondered this   the sun shook off a last heavy
Hotel   and she leapt and was in the fragile green pool as though
I were still sleeping it off eleven floors under her: she turned in a water
Ballet by herself   graceful   unredeemable   her tough face exactly
As beautiful and integral as the sun come out of the city.   Vulnerable,
Hurt in my country's murderous speed, she moved   and I would have taken
Her in my arms in water throbbing with the passion of travelling men,
Unkillable, both of us, at forty stories in the morning   and could have
Flown with her   our weightlessness preserved by the magic pool drawn from
Under the streets   out of that pond   passing over the meaningless
Guardrail   feeling the whole air pulse like water sleepless with desperate
Love-making   lifting us out of sleep into the city summer dawn
Of hundreds of feet of gray space spinning with pigeons now under

Us   among new panels of sun in the buildings blasting light silently
Back and forth across streets between them: could have moved with her
In all this   over the floods of glare raised up in sheets   the gauze
Distances where warehouses strove to become   over the ship I had ridden
Home in   riding gently   whitely   beneath.   Ah, lift us, green
City water, as we turn the harbor around with our legs   lazily changing
The plan of the city with motions like thistles   like the majestic swirl
Of soot   the winged seed of pigeons   and so would have held her
As I held my head   a-stammer with light   defending it against the terrible
Morning sun of drinkers   in that pain, exhalting in the blind notion
Of cradling her somewhere above ships and buses   in the air like a water
Ballet   dancing deep among the dawn buildings in a purely private
Embrace of impossibility   a love that could not have been guessed:
Woman   being   idea   temple dancer   tough girl from Bensonhurst
With a knee rebuilt out of sunlight   returned-to amazement   O claspable
Symbol   the unforeseen on home ground   The thing that sustains us forever
in other places!

The Birthday Dream

At the worst place in the hills above the city
Late at night I was driving   cutting through
The overbalancing slums. There was no soul or body
In the streets. I turned right   then left somewhere
Near the top, dead-ending into a wall. A car
Pulled out and blocked me. Four men detached from it.
I got out too. It was Saturday night   the thrill
Of trouble shimmered on the concrete. One shadow
Had a bottle of wine. I stood and said, say, Buddy,
Give me a drink of that wine   not at all fearing
Shaking   as on anything but dream bones   dream
Feet I would have. He said, We're looking for somebody
To beat up. It won't be me, I said   and took him
By the arm with one hand and tossed him into the air.
Snow fell from the clearness in time for there
To be a snowbank for him to fall into elbow-first.
He got up, holding the wine. This guy is too big,
He said, he is too big for us; get the Professor.
Four of us stood together as the wind blew and the snow

Disappeared   and watched the lights of the city
Shine   some others appearing   among them   some
Going out   and watched the lava-flow of headlights off
In the valley. Like a gunshot in the building next to us
A light went out   and down came a middle-aged man
With a hairy chest; his gold-trimmed track shorts had
YMCA Instructor on them   and I knew it was time
For the arm game. We stretched out on our stomachs
On top of the dead-end wall. On one side was the drop
We had all been looking into   and the other side sank
Away with my car   with the men: two darks lifted
Us toward the moon. We put our elbows on the wall
And clasped palms. Something had placed gold-rimmed
Glasses of wine beside us   apartment lights hung in them
Loosely   and we lay nose to nose at the beginning
Of that ceremony; I saw the distant traffic cross him
From eye to eye. Slowly I started to push   and he
To push. My body grew as it lay   forced against his
But nothing moved. I could feel the blood vessels
In my brow distend   extend   grow over the wall like vines
And in my neck   swell like a trumpet player's: I gritted
Into his impassive face   where the far lights moved   this is
What I want   this is what I came for. The city pulsed
And trembled in my arm   shook with my effort   for miles
In every direction   and from far below in the dark
I heard the voices of men raised up in a cry of wild
Encouragement   of terror   joy   as I strained to push
His locked hand down. I could not move him   did not want
To move him   would not yield. The world strove with my body
To overcome   the highways shuddered   writhed   came apart
At the centerline   far below us a silent train went by
A warning light   and slowly from the embodying air was loaded
With thousands of ghostly new cars   in tiered racks
The light like pale wine in their tinted windshields.
The culture swarmed around me like my blood   transfigured
By force. I put my head down and pushed with all my life
And writing sprang under my forehead   onto the concrete:
Graffitti scratched with a nail   a boot heel   an ice pick
A tire iron   a scrap of metal from a stolen car   saying
You are here   and I woke

Entangled with my wife, who labored   pled   screamed
To bring me forth. The room was full of mildness. I was forty.

False Youth: Two Seasons

SUMMER

I have had my time   dressed up as something else,
Have thrown time off my track by my disguise.
This can happen when one puts on a hunter's cap,
An unearned cowboy hat   a buckskin coat   or something
From outer space, that a child you have got has got
For Christmas. It is oddest and best in the uniform
Of your country   long laid in boxes and now let out
To hold the self-betrayed form in the intolerant shape
Of its youth.   I have had my time doing such,

Sitting with Phyllis Huntley as though I were my own
Son surrounded by wisteria   hearing mosquitoes without
The irritation middle age puts on their wings: have sat
By a big vine going round the rotten, imperial pillars
Of southern Mississippi. All family sounds drew back

Through the house in time to leave us hanging
By rusty chains. In the dark, dressed up in my militant youth,
I might have just come down from the black sky   alive
With an ancient war   dead with twenty million   twenty
Years ago   when my belt cried aloud for more holes
And I soft-saluted every changing shape   that saluted me,
And many that did not: every tree   pole   every bush
Of wisteria   as I came down from the air toward some girl

Or other. Decked out in something strange my country
Dreamed up   I have had my time in that swing,
The double chair that moves at the edge of dark
Where the years stand just out of range of house-
light, their hands folded at their fat waists, respectful
As figures at a funeral. And from out of the air an enormous
Grin came down, to remake my face   as I thought of children
Of mine almost her age   and a mosquito droned like an immortal
Engine. I have had my time of moving back and forth

With Phyllis Huntley   and of the movement of her small hand
Inside mine, as she told me how she learned to work
An electric computer in less than two afternoons of her job
At the air base. The uniform tightened as I sat
Debating with a family man away from home. I would not listen
To him, for what these boys want is to taste a little life
Before they die: that is when their wings begin to shine
Most brilliantly from their breasts into the darkness
And the beery breath of a fierce boy demands of the fat man
He's dying of   more air   more air   through the tight belt
Of time   more life   more now   than when death was faced
Less slowly   more now than then   more now.

WINTER

Through an ice storm in Nashville I took a student home,
Sliding off the road twice or three times; for this
She asked me in. She was a living-in-the-city
Country girl   who on her glazed porch broke off
An icicle, and bit through its blank bone: brought me
Into another life   in the shining-skinned clapboard house
Surrounded by a world where creatures could not stand,
Where people broke hip after hip. At the door my feet
Took hold, and at the fire I sat down with her blind
Grandmother. All over the double room were things
That would never freeze, but would have taken well
To ice: long tassels hanging from lamps   curtains
Of beads   a shawl on the mantel   all endless things
To touch   untangle   all things intended to be
Inexhaustible to hands. She sat there, fondling
What was in reach   staring into the fire with me
Never batting a lid. I talked to her easily   eagerly
Of my childhood   my mother whistling in her heartsick bed
My father grooming his gamecocks. She rocked, fingering
The lace on the arm of the chair   changing its pattern
Like a game of chess. Before I left, she turned and raised
Her hands, and asked me to bend down. An icicle stiffened
In my stomach   as she drew on my one lock of hair
Feeling the individual rare strands   not pulling any
Out. I closed my eyes as she put her fingertips lightly
On them   and saw, behind sight   something in me   fire

Swirl in a great shape like a fingerprint   like none other
In the history of the earth   looping   holding its wild lines
Of human force. Her forefinger   then her keen nail
Went all the way along the deep middle line of my brow
Not guessing but knowing   quivering   deepening
Whatever I showed by it. She said, you must laugh a lot
Or be in the sun, and I began to laugh quietly against
The truth, so she might feel what the line she followed
Did then. Her hands fell   and she said to herself, My God,
To have a growing boy. You cannot fool the blind, I knew
As I battled for air   standing   laughing a lot as she
Said I must do   squinting also as in the brightest sun
In Georgia   to make good   to make good the line in my head.
She lifted her face like a swimmer; the fire swarmed
On my false, created visage   as she rocked and took up
The tassel of a lamp. Some kind of song may have passed
Between our closed mouths as I headed   into the ice.
My face froze with the vast world of time   in a smile
That has never left me since my thirty-eighth year
When I skated like an out-of-shape bear to my Chevrolet
And spun my wheels on glass: that time when age was caught
In a thaw in a ravelling room   when I conceived of my finger
Print as a shape of fire   and of youth as a lifetime search
For the blind.

PART THREE

MAY DAY SERMON

May Day Sermon to the Women of Gilmer County, Georgia, by a Woman Preacher Leaving the Baptist Church

Each year at this time I shall be telling you of the Lord
—Fog, gamecock, snake and neighbor—giving men all the help they need
To drag their daughters into barns. Children, I shall be showing you
The fox hide stretched on the door   like a flying squirrel   fly
Open   to show you the dark where the one pole of light is paid out
In spring by the loft, and in it the croker sacks sprawling and shuttling
Themselves into place as it comes   comes   through spiders dead
Drunk on their threads   the hogs' fat bristling   the milk
Snake in the rafters unbending through gnats to touch the last place
Alive on the sun with his tongue   I shall be flickering from my mouth
Oil   grease cans   lard cans   nubbins   cobs   night
Coming   floating   each May with night coming I cannot help
Telling you how he hauls her to the centerpole   how the tractor moves
Over as he sets his feet and hauls   hauls   ravels her arms and hair
In stump chains: Telling: telling of Jehovah come and gone
Down on His belly   descending   creek-curving   blowing His legs

Like candles, out   putting North Georgia copper on His head
To crawl in under the door in dust red enough to breathe
The breath of Adam into: Children, be brought where she screams and begs
To the sacks of corn and coal   to nails   to the swelling ticks
On the near side of mules, for the Lord's own man has found the limp
Rubber that lies in the gulley   the penis-skin like a serpent
Under the weaving willow.
                            Listen: often a girl in the country,
Mostly sweating   mostly in spring, deep enough in the holy Bible
Belt, will feel her hair rise up   arms rise, and this not any wish

Of hers, and clothes like lint shredding off her   abominations
In the sight of the Lord: will hear the Book speak like a father
Gone mad: each year at this time will hear the utmost sound
Of herself, as her lungs cut, one after one, every long track
Spiders have coaxed from their guts   stunned spiders fall
Into Pandemonium   fall   fall   and begin to dance like a girl
On the red clay floor of Hell   she screaming   her father screaming
Scripture   CHAPter and verse   beating it into her with a weeping
Willow branch   the animals stomping   she prancing and climbing
Her hair   beasts shifting from foot to foot about the stormed
Steel of the anvil   the tractor gaslessly straining   believing
It must pull up a stump   pull   pull down the walls of the barn
Like Dagon's temple   set the Ark of the Lord in its place   change all
Things for good, by pain. Each year at this time you will be looking up
Gnats in the air   they boil   recombine   go mad with striving
To form the face of her lover, as when he lay at Nickajack Creek
With her by his motorcycle   looming   face trembling with exhaust
Fumes   humming insanely—each May you hear her father scream like God
And King James as he flails   cuds richen   bulls chew themselves whitefaced
Deeper into their feed bags, and he cries something the Lord   cries
Words! Words! Ah, when they leap   when they are let out of the Bible's
Black box   they whistle   they grab the nearest girl and do her hair up
For her lover in root-breaking chains   and she knows she was born to hang
In the middle of Gilmer County   to dance, on May Day, with holy
Words all around her   with beasts with insects   O children NOW
In five bags of chicken-feed the torsos of prophets form   writhe
Die out as her freckled flesh   as flesh and the Devil twist and turn
Her body to love   cram her mouth with defiance   give her words
To battle with the Bible's in the air: she shrieks sweet Jesus and God
I'm glad   O my God-darling   O lover   O angel-stud   dear heart
Of life put it in me *give*   you're killing   KILLING: each
Night each year at this time I shall be telling you of the snake-
doctor drifting from the loft, a dragonfly, where she is wringing
Out the tractor's muddy chains   where her cotton socks prance,
Where her shoes as though one ankle were broken, stand with night
Coming   and creatures drawn by the stars, out of their high holes
By moon-hunger driven   part the leaves   crawl out of Grimes Nose
And Brasstown Bald: on this night only I can tell how the weasel pauses
Each year in the middle of the road   looks up at the evening blue
Star   to hear her say again   O again   YOU CAN BEAT ME TO DEATH

And I'll still be glad:
                    Sisters, it is time to show you rust
Smashing the lard cans more in   spring after spring   bullbats
Swifts   barn swallows   mule bits clashing on walls   mist turning
Up white out of warm creeks: all over, fog taking the soul from the body
Of water   gaining   rising up trees   sifting up through smoking green
Frenzied levels of gamecocks sleeping from the roots   stream-curves
Of mist: wherever on God's land is water, roads rise up the shape of rivers
Of no return: O sisters, it is time   you cannot sleep with Jehovah

Searching for what to be, on ground that has called Him from His Book:
Shall He be the pain in the willow, or the copperhead's kingly riding
In kudzu, growing with vines toward the cows   or the wild face working over
A virgin, swarming like gnats   or the grass of the west field, bending
East, to sweep into bags and turn brown   or shall He rise, white on white,
From Nickajack Creek as a road?   The barn creaks like an Ark   beasts
Smell everywhere the streams drawn out by their souls   the flood-
sigh of grass in the spring   they shall be saved   they know as she screams
Of sin   as the weasel stares   the hog strains toward the woods
That hold its primeval powers:
                              Often a girl in the country will find herself
Dancing with God in a mule's eye, twilight drifting in straws from the dark
Overhead of hay   cows working their sprained jaws sideways at the hour
Of night all things are called: when gnats in their own midst and fury
Of swarming-time, crowd into the barn   their sixty-year day consumed
In this sunset   die in a great face of light that swarms and screams
Of love.
            Each May you will crouch like a sawhorse to make yourself
More here   you will be cow chips   chickens croaking for her hands
That shook the corn over the ground   bouncing   kicked this way
And that, by the many beaks   and every last one of you will groan
Like nails barely holding   and your hair be full of the gray
Glints of stump chains.   Children, each year at this time you shall have
Back-pain, but also heaven   but also   also this lovely other life-
pain between the thighs: woman-child or woman in bed in Gilmer
County   smiling in sleep like blood-beast and Venus together
Dancing the road as I speak, get up   up in your socks and take
The pain you were born for: that rose through her body straight
Up from the earth like a plant, like the process that raised overhead
The limbs of the uninjured willow.
                              Children, it is true

That the kudzu advances, its copperheads drunk and tremendous
With hiding, toward the cows   and wild fences cannot hold the string
Beans as they overshoot their fields: that in May the weasel loves love
As much as blood   that in the dusk bottoms young deer stand half
In existence, munching cornshucks   true that when the wind blows
Right   Nickajack releases its mist   the willow-leaves stiffen once
More   altogether   you can hear   each year at this time you can hear
No   Now, no   Now   Yes   Again   More   O   O my God
I love it   love you   don't leave   don't   don't stop O GLORY
Be:
          More dark   more coming   fox-fire crawls over the okra-
patch   as through it a real fox creeps to claim his father's fur
Flying on doornails   the quartermoon on the outhouse begins to shine
With the quartermoonlight of this night   as she falls and rises,
Chained to a sapling like a tractor   WHIPPED for the wind in the willow
Tree   WHIPPED for Bathsheba and David   WHIPPED for the woman taken
Anywhere   anytime   WHIPPED for the virgin sighing   bleeding
From her body   for the sap and green of the year   for her own good
And evil:
          Sisters, who is your lover? Has he done nothing but come
And go?   Has your father nailed his cast skin to the wall as evidence
Of sin?   Is it flying like a serpent in the darkness   dripping pure radiant venom
Of manhood?
          Yes, but *he* is unreeling in hills between his long legs
The concrete of the highway   his face in the moon beginning
To burn   twitch   dance like an overhead swarm   he feels a nail
Beat through his loins far away   he rises in pain and delight, as spirit
Enters his sex   sways   forms   rises with the forced, choked, red
Blood of her red-headed image, in the red-dust, Adam-colored clay
Whirling and leaping   creating   calling: O on the dim, gray man-
track of cement flowing into his mouth   each year he turns the moon back
Around on his handlebars   her image going all over him like the wind
Blasting up his sleeves. He turns off the highway, and
                                        Ah, children,
There is now something élse to hear: there is now this madness of engine
Noise in the bushes   past reason   ungodly   squealing   reverting
Like a hog turned loose in the woods   Yes, as he passes the first
Trees of God's land   game-hens overhead   and the farm is ON
Him   everything is more   *more*   MORE as he enters the black
Bible's white swirling ground   O daughters   his heartbeat great

With trees   some blue leaves coming   NOW   and right away fire
In the right eye   Lord   more   MORE   O Glory   land
Of Glory: ground-branches hard to get through   coops where fryers huddle
To death, as the star-beast dances and scratches at their home-boards,
His rubber stiffens on its nails: Sisters, understand about men and sheaths:

About nakedness: understand how butterflies, amazed, pass out
Of their natal silks   how the tight snake takes a great breath   bursts
Through himself and leaves himself behind   how a man casts finally
Off everything that shields him from another   beholds his loins
Shine with his children forever   burn with the very juice
Of resurrection: such shining is how the spring creek comes
Forth from its sunken rocks   it is how the trout foams and turns on
Himself   heads upstream, breathing mist like water, for the cold
Mountain of his birth   flowing   sliding in and through the ego-
maniacal sleep of gamecocks   shooting past a man with one new blind
Side   who feels his skinned penis rise like a fish through the dark
Woods, in a strange lifted-loving form   a snake about to burst
Through itself on May Day   and leave behind on the ground   still
Still   the shape of a fooled thing's body:

                                          he comes on,   comes
Through the laurel, wiped out on his right by an eye-twig   now he
Is crossing the cow track   his hat in his hand going on before
His face   then up   slowly over   over like the Carolina moon
Coming into Georgia   feels the farm close its Bible and ground-
fog over him   his dark side blazing   something whipping
By, beyond sight: each year at this time I shall be letting you
Know when she cannot stand   when the chains fall back on
To the tractor   when you should get up   when neither she nor the pole
Has any more sap   and her striped arms and red hair must keep her
From falling   when she feels God's willow laid on her, at last,
With no more pressure than hay, and she has finished crying to her lover's
Shifting face   and his hand when he gave it   placed it, unconsumed,
In her young burning bush.   Each year by dark she has learned

That home is to hang in   home is where your father cuts the baby
Fat from your flanks for the Lord, as you scream for the viny foreskin
Of the motorcycle rider. Children, by dark   by now, when he drops
The dying branch and lets her down   when the red clay flats
Of her feet hit the earth   all things have heard   fog, gamecock
Snake and lover—and we listen: Listen, children, for the fog to lift

The form of sluggish creeks into the air: each spring, each creek
On the Lord's land flows in two   O sisters, lovers, flows in two
Places: where it was, and in the low branches of pines where chickens
Sleep in mist   and that is where you will find roads floating free
Of the earth   winding   leading unbrokenly out of the farm of God
The father:
                    Each year at this time she is coming from the barn   she
Falls once, hair hurting her back   stumbles walking naked
With dignity   walks with no help to the house   lies face down
In her room, burning   tuning in   hearing in the spun rust-
groan of bedsprings, his engine root and thunder like a pig,
Knowing who it is   must be   knowing that the face of gnats will wake
In the woods, as a man: there is nothing else this time of night
But her dream of having wheels between her legs: tires, man,
Everything she can hold, pulsing together   her father walking
Reading   intoning   calling   his legs blown out by the ground-
fogging creeks of his land: Listen   listen like females each year
In May   O glory   to the sound   the sound of your man gone wild
With love in the woods   let your nipples rise   and leave your feet
To hear: This is when moths flutter in from the open, and Hell
Fire of the oil lamp shrivels them   and it is said
To her: said like the Lord's voice trying to find a way
Outside the Bible   O sisters   O women and children who will be
Women of Gilmer County   you farm girls and Ellijay cotton mill
Girls, get up   each May Day   up in your socks   it is the father
Sound   going on about God   making, a hundred feet down,
The well beat its bucket like a gong: she goes to the kitchen,
Stands with the inside grain of pinewood whirling on her like a cloud
Of wire   picks up a useful object   two   they are not themselves
Tonight   each hones itself as the moon does   new by phases
Of fog   floating unchanged into the house   coming atom
By atom   sheepswool   different smokes   breathed like the Word
Of nothing, round her seated father. Often a girl in the country,
Mostly in spring   mostly bleeding   deep enough in the holy Bible
Belt   will feel her arms rise up   up   and this not any wish
Of hers   will stand, waiting for word.   O daughters, he is rambling
In Obadiah   the pride of thine heart hath deceived thee, thou
That dwelleth in the clefts of the rock, whose habitation is high
That saith in his heart   O daughters   who shall bring me down
To the ground?   And she comes down   putting her back into

The hatchet   often   often   he is brought down   laid out
Lashing   smoking   sucking wind: Children, each year at this time
A girl will tend to take an ice pick in both hands   a lone pine
Needle   will hover   hover: Children, each year at this time
Things happen quickly   and it is easy for a needle to pass
Through the eye of a man bound for Heaven   she leaves it   naked goes
Without further sin through the house   floating in and out of all
Four rooms   comes onto the porch on cloud-feet   steps down and out
And around to the barn   pain changing   her old screams hanging
By the hair around her: Children, in May, often a girl in the country
Will find herself lifting wood   her arms like hair rising up
To undo locks   raise latches   set gates aside   turn all things
Loose   shoo them out   shove   pull   O hogs are leaping ten
Million years back through fog   cows walking worriedly   passing out
Of the Ark   from stalls where God's voice cursed and mumbled
At milking time   moving   moving   disappearing   drifting
In cloud   cows in the alders already lowing far off   no one
Can find them each year: she comes back to the house and grabs double
Handfuls of clothes
                           and her lover, with his one eye of amazing grace
Of sight, sees her coming as she was born   swirling   developing
Toward him   she hears him grunt   she hears him creaking
His saddle   dead-engined   she conjures one foot whole from the ground-
fog to climb him behind   he stands up   stomps   catches   roars
Blasts the leaves from a blinding twig   wheels   they blaze up
Together   she breathing to match him   her hands on his warm belly
His hard blood renewing like a snake   O now   now as he twists
His wrist, and takes off with their bodies:
                                             each May you will hear it
Said that the sun came as always   the sun of next day burned
Them off with the mist: that when the river fell back on its bed
Of water   they fell from life   from limbs   they went with it
To Hell   three-eyed   in love, their legs around an engine, her arms
Around him.   But now, except for each year at this time, their sound
Has died: except when the creek-bed thicks its mist   gives up
The white of its flow to the air   comes off   lifts into the pinepoles
Of May Day   comes back as you come awake in your socks and crotchhair
On new-mooned nights of spring   I speak   you listen and the pines fill
With motorcycle sound as they rise, stoned out of their minds on the white
Lightning of fog   singing   the saddlebags full of her clothes

Flying   snagging   shoes hurling away   stockings grabbed-off
Unwinding and furling on twigs: all we know   all we could follow
Them by was her underwear   was stocking after stocking where it tore
Away, and a long slip stretched on a thorn   all these few gave
Out. Children, you know it: that place was where they took
Off into the air   died   disappeared   entered my mouth   your mind
Each year   each pale, curved breath   each year as she holds him
Closer wherever he hurtles   taking her   taking her   she going forever
Where he goes   with the highways of rivers   through one-eyed
Twigs   through clouds of chickens   and grass with them bends
Double   the animals lift their heads   peanuts and beans exchange
Shells in joy   joy like the speed of the body and rock-bottom
Joy: joy by which the creek bed appeared to bear them out of the Bible
's farm   through pine-clouds of gamecocks where no earthly track
Is, but those risen out of warm currents   streams born to hang
In the pines of Nickajack Creek: tonight her hands are under
His crackling jacket   the pain in her back enough to go through
Them both   her buttocks blazing in the sheepskin saddle: tell those
Who look for them   who follow by rayon stockings   who look on human
Highways   on tracks of cement and gravel   black weeping roads
Of tar: tell them that she and her rider have taken no dirt
Nor any paved road   no path for cattle   no county trunk or trail
Or any track upon earth, but have roared like a hog on May Day
Through pines and willows: that when he met the insane vine
Of the scuppermong   he tilted his handlebars back and took
The road that rises in the cold mountain spring from warm creeks:
O women in your rayon from Lindale, I shall be telling you to go
To Hell   by cloud   down where the chicken walk is running
To weeds   and anyone can show you where the tire marks gave out
And her last stocking was cast   and you stand as still as a weasel
Under Venus   before you dance   dance yourself blue with blood-
joy looking into the limbs   looking up into where they rode
Through cocks tightening roots with their sleep-claws. Children,
They are gone: gone as the owl rises, when God takes the stone
Blind sun off its eyes, and it sees   sees hurtle in the utter dark
Gold of its sight, a boy and a girl buried deep in the cloud
Of their speed   drunk, children   drunk with pain and the throttle
Wide open, in love   with a mindless sound   with her red hair
In the wind streaming gladly for them both   more than gladly
As the barn settles under the weight of its pain   the stalls fill once

More with trampling like Exodus   the snake doctor gone the rats beginning
On the last beans   and all the chicks she fed, each year at this time
Burst from their eggs as she passes:
                                        Children, it is true that mice
No longer bunch on the rafters, but wade the fields like the moon,
Shifting in patches   ravenous   the horse floats, smoking with flies,
To the water-trough   coming back less often   learning to make
Do with the flowing drink of deer   the mountain standing   cold
Flowing into his mouth   grass underfoot   dew   horse or what
ever he is now   moves back into trees where the bull walks
With a male light spread between his horns   some say screams like a girl
And her father yelling together:
                                        Ah, this night in the dark laurel
Green of the quartermoon I shall be telling you that the creek's last
Ascension is the same   is made of water and air   heat and cold
This year as before: telling you not to believe every scream you hear
Is the Bible's: it may be you or me   it may be her sinful barn-
howling for the serpent, as her father whips her, using the tried
And true rhythms of the Lord.   Sisters, an old man at times like this
Moon, is always being found   yes found with an ice-pick on his mind,
A willow limb in his hand.   By now, the night-moths have come
Have taken his Bible and read it   have flown, dissolved, having found
Nothing in it for them.   I shall be telling you at each moon   each
Year at this time, Venus rises   the weasel goes mad at the death
In the egg, of the chicks she fed for him by hand: mad in the middle
Of human space he dances   blue-eyed   dances with Venus rising
Like blood-lust over the road   O tell your daughters   tell them
That the creek's ghost can still   O still can carry double
Weight of true lovers   any time   any night as the wild turkeys claw
Into the old pines of gamecocks   and with a cow's tongue, the Bible calls
For its own, and is not heard   and even God's unsettled great white father-
head with its ear to the ground, cannot hear   know   cannot pick
Up where they are   where her red hair is streaming through the white
Hairs of His centerless breast: with the moon   He cries with the cow all
Its life penned up with Noah in the barn   talk of original
Sin as the milk spurts   talk of women   talk of judgment and flood
And the promised land:
                                        Telling on May Day, children: telling
That the animals are saved without rain   that they are long gone
From here   gone with the sun   gone with the woman taken

In speed   gone with the one-eyed mechanic   that the barn falls in
Like Jericho at the bull's voice   at the weasel's dance   at the hog's
Primeval squeal   the uncut hay walks when the wind prophesies in the west
Pasture   the animals move   roam, with kudzu creating all the earth
East of the hayfield: Listen: each year at this time the county speaks
With its beasts and sinners   with its blood: the county speaks of nothing
Else each year at this time: speaks as beasts speak to themselves
Of holiness learned in the barn: Listen   O daughters   turn   turn
In your sleep   rise with your backs on fire   in spring   in your socks
Into the arms of your lovers: every last one of you, listen one-eyed
With your man   in hiding   in fog where the animals walk through
The white breast of the Lord   muttering   walk with nothing
To do but be   in the spring laurel in the mist and self-sharpened
Moon   walk through the resurrected creeks   through the Lord
At their own pace   the cow shuts its mouth and the Bible is still
Still open at anything   we are gone   the barn wanders over the earth.

THE EYE-BEATERS, BLOOD, VICTORY, MADNESS, BUCK-HEAD AND MERCY

Diabetes

One night I thirsted like a prince
Then like a king
Then like an empire   like a world
On fire. I rose and flowed away and fell
Once more to sleep. In an hour I was back
In the kingdom   staggering, my belly going round with self-
Made night-water, wondering what
The hell. Months of having a tongue
Of flame convinced me: I had better not go
On this way. The doctor was young

And nice. He said, I must tell you,
My friend, that it is needles moderation
And exercise. You don't want to look forward
To gangrene and kidney

Failure   boils blindness infection skin trouble falling
Teeth coma and death.
                         O.K.
                               In sleep my mouth went dry
With my answer   and in it burned the sands
Of time with new fury. Sleep could give me no water
But my own. Gangrene in white
Was in my wife's hand at breakfast
Heaped like a mountain. Moderation, moderation,
My friend, and exercise. Each time the barbell
Rose   each time a foot fell
Jogging, it counted itself
One death   two death   three death and resurrection
For a little while. Not bad! I always knew it would have to be
                                       somewhere around
The house: the real
Symbol of Time I could eat
And live with, coming true when I opened my mouth:
True in the coffee and the child's birthday
Cake   helping sickness be fire-
tongued, sleepless and water-

logged   but not bad, sweet sand
Of time, my friend, an everyday—
A livable death at last.

II

UNDER BUZZARDS

[for Robert Penn Warren]

Heavy summer. Heavy. Companion, if we climb our mortal bodies
High with great effort, we shall find ourselves
Flying with the life
Of the birds of death. We have come up
Under buzzards   they face us

Slowly   slowly circling   and as we watch them they turn us
Around, and you and I spin
Slowly, slowly rounding
Out the hill. We are level
Exactly on this moment; exactly on the same bird-

plane with those deaths. They are the salvation of our sense
Of glorious movement. Brother, it is right for us to face
Them every which way, and come to ourselves and come
From every direction
There is. Whirl and stand fast!
Whence cometh death, O Lord?
On the downwind, riding fire,

Of Hogback Ridge.
But listen: what is dead here?
They are not falling but waiting   but waiting
Riding, and they may know
The rotten, nervous sweetness of my blood.

Somewhere riding the updraft
Of a far forest fire, they sensed the city sugar
The doctors found in time.
My eyes are green as lettuce with my diet,
My weight is down,

One pocket nailed with needles and injections, the other dragging
With sugar cubes to balance me in life
And hold my blood

Level, level. Tell me, black riders, does this do any good?
Tell me what I need to know about my time
In the world. O out of the fiery

Furnace of pine-woods, in the sap-smoke and crownfire of needles,
Say when I'll die. When will the sugar rise boiling
Against me, and my brain be sweetened
to death?
In heavy summer, like this day.
All right! Physicians, witness! I will shoot my veins
Full of insulin. Let the needle burn
In. From your terrible heads
The flight-blood drains   and you are falling back
Back to the body-raising

Fire.
Heavy summer. Heavy. My blood is clear
For a time. Is it too clear? Heat waves are rising
Without birds. But something is gone from me,
Friend. This is too sensible. Really it is better
To know when to die   better for my blood
To stream with the death-wish of birds.
You know, I had just as soon crush
This doomed syringe
Between two mountain rocks, and bury this needle in needles

Of trees. Companion, open that beer.
How the body works   how hard it works
For its medical books is not
Everything: everything is how
Much glory is in it: heavy summer is right.

For a long drink of beer. Red sugar of my eyeballs
Fells them turn blindly
In the fire   rising   turning   turning
Back to Hogback Ridge, and it is all
Delicious, brother: my body is turning   is flashing unbalanced
sweetness everywhere, and I am calling my birds.

Messages

[to and from my sons]

I
BUTTERFLIES

Over and around   grass banked and packed short and holding back
Water, we have been
Playing, my son, in pure abandon,
And we still are. We play, and play inside our play and play
Inside of that, where butterflies are increasing
The deeper we get
And lake-water ceases to strain. Ah, to play in a great field of light
With your son, both men, both
Young and old! Ah, it was then, Chris,

As now! You lay down on the earth
Dam, and I rambled forth and did not look and found
And found like a blueprint of animal
Life, the whole skeleton of a cow. O son, left
In pure abandon, I sat down inside the bones in the light
Of pine trees, studying the tiny holes
In the head, and where the ants
Could not get through, the nerves had left
Their messages. I sat in the unmoving hearse
Flying, carried by cow-bones in pure
Abandon, back to you. I picked up the head
And inside the nose-place were packets
And whole undealt decks
Of thin bones, like shaved playing cards.
I won the horns. They twisted loose from the forehead
And would not twist back   as I gambled and rocked
With the skull in my lap,
The cow not straining to live. In that car I rode
Far off
and in
and in
While you were sleeping off the light
Of the world.
And when I came
From the bone dust in pure abandon, I found you lying on the earth

Dam, slanted in the grass that held back
The water, your hands behind your head,
Gazing through your eyelids into the universal
Light, and the butterflies were going

. . . Here

                              here

            here
            here

                         from here

    madly over

                    to

        here

                              here.

They went over you   here   and through you
            Here   no   yes and tattered apart,
            Beat out over water and back
            To earth, and over my oldest
    Son asleep: their ragged, brave wings
Pulsed on the blue flowers   shook like the inmost
    Play   and blazed all over and around
            Where you slept holding back
Water without strain.
                         That is all, but like all joy

On earth and water,

                   in bones and in wings and in light
          It is a gamble. It is play, son, now
      As then. I put the horns beside you in the grass
      And turned back to my handsprings and my leaps.

II
GIVING A SON TO THE SEA

    Gentle blondness and the moray eel go at the same time
    On in my mind as you grow, who fired at me at the age
            Of six, a Christmas toy for child
          Spies: a bullet with a Special Secret
Message Compartment. My hands undid the bullet meant
           For my heart, and it read aloud
        "I love you." That message hits me most
    When I watch you swim, that being your only talent.
    The sea obsesses you, and your room is full of it:

          Your room is full
        Of flippers and snorkels and books
          On spearfishing.
                O the depths,
    My gentle son. Out of that room and into the real
        Wonder and weightless horror
    Of water   into the shifts of vastness
    You will probably go, for someone must lead
      Mankind, your father and your sons,
        Down there to live, or we all die
          Of crowding. Many of yóu
          Will die, in the cold roll
      Of the bottom currents, and the life lost
    More totally than anywhere, there in the dark
Of no breath at all.
             And I must let you go, out of your gentle
      Childhood into your own man suspended
        In its body, slowly waving its feet
    Deeper and deeper, while the dark grows, the cold
        Grows careless, the sun is put
         Out by the weight of the planet
    As it sinks to the bottom. Maybe you will find us there
      An agonizing new life, much like the life

Of the drowned, where we will farm eat sleep and bear children
    Who dream of birds.
                            Switch on your sea-lamp, then,
    And go downward, son, with your only message
    Echoing. Your message to the world, remember,
                Came to your father
    At Christmas like a bullet. When the great fish roll
    With you, herded deep in the deepest dance,
    When the shark cuts through your invisible
                Trail, I will send back
    That message, though nothing that lives
                Underwater will ever receive it.
    That does not matter, my gentle blond
        Son. That does not matter.

Mercy

        Ah, this night   this night mortality wails out
Over Saint Joseph's   this night and every   over Mercy   Mercy
Mercy Manor. Who can be dressed right for the long cry?
Who can have his tie knotted to suit the cinder Doctors'
        Parking Lot? O yes I'm walking   and we go   I go
                In   into a whorehouse
                And convent rolled
        Into   into something   into the slant streets of slum
            Atlanta. I've brought the House Mother
            A bottle of gin. She goes for ice
        Rattling the kitchen somewhere over   under
            The long cry. Fay hasn't come in
                Yet; she's scrubbing
        For Doctor Evans. Television bulks as the girls pass
                In, rising
            Up the stairs, and one says to me, What
    Say, Good Loking. Something wails like a held-down saint
    In Saint Joseph's. The kids, the Mother   the House
Mother says, all act like babies these days. Some of them are, I say
            In a low scream. Not all, she says, not all.
                You ever been a nurse?
        I ask. No; my husband was in wholesale furniture.

Passed away last year of a kidney
Disease; they couldn't do anything for him
At all: he said you go and work
With those girls who've been so good
To me. And here I am, Good
Looking. Fay ought to be
Here in a little while.
                    The girls that went up are coming
Down, turning the leaves
Of the sign-out book. You waiting for Fay? Yes.
She'll be a little while. O.K.
More ice, to ice-pack
The gin. The last door opens.
It is Fay. This night mortality wails out. Who died,
My love? Whom could you not do anything for? Is that some stranger's
Blood on your thigh? O love I know you by the lysol smell you give
Vaseline. Died   died
On the table.
                    She'll just be a minute. These are good girls, the Mother
Says. Fay's a good girl. She's been married; her aunt's
Keeping the kids. I reckon you know that, though. I do,
And I say outside
Of time, there must be some way she can strip
Blood off   somebody's blood   strip and comb down and out
That long dark hair. She's overhead
Naked she's streaming
In the long cry   she has her face in her hands
In the shower, thinking of children
Her children in and out
Of Saint Joseph's   she is drying   my eyes burn
Like a towel   and perfume and disinfectant battle
In her armpits   she is stamping
On the ceiling to get her shoes to fit: Lord, Lord, where are you,
Fay? O yes, you big cow-bodied
Love o yes you have changed
To black   you are in deep
Dark and your pale face rages
With fatigue. Mother   Mother   House
Mother of Mercy
Manor, you can have the rest

Of the gin. The cinders of the parking lot are blazing all around
Saint Joseph's; the doctors are leaving. Turn out the light as you go up
To your husband's furniture, and come
Here to me, you big
Bosomed hard handed hard
Working worker for Life, you. I'll give you something
Good   something like a long cry
Out over the ashes of cars   something like a scream through
                                        hundreds of bright
Bolted-down windows. O take me into
Your black. Without caring, care
For me. Hold my head in your wide scrubbed
Hands bring up
My lips. I wail like all
Saint Joseph's   like mortality
This night   and I nearly am dead
In love   collapsed on the street   struck down
By my heart, with the wail
Coming to me, borne in ambulances voice
By voice into Saint Joseph's   nearly dead
On arrival   on the table beyond
All help: She would bend
Over me like this   sink down
With me in her white dress
Changing to black   we sink
Down flickering
Like television   like Arthur Godfrey's face
Coming on   huge   happy
About us   happy
About everything   O bring up
My lips   hold them down don't let them cry
With the cry   close   closer   eyeball to eyeball
In my arms, O queen of death
Alive, and with me at the end.

Two Poems of Going Home

I

LIVING THERE

The Keeper
Is silent   is living in the air not
Breathable, of time. It is gray
Winter in the woods where he lives.
They've been cut down; you can see through
What he is keeping   what used to be a room
In a house with one side turned
To trees. There are no woods now, only other
Houses. Old Self like a younger brother, like a son, we'd come rambling
Out of the house in wagons, turn off the back
Driveway and bump at full bump-speed down
Through the woods, the branches flickering
With us, with the whole thing of home
A blur, gone rolling in leaves. But people are always coming

To know woods   to know rooms in houses
That've been torn down. Where we live, you and I,
My youth and my middle
Age   where we live with our family, miles away
From home, from my old home,
I have rooms
I keep, but this old one, the one where I grew
Up, is in the air
Of winter it is over
Other houses like a ghost. The house lives only
In my head while I look and the sun sinks
Through the floors that were here: the floors
Of time. Brother, it is a long way to the real

House I keep. Those rooms are growing
Intolerable in minds I made
Up, though all seems calm when I walk
Into them as though I belonged there. Sleepers are stirring   an arm lies
Over a face, and the lights are burning
In the fish tank. It is not like this,
But it will be. One day those forms will rise
And leave   and age

And come back   and that house will flame like this
In the Keeper's head
With the last sun; it will be gone,
And someone will not be able
To believe there is only nothing

Where his room was, next to his father's
Blue-eyed   blue-eyed   the fixer   the wagon-master
Blazing in death
With life: will not be able to look
Into windows of the room where he saw,
For the first time, his own blood.
That room fills only with dying
Solar flame   with only the backyard wind
Only the lack
Of trees, of the screech-owl my mother always thought
Was a hurt dog. And tell me for the Lord God
's sake, where are all our old
Dogs?
Home?
Which way is that?
Is it this vacant lot? These woven fences?
Or is it hundreds

Of miles away, where I am the Keeper
Of rooms turning night and day
Into memory? Is it the place I now live
And die in   the place I manage
In? Is it with those people who never knew
These people, except for me? Those people sleeping
Eating my food   loading
Their minds with love   their rooms with what they love
And must lose, and cannot forget? Those fish
Tanks   those James Bond posters   those telescopes
And microscopes and the hidden pictures
Of naked girls? Who are they? And will they come foolishly
Back to stare at nothing
But sunset, where the blood flowed and the wagon wheel grew whole in the hands
Of the bald-headed father? Will they look into those rooms where now
They sleep, and see nothing but moonlight   nothing but everything
Far and long

Gone, long gone? Why does the Keeper go blind
With sunset? The mad, weeping Keeper who can't keep
A God-damned thing   who knows he can't keep everything
Or anything alive: none of his rooms, his people
His past, his youth, himself,
But cannot let them die? Yes, I keep
Some of those people, not in wagons but in the all-night glimmer
Of fish   in the secret glimmer
Of unfolding girls. I think I know—
I know them well. I call them, for a little while, sons.

II

LOOKING FOR THE BUCKHEAD BOYS

Some of the time, going home, I go
Blind and can't find it.
The house I lived in growing up and out
The doors of high school is torn
Down and cleared
Away for further development, but that does not stop me.
First in the heart
Of my blind spot are
The Buckhead Boys. If I can find them, even one,
I'm home. And if I can find him   catch him in or around
Buckhead, I'll never die; it's likely my youth will walk
Inside me like a king.

First of all, going home, I must go
To Wender and Roberts' Drug Store, for driving through I saw it
Shining   renewed   renewed
In chromium, but still there.
It's one of the places the Buckhead Boys used to be, before
Beer turned teen-ager.
Tommy Nichols
Is not there. The Drug Store is full of women
Made of cosmetics. Tommy Nichols has never been
In such a place: he was the Number Two Man on the Mile
Relay Team in his day.
What day?
My day. Where was I?
Number Three, and there are some sunlit pictures
In the Book of the Dead to prove it: the 1939

North Fulton High School Annual. Go down,
Go down

To Tyree's Pool Hall, for there was more
Concentration of the spirit
Of the Buckhead Boys
In there, than anywhere else in the world.
Do I want some shoes
To walk all over Buckhead like a king
Nobody knows? Well, I can get them at Tyree's;
It's a shoe store now. I could tell you where every spittoon
Ought to be standing. Charlie Gates used to say one of these days
I'm gonna get myself the reputation of being
The bravest man in Buckhead. I'm going in Tyree's toilet
And pull down my pants and take a shit.
Maybe
Charlie's the key: the man who would say that would never leave
Buckhead. Where is he? Maybe I ought to look up
Some Old Merchants. Why didn't I think of that
Before?
Lord, Lord! Like a king!

Hardware. Hardware and Hardware Merchants
Never die, and they have everything on hand
There is to know. Somewhere in the wood-screws Mr. Hamby may have
My Prodigal's Crown on sale. He showed up
For every football game at home
Or away, in the hills of North Georgia. There he is, as old
As ever.
Mr. Hamby, remember me?
God A'Mighty! Ain't you the one
Who fumbled the punt and lost the Russell game?
That's right.
How're them butter fingers?
Still butter, I say,
Still fumbling, But what about the rest of the team? What about Charlie
Gates?
He the boy that got lime in his eye from the goal line
When y'all played Gainesville?
Right.
I don't know. Seems to me I see . . .

See? See? What does Charlie Gates see in his eye burning
With the goal line? Does he see a middle-aged man from the Book
Of the Dead looking for him in magic shoes
From Tyree's disappeared pool hall?

Mr. Hamby, Mr. Hamby,

Where? Where is Mont Black?

Paralyzed. Doctors can't do nothing.

Where is Dick Shea?

Assistant Sales Manager

Of Kraft Cheese.

How about Punchy Henderson?

Died of a heart attack

Watching high school football

In South Carolina.

Old Punchy, the last
Of the windsprinters, and now for no reason the first
Of the heart attacks.

Harmon Quigley?

He's up at County Work Farm

Sixteen. Doing all right up there; be out next year.

Didn't anybody get to be a doctor

Or lawyer?

Sure. Bobby Laster's a chiropractor. He's right out here

At Bolton; got a real good business.

Jack Siple?

Moved away.

Gordon Hamm?

Dead

In the war.

O the Book
Of the Dead, and the dead bright sun on the page
Where the team stands ready to explode
In all directions with Time. Did you say you see Charlie

Gates every now and then?

Seems to me.

Where?

He may be out yonder at the Gulf Station between here and Sandy
Springs.

Let me go pull my car out
Of the parking lot in back
Of Wender and Roberts'. Do I need gas? No; let me drive around the block
Let me drive around Buckhead
A few dozen times   turning   turning in my foreign
Car till the town spins   whirls till the chrome vanishes
From Wender and Roberts'   the spittoons are remade
From the sun itself   the dead pages flutter the hearts rise up, that lie
In the ground, and Bobby Laster's backbreaking fingers
Pick up a cue-stick   Tommy Nichols and I rack the balls
And Charlie Gates walks into Tyree's un-
imaginable toilet.
I go north
Now, and I can use fifty
Cents' worth of gas.
It is Gulf. I pull in and praise the Lord Charlie
Gates comes out. His blue shirt dazzles
Like a baton-pass. He squints he looks at me
Through the goal line. Charlie, Charlie, we have won away from
We have won at home
In the last minute. Can you see me? You say
What I say: where in God
Almighty have you been all this time? I don't know,
Charlie. I don't know. But I've come to tell you a secret
That has to be put into code. Understand what I mean when I say
To the one man who came back alive
From the Book of the Dead   to the bravest man
In Buckhead   to the lime-eyed ghost
Blue-wavering in the fumes
Of good Gulf gas, "Fill 'er up."
With wine? Light? Heart-attack blood? The contents of Tyree's toilet? The beer
Of teen-age sons? No; just
"Fill 'er up. Fill 'er up, Charlie."

The Place

We are nerve-blowing now. Unspeaking and whiteness around. Warm wind
Was never here. Snow has no move. So this
Has placed us. Dark is with it nearly, for this last of day-

Shaking of shores.

Night is down on us; hold me with all your fur.
These waters have put every grain of their ice
Into our red hand-marrow. Statue-faced, let us breathe
On each other   let us breathe the ice

Sweeping into the air, for it has crossed to
Within us, rigidly airborne, impassable from crossing
Miles of lake-freeze in our
Overwhelming direction. They hang true lovers with thread-

steel through the nose. It hurts straight up and down
Inside us. This is where we come, and we are cross-
eyed with love and every tooth
root aches. Lover, this is where:

I can tell you here.

Apollo

. . . whoever lives out there in space must surely
call Earth "the blue planet" . . . —*Ed White*

I. FOR THE FIRST MANNED MOON ORBIT

So long
So long as the void
Is hysterical, bolted out, you float on nothing

But procedure alone,

Eating, sleeping like a man
Deprived of the weight of his own
And all humanity in the name

Of a new life
and through this, making new
Time slowly, the moon comes.
Its mountains bulge
They crack they hold together
Closer   spreading   smashed crust
Of uncanny rock   ash-glowing   alchemicalizing the sun
With peace: with the peace of a country

Bombed-out by the universe.
                                You lean back from the great light-
                        shattered face   the pale blaze
                          Of God-stone coming

                Close   too close, and the dead seas turn
                          The craters hover   turn
                          Their dark side to kill
                          The radio, and the one voice
        Of earth.
                          You and your computers have brought out
                          The silence of mountains the animal
                          Eye has not seen since the earth split.
                          Since God first found geometry
                              Would move   move
                          In mysterious ways. You hang

        Mysteriously, pulling   the moon-dark pulling,
                          And solitude breaks down
                Like an electrical system: it is something

                          Else: nothing is something
                          Something I am trying

                          To say O God

Almighty! To come back! To complete the curve   to come back
    Singing with procedure   back through the last dark
        Of the moon, past the dim ritual
Random stones of oblivion, and through the blinding edge
        Of moonlight into the sun

           And behold

    The blue planet steeped in its dream

  Of reality, its calculated vision shaking with
        The only love.

II. THE MOON GROUND

       You look as though
You know me, though the world we came from is striking
    You in the forehead like Apollo. Buddy,
We have brought the gods. We know what it is to shine
    Far off, with earth. We alone

Of all men, could take off
Our shoes and fly. One-sixth of ourselves, we have gathered,
Both of us, under another one
Of us overhead. He is reading the dials he is understanding
Time, to save our lives. You and I are in earth
light and deep moon
shadow on magic ground
Of the dead new world, and we do not but we could
Leap over each other, like children in the universal playground
of stones
but we must not play
At being here: we must look
We must look for it: the stones are going to tell us
Not the why but the how of all things. Brother, your gold face flashes
On me. It is the earth. I hear your deep voice rumbling from the body
Of its huge clothes   Why did we come here
It does not say, but the ground looms, and the secret
Of time is lying
Within amazing reach. It is everywhere
We walk, our glass heads shimmering with absolute heat
And cold. We leap slowly
Along it. We will take back the very stones
Of Time, and build it where we live. Or in the cloud
striped blue of home, will the secret crumble
In our hands with air? Will the moon-plague kill our children
In their beds? The Human Planet trembles in its black
Sky with what we do   I can see it hanging in the god-gold only
Brother of your face. We are this world: we are
The only men. What hope is there at home
In the azure of breath, or here with the stone
Dead secret? My massive clothes bubble around me
Crackling with static and Gray's
Elegy helplessly coming
From my heart, and I say I think something
From high school I remember Now
Fades the glimmering landscape on the sight, and all the air
A solemn stillness holds. Earth glimmers
And in its air-color a solemn stillness holds
It. O brother! Earth-faced god! APOLLO! My eyes blind
With unreachable tears   my breath goes all over

Me and cannot escape. We are here to do one
Thing only, and that is rock by rock to carry the moon to take it
Back. Our clothes embrace we cannot touch we cannot
Kneel. We stare into the moon
dust, the earth-blazing ground. We laugh, with the beautiful craze
Of static. We bend, we pick up stones.

The Cancer Match

Lord, you've sent both
And may have come yourself. I will sit down, bearing up under
The death of light very well, and we will all
Have a drink. Two or three, maybe.
I see now the delights

Of being let "come home"
From the hospital.
Night!
I don't have all the time
In the world, but I have all night.
I have space for me and my house,
And I have cancer and whiskey

In a lovely relation.
They are squared off, here on my ground. They are fighting,
Or are they dancing? I have been told   and told
That medicine has no hope, or anything
More to give,

But they have no idea
What hope is, or how it comes, You take these two things:
This bourbon and this thing growing. Why,
They are like boys! They bow
To each other

Like judo masters,
One of them jumping for joy, and I watch them struggle
All around the room, inside and out
Of the house, as they battle
Near the mailbox

And superbly
For the street-lights! Internally, I rise like my old self
To watch: and remember, ladies and gentlemen,
We are looking at this match
From the standpoint

Of tonight
Alone. Swarm over him, my joy, my laughter, my Basic Life
Force! Let your bright sword-arm stream
Into that turgid hulk, the worst
Of me, growing:

Get 'im, O Self
Like a belovèd son! One more time! Tonight we are going
Good   better and better   we are going
To win, and not only win but win
Big, win big.

Venom

[for William Haast]

Forever, it comes from the head. *Where does it end?*
In life-blood. All over it, in fact, like thrown
Off and thrown-again light. There is little help
For it, but there is some.

*The priest of poison: where is he? Who is
His latest snake? How does he work?*

He has taken it all, brother, and his body lies
With its hand in ice, in a lung

Of iron
but at last he rises, his heart changing
What the snake thought. Tooth-marks all over
Him are chattering of life, not death, not
What God gave them. He shimmers

With healing. He will lie down again
With him the snake has entered.
His blood will flow the length
Of the veins of both. They will clasp arms and double-dream

Of the snake in the low long smothering
Sun. Look down! They stretch out giving
And taking. Clouds of family beat the windows
Of doctors with their breath. Here lies

The man made good by a hundred
Bites. It is not God but a human
Body they pray to: Turn the poison
Round turn it back on itself O turn it

Good: better than life they whisper:
Turn it, they hammer whitely:
Turn it, turn it,
Brother.

Blood

In a cold night
Of somebody. Is there other
Breath? What did I say?
Or do?

Mercy.
MERCY!

There is nothing,
But did I do it? I did something.
Merciful, merciful
O God, what? And

Am I still drunk?
Not enough O

Is there any light O where
Do you *touch* this room?
O father

Of Heaven my head cannot
Lift but my hand maybe—
Nobody is breathing   what weapon
was it? Light smashes

Down there is nothing but
Blood blood all over

Me and blood. Her hair is smeared.
My God what has got loose
In here at last? Who *is*

This girl? She is
Some other town some far
From home: knife
Razor, fingernails O she has been opened
Somewhere and yet

She sighs she turns in the slaughtered sheets
To me in the blood of her children.
Where in what month?

In the cold in the blood
Of life, she turns
To me, and my weapon
Will never recover its blood.
Who is

This woman? No matter; she is safe.
She is safe with me.

In the Pocket

NFL

Going backward
All of me and some
Of my friends are forming a shell   my arm is looking
Everywhere and some are breaking
In   breaking down
And out   breaking
Across, and one is going deep   deeper
Than my arm. Where is Number One hooking
Into the violent green alive
With linebackers? I cannot find him he cannot beat
His man   I fall back more
Into the pocket   it is raging and breaking

Number Two has disappeared into the chalk
Of the sideline   Number Three is cutting with half
A step of grace   my friends are crumbling
Around me the wrong color
Is looming   hands are coming
Up and over between
My arm and Number Three: throw it hit him in the middle
Of his enemies   hit move scramble
Before death and the ground
Come up   LEAP STAND KILL DIE STRIKE

Now.

Knock

Sharing   what sharing   quickly who
Is outside   in   both you together here
And unseen out   let the bed huddle and jump

Naked in the quick dead middle
Of the night, making what is to be
There   you being broken by something

Open where the door thins out
Making frames of the room's early-
warning wood   is the code still

The same can the five fingers
Of the hand still show against
Anything? Have they come for us?

Victory

By September *3rd* I had made my bundle
Of boards and a bag of nails. America, I was high
On Okinawa, with the fleet lying on its back
Under me, whispering "I can't help it"
                                    and all ships firing up fire
Fighting liquids   sucking seawater, hoses climbing and coloring
The air, for Victory. I was clear-seeing

The morning   far-seeing backward
And forward from the cliff. I turned on the ground
And dug in, my nails and bag of magic
Boards from the tent-floor trembling to be
A throne. I was ready to sail
The island toward life
After death, left hand following right into the snail
shelled ground, then knocking down and nailing down my chair like a box
seat in the worldwide window of peace   and sat and lay down my arms
On the stomped grains of ammo-crates heavy with the soles
Of buddies who had helped me wreck the tent
In peace-joy, and of others long buried
At sea. The island rocked with the spectrum
Bombardment of the fleet   and there I was
For sure   saved and plucked naked to my shirt
And lids. I raised my head to the sun.
What I saw was two birthdays

Back, in the jungle, before I sailed high on the rainbow
Waters of victory   before the sun
Of armistice morning burned into my chest
The great V of Allied Conquest. Now it was not here
With the ships sucking up fire
Water and spraying it wild
Through every color, or where, unthreatened, my navel burned
Burned like an entry-wound. Lord, I deepened
Memory, and lay in the light high and wide
Open, murmuring "I can't help it" as I went
South in my mind

Yes Mother
there were two fine hands
Driving the jeep: mine, much better than before, for you had sent
Whiskey. What could I do but make the graveyards soar! O you coming
Allied Victory, I rambled in the night of two birthdays
Ago, the battle of Buna stoned
In moonlight   stone-dead left and right   going nowhere
Near friend or foe, but turned off into the thickest
Dark. O yes, Mother, let me tell you: the vines split and locked:
About where you'd never know me is
Where I stalled
and sat bolt up-

                    right in the moonlit bucket
         Seat throne of war
                              cascading the bottle to drink
      To victory, and to what I would do, when the time came,
         With my body. The world leapt like the world
Driving nails, and the moon burned with the light it had when it split

              From the earth. I slept and it was foretold
              That I would live. My head came true
     In a great smile. I reached for the bottle. It was dying and the moon
              Writhed closer to be free; it could answer
    My smile of foreknowledge. I forgot the mosquitoes that were going
         Mad on my blood, of biting me once too often on the bites
    Of bites. Had the Form in the moon come from the dead soldier
         Of your bottle, Mother? Let down in blocked
         Out light, a snakehead hung, its eyes putting into mine
    Visions of a victory at sea. New Guinea froze. Midair was steady

              Between. Snake-eyes needle-eyed   its
              Lips halving its head
              Stayed shut. I held up the last drop
              In the bottle, and invited him
              To sin   to celebrate
    The Allied victory to come. He pulled back a little over
              The evil of the thing I meant
    To stand for brotherhood. Nightshining his scales on Detroit
              Glass, he stayed on and on
              My mind. I found out the angel
         Of peace is limbless and the day will come
         I said, when no difference is between
              My skin and the great fleets
Delirious with survival. Mother, I was drunk enough on your birthday
         Present, not to die there. I backed the jeep out
    Of the Buna weeds
                         and, finally, where the sun struck
    The side of the hill, there I was
                              back from the dark side
Of the mind, burning like a prism over the conquering Catherine
         Wheel of the fleet. But ah, I turned

              I sank I lay back dead
         Drunk on a cold table   I had closed my eyes

And gone north   and lay to change
Colors all night. Out of the Nothing of occupation
Duty, I must have asked for the snake: I asked or the enemy told
Or my snakeskin told
Itself to be. Before I knew it in Yokahama, it was at my throat
Beginning with its tail, cutting through the world
wide Victory sign   moving under
My armpit like a sailor's, scale
By scale. Carbon-arc-light spat in the faces of the four
Men who bent over me, for the future lay brilliantly in
The needles of the enemy. Naked I lay on their zinc
Table, murmuring "I can't help it."
He coiled around me, yet

Headless   I turned with him side
To side, as the peaceful enemy
Designed   a spectrum of scales O yes
Mother I was in the tattoo parlor to this day
Not knowing how I got there as he grew,
Red scales sucking up color   blue
White with my skin running out of the world
Wide sun. Frothing with pinpricks, filling with ink
I lay and it lay
Now over my heart   limbless I fell and moved like moonlight
On the needles   moving to hang my head
In a drunk boy's face, and watch him while he dreamed
Of victory at sea. I retched but choked
It back, for he had crossed my breast, and I knew that many-
colored snakeskin was living with my heart   our hearts
Beat as one   port-of-call red   Yokahoma blue
O yes and now he lay low

On my belly, and gathered together the rainbow
Ships of Buckner Bay. I slumbered deep and he crossed the small
Of my back   increased
His patchwork hold on my hip   passed through the V between
My legs, and came
Around once more   all but the head   then I was turning   the snake
Coiled round my right thigh and crossed
Me with light hands   I felt myself opened
Just enough, where the serpent staggered on his last

Colors   needles gasping for air   jack-hammering
My right haunch burned by the hundreds
Of holes, as the snake shone on me complete   escaping
Forever   surviving   crushing   going home
To the bowels of the living,
His master, and the new prince of peace.

The Lord in the Air

> . . . If the spectator could . . . make a
> friend & companion of one of these Images
> of wonder . . . then would he meet the Lord
> in the air & . . . be happy. —*Blake*

Shook down   shook up on these trees they have come
From moment to this moment floating on   in   and this
Moment changes now not with the light for my son
Has come   has come out with one crow floating
Off a limb   back on and off   off a limb in other
Sunlight turning and making him call himself

Blacker   then settles back   back into the other
Moment. They hunch and face in. O yes they are all in
These very trees of the son-faced and fenced-
in backyard   waiting for my boy and the Lord
In the air. O parents great things can be released
From your left-handed son's left hand! They don't know

It, but he has them all in his palm, and now puts them
All in his mouth. Out by the blue swoon of the pool
He lifts the wood whistle to his blond lips. A scratch-
long sound rises out of him   the trees flap and fall
Back, and ah there are crows dealt out all over inside
The light   they mix and mingle   dive   swerve throughout

Themselves   calling   self-shuffling   saying
With my boy's other tongue   sailing   meeting the Lord
Of their stolen voice in the air   and more incoming from miles
Away are here   they wheel in blast after blast
In the child's lungs, as he speaks to them in the only
Word they understand   the *one*   the syllable that means

Everything to them   he has them cold: their several
Accents   they cry with him they know more than all
They have known   fear grief good danger love and marriage
With the Lord in the air. The pool trembles   my boy falls
From his voice   falls in stitches to the concrete   one
More word he says   not intended   never heard   he gives

Them a tone never struck in the egg   in the million years
Of their voice   the whole sky laughs with crows   they creak
And croak with hilarity   black winged belly-laughs they tell
Each other   the great joke of flight   sound living
Deep in the sun and waiting   a sound more or less   or more
Like warning, like marriage. O Chris come in, drop off now

Black birds from your tongue of wood, back into our neighbor
Trees   into other dimensions, their added-to moment and light
Plays over the pool in lovely silence like new   surely like new
Power over birds and beasts: something that has come in
From all over   come out but not for betrayal, or to call
Up death or desire, but only to give   give what was never.

Pine

successive apprehensions

I

Low-cloudly it whistles, changing heads
On you. How hard to hold and shape head-round.
So any hard hold
Now loses; form breathes near. Close to forest-form
By ear, so landscape is eyelessly
Sighing through needle-eyes. O drawn off
The deep end, step right up
And be where. It could be a net
Spreading field: mid-whistling crossed with an edge and a life
Guarding sound. Overhead assign the bright and dark
Heels distance-running from all   overdrawing the only sound
Of this sound   sound of a life-mass
Drawn in long lines in the air   unbroken   brother-saving
Sound merely soft

And loudly soft just in time   then nothing and then
Soft   soft and a little caring-for   sift-softening
And soared-to. O ankle-wings lightening and fleeing
Brothers sending back for you
To join the air and live right: O justice-scales leaning toward mercy
Wherever. Justice is exciting in the wind
As escape continuing   as an ax hurling
Toward sound and shock. Nothing so just as wind
In its place in low cloud
Of its tree-voice stopped and on-going   footless flight
Sound like brothers coming on as
All-comers coming and fleeing
From ear-you and pine, and all pine.

II

What mainly for the brow-hair
Has been blowing, dimensions and glows in:
Air the most like
Transfusion expands and only
There it is fresh
From overhead, steep-brewing and heavy from deep
Down upcoming new
To the lungs like a lean cave swimming—
Throat-light and iron
Warm spray on the inside face
Cutting often and cooling-out and brow
Opening and haunting freshly. So have you changed to this
You like a sea-wall
Tarred as a stump and blowing
Your skull like clover   lung-swimming in rosin
Dwelling
by breath
breath:
Whose head like a cave opens living
With eddies   needle-sapped out
Of its mind by this face-lifting
Face like a tree-beast
Listening, resetting the man-broken nose
bones on wine
Currents, as taste goes wild

And wells up   recalls   recovers and calls
For its own, for pure spirit
Food: windfalls and wavers out again
From nothing, in green sinus-packs.

III

More and more, through slow breaks
In the wind   no a different no this
Wind, another life of you rises,
A saliva-gland burns like a tree.
You are what you eat
                    and what will flutter
Like food if you turn completely
To your mouth, and stand wide open?
A wafer of bark, another
Needle, bitter rain by the mouthful coming.
Hunger swirls and slowly down
Showers   and are your children
What you eat? What green of horror
And manna in the next eye
To come from you? And will he whistle
From head to foot?

Bitter rain by the mouthful coming.

IV

More hands on the terrible rough.
More pain but more than all
Is lodged in the leg-insides. More holding,
Though, more swaying. Rise and ride
Like this and wear and ride
Away with a passionate faceful
Of ply and points. The whole thing turns
On earth, throwing off a dark
Flood of four ways
Of being here blind and bending
Blacked-out and framed
Suspended and found alive in the rough palm-
And thigh-fires of friction, embracing in the beyond
It all, where,

Opening one by one, you still can open
One thing more. A final form
And color at last comes out
Of you alone putting it all
Together like nothing
Here like almighty

Glory.

Madness

(Time: Spring. Place: Virginia. A domestic dog wanders
from the house, is bitten by a rabid female fox, runs mad
himself, and has to be hunted down, killed, and beheaded.)

Lay in the house mostly living
With children when they called   mostly
Under the table begging for scraps lay with the head
On a family foot
Or stretched out on a side,
Firesided. Had no running
Running, ever.
Would lie relaxed, eyes dim

With appreciation, licking the pure contentment
Of long   long notched
Black lips. Would lap up milk like a cat and swim clear
In brown grateful eyes. That was then, before the Spring
Lay down and out
Under a tree, not far but a little far and out
Of sight of the house.
Rain had sown thick and gone

From the house where the living
Was done, where scraps fell and fire banked full
On one sleeping side of the spirit
Of the household
                    and it was best
To get up and wander
Out, out of sight. Help me was shouted

To the world of females   anyone will do
To the smoking leaves.

Love could be smelt. All things burned deep
In eyes that were dim from looking
At the undersides of tables   patient with being the god
Of small chidlren. In Spring it is better with no
Doors which the god
Of households must beg at   no locks where the winds blows
The world's furry women
About in heat. And there

She lay, firesided, bushy-assed, her head
On the ground wide open, slopping soap:
Come   come close
She said like a god's
Wild mistress said come
On boy, I'm what you come

Out here in the bushes for. She burned alive
In her smell, and the eyes she looked at burned
With gratitude, thrown a point-eared scrap
Of the world's women, hot-tailed and hunted: she bit down
Hard on a great yell
To the house being eaten alive
By April's leaves. Bawled; they came and found.
The children cried

Helping tote to the full moon
Of the kitchen   "I carried the head"   O full of eyes
Heads kept coming across, and friends and family
Hurt   hurt
The spirit of the household, on the kitchen
Table being thick-sewed   they saying it was barbed
Wire looked like
It got him, and he had no business running

Off like that. Black lips curled as they bathed off
Blood, bathed blood. Staggered up under
The table making loud
A low-born sound, and went feeling

For the outer limits
Of the woods   felt them break and take in
The world   the frame turn loose and the house
Not mean what it said it was. Lay down and out
Of sight and could not get up
The head, lying on God's foot firesided
Fireheaded   formed a thought
Of Spring   of trees in wildfire
Of the mind speeded up   and put all thirst

Into the leaves. They grew
Unlimited. Soap boiled
Between black lips: the house
Spirit jumped up beyond   began to run   shot
Through the yard and bit down
On the youngest child. And when it sprang down
And out across the pasture, the grains of its footprints leapt
Free, where horses that shied from its low

New sound were gathered, and men swung themselves
Up to learn what Spring
Had a new way to tell, by bringing up
And out the speed of the fields. A long horn blew
Firesided   the mad head sang
Along the furrows   bouncing and echoing from earth
To earth through the body
Turning   doubling back
Through the weather of love running wild and the horses full

Of strangers coming after. Fence wire fell and rose
Flaming with messages as the spirit ran
Ran with house-hair
Burr-picking madly   and after came

Men   horses   spirits
Of households leaping crazily beyond
Their limits, dragging their bodies by the foaming throat through grass
And beggar-lice and by the red dust
Road where men blazed and roared
With their shoulders   blew it down and apart where it ran
And lay down on the earth of God's

One foot and the foot beneath the table kicked
The white mouth shut: this was something

In Spring in mild brown eyes   as strangers
Cut off the head and carried and held it
Up, blazing with consequence   blazing
With freedom saying   bringing
Help   help   madness   help.

The Eye-Beaters

[for Mary Bookwalter]

A man   Come something   come blood sunlight   come and they break
visits a   Through the child-wall, taking heart from the two left feet
Home for
children in   Of your sound: are groping for the Visitor in the tall corn
Indiana,   Green of Indiana. You may be the light, for they have seen it coming
some of
whom have   From people: have seen it on cricket and brick have seen it
gone blind   Seen it fade   seen slowly the edge of things fail   all corn
there.
     Green fail   heard fields grind   press with insects and go round
     To the back of the head. They are blind. Listen   listen well
A therapist   To your walking that gathers the blind in bonds   gathers these
explains   Who have fought with themselves   have blacked their eyes wide
why the
children   Open, toddling like dolls and like penguins   soft-knotted down,
strike   Protected, arms bound to their sides in gauze, but dark is not
their eyes.   To be stood in that way: they holler   howl till they can shred
     Their gentle ropes   whirl and come loose. They *know* they should see
     But *what*, now? When their fists smash their eyeballs, they behold no
     Stranger giving light from his palms. What they glimpse has flared
     In mankind from the beginning. In the asylum, children turn to go back
     Into the race: turn their heads without comment into the black magic
     Migraine of caves. Smudge-eyed, wide-eyed, gouged, horned, caved-
     in, they are silent: it is for you to guess what they hold back inside
     The brown and hazel   inside the failed green   the vacant blue-
The Visitor   eyed floating of the soul. Was that lightning   was that a heart-
begins to   struck leap   somewhere before birth? Why do you eat the green summer
invent a
fiction to   Air like smoky meat? Ah, Stranger, you do not visit this place,
save his   You live or die in it   you brain-scream you beat your eyes to see
mind.   The junebug take off backwards   spin   connect his body-sound

To what he is in the air. But under the fist, on the hand-stomped bone,
A bison leaps out of rock   fades   a long-haired nine-year-old clubs
Her eye, imploding with vision   dark   bright again   again again
A beast, before her arms are tied. Can it be? Lord, when they slug
Their blue cheeks blacker, can it be that they do not see the wings
And green of insects   or the therapist suffering kindly   but a tribal light old

*He tries to
see what
they see
when they
beat their
eyes.*

Enough to be seen without sight? There, quiet children stand watching
A man striped and heavy with pigment, lift his hand with color coming
From him. Bestial, working like God, he moves on stone he is drawing
A half-cloud of beasts on the wall. They crane closer, helping, beating
Harder, light blazing inward from their fists   and see   see leap
From the shocked head-nerves, great herds of deer on the hacked glory plain
Of the cave wall: antelope   elk: blind children strike for the middle
Of the brain, where the race is young. Stranger, they stand here
And fill your mind with beasts: ibex   quagga   rhinoceros of wool-
gathering smoke: cave bear   aurochs   mammoth: beings that appear
Only in the memory of caves   the niches filled, not with Virgins,
But with the squat shapes of the Mother. In glimmers of mid-brain pain
The forms of animals are struck like water from the stone   where hunger
And rage   where the Visitor's helplessness and terror   all
Move on the walls and create.

                (Look up: the sun is taking its stand on four
   o'clock of Indiana time, painfully blazing   fist of a ball of fire
God struck from His one eye).

                  No; you see only dead beasts playing
In the bloody handprint on the stone where God gropes like a man
Like a child, for animals   where the artist hunts and slashes, glowing
Like entrail-blood, tracking the wounded game across the limestone
As it is conceived. The spoor leads   his hand changes   grows
Hair like a bison   horns like an elk   unshapes   in a deer-leap emerges
From the spear-pitted rock, becoming what it can make unrolling
Not sparing itself clenching re-forming rising   beating
For light.

          Ah, you think it, Stranger: you'd like that you try hard

*His Reason
argues
with his
invention.*

*To think it, to think for them. But what you see, in the half-inner sight
Of squinting, are only fields   only children whose hands are tied away
From them for their own good   children waiting to smash their dead
Eyes, live faces, to see nothing.* As before, they come to you smiling,
Using their strange body-English. *But why is it this they have made up
In your mind? Why painting and Hunting? Why animals showing how God*

Is subject to the pictures in the cave   their clotted colors like blood
On His hands as the wild horse burns   as the running buck turns red
From His palm, while children twist in their white ropes, eyes wide,
Their heads in the dark meat of bruises?
                                   And now, blind hunters,
Swaying in concert like corn   sweet-faced   tribe-swaying at the red wall
Of the blind like a cooking-fire   shoulder-moving, moaning as the cave-
artist moaned when he drew the bull-elk to the heart   come ring
Me round. I will undo you. Come, and your hands will be free to fly
Straight into your faces, and shake the human vision to its roots
Flint-chipping sparks spring up: I can see   feel   see another elk
Ignite with his own becoming: it is time.
                                        Yes, indeed I know it is not
So   I am trying to make it   make something   make them make me
Re-invent the vision of the race   knowing the blind must see
By magic or nothing. Therapists, I admit it; it helps me to think
That they can give themselves, like God from their scabby fists, the original
Images of mankind: that when they beat their eyes, I witness how
I survive, in my sun-blinded mind: that the beasts are calling to God
And man for art, when the blind open wide and strike their incurable eyes
In Indiana. *And yet, O Stranger, those beasts and mother-figures are all*
Made up by you. They are your therapy. There is nothing inside their dark,
Nothing behind their eyes but the nerve that kills the sun above the corn
Field   no hunt no meat no pain-struck spark no vision   no pre-history
For the blind   nothing but blackness forever   nothing but a new bruise
Risen upon the old.

The children retire, but he hears them behind their wall.

                        They have gone away; the doors have shut shut on you
And your makeshift salvation. Yet your head still keeps what you would
    put in theirs
If you were God. Bring down your lids like a cave, and try to see
By the race alone. Collective memory stirs   herd-breathes   stamps
In snow-smoke, as the cave takes hold. You are artist and beast and
The picture of the beast: you are a ring of men and the stampeded bones
Tumbling into the meat-pit. A child screams out in fury, but where,
In the time of man? O brother, quiver and swear: It is true that no thing
Anyone can do is good enough for them: not Braille not data
Processing   not "learning TV repair" not music   no, and not not being
"A burden": none of these, but only vision: what they see must be crucial

To the human race. It is so; to let you live with yourself after seeing
Them, they must be thought to see by what has caused   is causing us all
To survive. In the late sun of the asylum, you know nothing else will do
You; the rest is mere light. In the palm of the hand the color red is calling
For blood   the forest-fire roars on the cook-stone, smoke-smothered and
   lightning-
born   and the race hangs on meat and illusion   hangs on nothing
But a magical art. Stranger, you may as well take your own life
Blood   brain-blood, as vision. Yes; that hammering on the door is not
Your heart, or the great pulse of insects; it is blind children beating
Their eyes to throw a picture on the wall. Once more you hear a child yell
In pure killing fury   pure triumph pure acceptance   as his hands burst
Their bonds. It is happening. Half-broken light flickers with agony
Like a head   throwing up the beast-paint the wall cannot shake
For a million years.
                    Hold on to your fantasy; it is all that can save
A man with good eyes in this place. Hold on, though doctors keep telling
You to back off   to be what you came as   back off from the actual
Wall of their screaming room, as green comes all around you with its ears
Of corn, its local, all-insect hum, given junebugs and flies wherever
They are, in midair. No;
                        by God. There is no help for this but madness,
Perversity. Think that somewhere under their pummeled lids they gather
At the wall of art-crazed beasts, and the sun blazing into the blackout
Of the cave, dies of vision. A spell sways in. It is time for the night
Hunt, and the wild meat of survival. The wall glimmers that God and man
Never forgot. I have put history out. An innocent eye, it is closed
Off, outside in the sun. Wind moans like an artist. The tribal children lie
On their rocks in their animal skins   seeing in spurts of eye-beating
Dream, the deer, still wet with creation, open its image to the heart's
Blood, as I step forward, as I move through the beast-paint of the stone,
Taken over, submitting, brain-weeping. Light me a torch with what we
   have preserved
Of lightning. Cloud bellows in my hand. God man hunter artist father
Be with me. My prey is rock-trembling, calling. Beast, get in
My way. Your body opens onto the plain. Deer, take me into your life-
lined form. I merge, I pass beyond in secret   in perversity and the sheer
Despair of invention   my double-clear bifocals off   my reason gone
Like eyes. Therapist, farewell at the living end. Give me my spear.

Turning Away
Variations on Estrangement

I

Something for a long time has gone wrong,
Got in between this you and that one other
And now   here   you must turn away.

Beyond! Beyond! Another life moves

In numbing clarity begins
By looking out the simple-minded window,
The face untimely relieved
Of living the expression of its love.

II

Shy, sad, adolescent   separated-out
The gaze stands alone in the meadow
Like a king starting out on a journey
Away from all things that he knows.
It stands there   there

With the ghost's will to see and not tell
What it sees with its nerveless vision
Of sorrow, its queen-killing glare:
The apple tree in the wind
Paling with noon sleep,
Light pouring down from the day-moon
White-hot inside the sun's mildness,

The eyes clamped by an ordinary meadow
As by the latest masterpiece
Under the sun.

III

For the face a studded look slowly
Arrives from a gulley of chickweed
Like a beard, come from something
Unwanted, that the face cannot help all its life.
Hair curls inside the jaws

Unstoppable   mindless   turns white
Turns straight   chokes
Helplessly, in more and more dangerous
Iron-masked silence.

I V

A deadly, dramatic compression
Is made of the normal brow. Because of it
The presence of the hand upon the sill
Calms and does not shake the thing beheld.
Every stone within sight stands ready
To give you its secret
Of impassivity, its unquestionable
Silence: you wear
Its reason for existence where you stand

So still   the tongue grows solid also
Holding back the rock speech.

V

A hooked shape threads
Through your nostrils, and you have
Caesar's eagle look, and nothing
For it to do,
Even though, on the golden
Imperial helmet, little doors close over
Your face, and your head is covered
With military flowers.

V I

Turning away,
You foresee the same fields you watch.
They are there an instant
Before they are ready: a stream being slowly suspended
Between its weeds, running where it once was,
Keeping its choir-sounds going
All like crowned boys
But now among grasses that are

An enormous green bright growing No
That frees forever.

VII

The mutual scar on the hand of man
And woman, earned in the kitchen,
Comes forth   rises for you to brush
Off like a cutworm
As the weed with wings explodes
In air, laying in front of you down
Cheap flowers by hundreds of thousands
And you try to get by heart
The words written after the end

Of every marriage manual, back
To the beginning, saying
Change; form again; flee.

VIII

Despair and exultation
Lie down together and thrash
In the hot grass, no blade moving,
A stark freedom primes your new loins:
Turning away, you can breed
With the farthest women

And the farthest also in time: breed
Through bees, like flowers and bushes:
Breed Greeks, Egyptians and Romans   hoplites
Peasants   caged kings   clairvoyant bastards:
The earth's whole history blazes
To become this light
For you are released to all others,

All places and times of all women,
And for their children hunger
Also: for those who could be half
You, half someone unmet,
Someone dead, immortal, or coming.

Near you, some being suddenly
Also free, is weeping her body away.

IX

The watched fields shake   shake
Half blind with scrutiny.
All working together, grasshoppers
Push on a stem apiece
And the breathless meadow begins
To sway   dissolve   revolve:

Faintness   but the brain rights
Itself with a sigh in the skull
And sees again nothing
But intensified grass. Listen:
When this much is wrong, one can fix one's head

In peacetime   turning away
From an old peaceful love
To a helmet of silent war
Against the universe   and see
What to do with it all: see with the eyes
Of a very great general
Roads ditches trees
Which have sunk their roots to provide
Not shade but covering-fire.

Somewhere in this guarded encampment
The soul stands stealthily up
To desert: stands up like the sex
About to run   running
Through pinewoods   creeks   changes of light   night
And day   the wide universe streaming over it
As it stands there panting   over-sensitized
Filled with blood from the feet

Heartbeating   surviving   in the last

Place   in cloud river meadowgrass or grave   waiting
For bird beast or plant to tell it

How to use itself   whom to meet   what to do
Which way to go to join
The most ineffectual army   the defiant, trembling
Corps of the unattached.

Fear passes
Into sweat hidden openly
In the instant new lines of the brow. The field
Deepens in peace, as though, even
Before battle, it were rich-
ening with a generation's
Thousand best, quietest men
In long grass bending east
To west. Turning away, seeing fearful
Ordinary ground, boys' eyes manlike go,
The middle-aged man's like a desperate
Boy's, the old man's like a new angel's

Beholding the river in all
White places   rushing
At and burning its boulders
Quietly   the current laid
In threads   as, idly, a conqueror's horse,

Ox-headed, is born of the shape of a cloud
That was an unnoticed
Deep-hanging bed.
Water waves in the air,
A slant, branded darkness
From a distant field full of horses
Uprisen into a cloud
That is their oversoul.

XII

Under the great drifting stallion
With his foreleg bloatedly cocked, the armed
Men who could spring from your teeth
Double their strength in your jaws:

XIII

So many battles
Fought in cow pastures   fought back
And forth over anybody's farm
With men or only
With wounded eyes—
Fought in the near yellow crops
And the same crops blue farther off.

XIV

Dead armies' breath like a sunflower
Stirs, where the loved-too-long
Lie with a whimper of scythes.
Coming to them, the seeds
Of distant plants either die
Or burn out when they touch
Ground, or are born in this place.
Rain is born rain: let tons of repossessed
Water walk to us!

XV

You may have swallowed a thistle
Or the first drop of rain;
You have been open-mouthed.
Now speak of battles that bring

To light no blood, but strew the meadows
With inner lives:
Speak now with the thistle's sharpness
Piercing   floating   descending
In flowers all over the field
With a dog-noise low in the calyx.

XVI

Like a hound, you can smell the earth change
As your cloud comes over the sun
Like a called horse.
The long field summons its armies
From every underground
Direction. Prepare to fight

The past   flee   lie down,
Heartbeat a noise in your head
Like knocking the rungs from a ladder:
So many things stand wide
Open! Distance is helplessly deep
On all sides   and you can enter, alone,
Anything   anything can go
On wherever it wishes   anywhere in the world or in time
But here and now.

XVII

Turning away, the eyes do not mist over
Despite the alien sobbing in the room.
Withhold! Withhold! Stand by this window
As on guard
Duty   rehearsing what you will answer
If questioned   stand

General   deserter   freed slave belovèd of all,
Giving off behind your back
Ridiculous energy   stand

Like a proof of character learned
From Caesar's *Wars*   from novels
Read in the dark,
Thinking of your life as a thing
That can be learned,
As those earnest young heroes learned theirs,
Later, much later on.

THE ZODIAC

This poem is based on another of the same title.

That one was written by Hendrik Marsman, who was killed by a torpedo in the North Atlantic in 1940.

It is in no sense a translation, for the liberties I have taken with Marsman's original poem are such that the poem I publish here, with the exception of a few lines, is completely my own.

Its twelve sections are the story of a drunken and perhaps dying Dutch poet who returns to his home in Amsterdam after years of travel and tries desperately to relate himself, by means of stars, to the universe.

—homage to Hendrik Marsman, lost at sea, 1940—

The Zodiac

I

          The Man I'm telling you about brought himself back alive
A couple of years ago.   He's here,
      Making no trouble
               over the broker's peaceful
    Open-bay office at the corner of two canals
        That square off and starfish into four streets
          Stumbling like mine-tunnels all over town.

  To the right, his window leaps and blinds
                   and sees
The bridges shrivel on contact with low cloud
                leaning to reach out
    Of his rent-range
         and get to feudal doors:
      Big-rich houses whose thick basement-stones
        Turn water into cement inch by inch
      As the tide grovels down.
                 When that tide turns
   Hé turns left   his eyes back-swivel into his head
        In hangover-pain like the flu   the flu
      Dizzy with tree-tops
            all dead, but the eye going
   Barely getting   but getting you're damn right but still
      Getting them.
              Trees, all right.   No leaves.   All right,

Trees, stand
                  and deliver.   They stand and deliver
          Not much: stand
          Wobble-rooted, in the crumbling docks.
                                                  So what?

The town square below, deserted as a Siberian crater, lies in the middle
Of his white-writing darkness   stroboscoped   red-stopped by the
                                                          stammering mess
          Of the city's unbombed neon, sent through rivers and many cities
                          By fourth-class mail from Hell.

All right, since you want to, look:

          Somebody's lugged a priest's failed prison-cell
          Swaybacked up the broker's cut-rate stairs.   He rents it on credit.

No picture
                  nothing but a bed and desk
          And empty paper.
                              A flower couldn't make it in this place.
          It couldn't live, or couldn't get here at all.
                              No flower could get up these steps,
                              It'd wither at the hollowness
Of these foot-stomping
                          failed creative-man's boards—
                          There's nothing to bring love or death

                              Or creative boredom through the walls.
                                                                  Walls,

                          Ah walls.   They're the whole place.   And any time,
                  The easting and westing city in the windows
                  Plainly are not true
                                        without a drink.   But the *walls*—
                  Weightless   ridiculous   bare
                          Are there just enough to be dreadful
Whether they're spinning or not.   They're there to go round him

          And keep the floor turning with the earth.
He moves among stars.
                          Sure.   We all do, but he is star-*crazed*, mad

With *Einfühlung*, with connecting and joining things that lay their meanings

          Over billions of light years
                              eons of time—Ah,

Years of light: billions of them: they are pictures

Of some sort of meaning.   He thinks the secret

Can be read.   But human faces swim through
Cancer   Scorpio   Leo   through all the stupefying design,

And all he can add to it or make of it, living or dead:
An eye lash-flicker, a responsive
light-year light
From the pit of the stomach, and a young face comes on,
Trying for the pit of his poem
strange   remembered
Comes on faintly, like the faint, structural light
Of Alnilam, without which Orion

Would have no center   the Hunter
Could not hunt, in the winter clouds.
The face comes on

Glowing with billions of miles   burning like nebulae,
Like the horse-head nebula in Orion—

She was always a little horse-faced,
At least in profile   she is some strange tint
Of second-order blue: intensity   she is eternal
As long as *he* lives—the stars and his balls meet
And she shows herself as any face does
That *is* eternal, raying in and out
Of the body of a man: in profile   sketched-in by stars
Better than the ones God set turning

Around us forever.
The trees night-pale

Out.   Vacuum.
Absolute living-space-white.   Only one way beyond

The room.
The Zodiac.
He must solve it   must believe it   learn to read it
No, wallow in it

As poetry.
He's drunk.   Other drunks, it's alligators

Or rats, their scales and eyes
Turning the cold moon molten on the floor.—   With him, it's his party-time arm

Of soldier ants; they march over
His writing hand, heading for the Amazon Basin.
He can take *them* . . .
He bristles   itches like a sawdust-pile

But something's more important than flesh-crawling
To gain an image
line by line: they give him an idea.   Suppose—

Well, let's just suppose I . . .

No ants.   No idea.   Maybe they'll come back
All wildly drunk, and dance
Into the writing.   It's worth a try.

Hot damn, here they come!   He knows them, name for name
As they surround his fingers, and carry the maze
Onto the paper: they're named for generals.
He thinks
That way: of history, with his skin
with everything

He has, including delirium tremens
staring straight

Into the lamp.   You are a strange creature,

Light,
he says to light.   Maybe one day I'll get something
Bigger than ants   maybe something from the sea.
Keep knocking back the *aquavit*. By the way, my man, get that *aqua*!
There's a time acoming when the life of the sea   when

The stars and their creatures get together.

Light
is another way. This is when the sun drifts in
Like it does in any window, but this sun is coming
From the east part of town.   Shit, I don't know where I am
This desk is rolling like the sea
Come home   come to my home—

I'll never make it to land.   I am alone:

                    I am my brother:

         I look at my own decoration
                  Outside of the page:
                              three rods: they're turning modernly—

A mobile he's got up
Above the bed, from splintered bottle-bits and coat-hangers:

   You know they are, there really *are*
                  Small, smashed greens revolving
In a room.
                  It all hangs together, and *you* made it:
            Its axis is spinning
Through the Zodiac.
                        He flicks it and sets the model
            For a universe of green, see-through stars
Going faster.   The white walls stagger
            With lights:
   He has to hold onto the chair: the room is pitching and rolling—
            He's sick   seasick with his own stars,
                        seasick and airsick   sick

      With the Zodiac.

                        Even drunk
Even in the white, whiskey-struck, splintered star of a bottle-room dancing,
            He knows he's not fooling himself   he knows

                  Not a damn thing of stars   of God   of space

Of time   love night death sex fire numbers signs words,

Not much of poetry.   But by God, we've got a *universe*

Here

         Those designs of time are saying *some*thing
         Or maybe something or *other*.

                        Night—

   Night tells us.   It's coming—

Venus shades it and breaks it.   Will the animals come back
Gently, creatively open,

   Like they were?

Yes.

The great, burning Beings   melt into place
A few billion-lighted inept beasts

Of God—

      What else is there?   What other signs   what other symbols

    Are *any*thing beside these?   If the thing hasn't been said
This way,   then God can't say it.
                  Unknown.   Unknown.
    His mobile made of human shattering-art

  Is idling through space, and also oddly, indifferently,
Supremely, through beauty as well.   Yes,

     Sideways through beauty.   He swirls in his man-made universe,

His room, his liquor, both the new bottle and the old
    Fragmented godlike one.
He never gets tired.   Through his green, moving speckles,

He looks sideways, out and up   and there it is:
    The perpetual Eden of space
                  there where you want it.

What animal's getting outlined?
      All space is being bolted
  Together: eternal blackness

               studded with creatures.
Stars.
      Beasts.   Nothing left but the void
         Deep-hammering its creatures with light-years.
Years made of light.
          Only light.

              Yes.

    But what about the damned *room*?
God-beast-stars   wine-bottle constellations   jack-off dreams
    And silence. That's about it.

              They're all one-eyed—
The Lion   the Scorpion   the others coming—
    Their one-eyed eyesight billions of years

In the making, making and mixing with his liquor-bottle green
Splintered shadows   *art*-shadows, for God's sake:

Look, stupid, get your nose out of the sky for once.
There're things that are *close* to you, too. Look at *them*!

Don't cringe: look right out over town.
Real birds. There they are in their curves, moving in their great element
That causes our planet to be blue and causes us all
To breathe.   Ah, long ghostly drift
Of wings.
Well, son of a bitch.
He sits and writes,
And the paper begins to run
with signs.
But he can't get rid of himself enough
To write poetry.   He keeps thinking Goddamn
I've misused myself   I've fucked up   I haven't worked—

I've traveled and screwed too much,
but   but by dawn, now   NOW
Something   coming   through-coming   down-coming   up
To me   ME!
His hand reaches, dazzling with drink   half alive,
for the half-dead vision.   That room and its page come in and
out
Of being.   You talk about *looking*:   would you look at *that*
Electric page!   What the hell did I say?   Did *I* say that?
You bastard, you. Why didn't you know that before?
Where the hell have you been with your *head*?
You and the paper should have known it, you and the ink: you write

Everybody writes

With blackness. Night. Why has it taken you all this time?
All this travel, all those lives
You've fucked up? All those books read
Not deep enough? It's staring you right in the face   The
secret—

Is whiteness.   You can do *anything* with that.   But no—
The secret is that on whiteness you can release
The blackness,

the night sky.   Whiteness is death   is dying
For human words to raise it from purity   from the grave
Of too much light.   Words must come to it
Words from *any*where   from   from
Swamps   mountains   mud   shit   hospitals   wars   travels   from

Stars

From the Zodiac.
You son of a bitch, you! Don't try to get away from yourself!
I won't have it! You know God-damned well I mean you! And you too,
Pythagoras!   Put down that guitar, lyre, whatever it is!
You've driven me nuts enough with your music of the spheres!
But I'll bet you know what to know:

Where God once stood in the stadium
Of European history, and battled mankind in the blue air
Of manmade curses, under the exploding flags
Of dawn,   I'd put something else now:
I'd put something overhead   something new: a new beast

For the Zodiac.   I'd say to myself like a man

Bartending for God,
What'll it be?
Great! The stars are mine, and so is
The imagination to work them—
To create.
Christ, would you tell me why my head
Keeps thinking up these nit-witted, useless images?

Whiskey helps.
But it does.   It does.   And now I'm working
With *constellations*! What'll it *be,* Heaven? What new creature
Would you *like* up there?   Listen, you universal son-of-a-bitch,
You're talking to a poet now, so don't give me a lot of shit.
My old man was a God-damned astronomer
Of sorts
—and didn't he say the whole sky's *invented*?
Well, I am now in*ven*ting.   You've *got* a Crab:
Especially tonight. I love to eat them: They scare me to death!
My head is smashed with *aquavit,*
And I've got a damn good Lobster in it   for   for

The Zodiac.   I'll send it right up.

And   listen now
I want *big* stars: some red   some white   also blue-white dwarves—
    I want *everybody* to see my lobster! This'll be a *healing* lobster:
  Not Cancer.   People will pray to him.   He'll have a good effect
On Time.
        Now what I want to do is stretch him out

    Jesus, Christ, I'm drunk

          I said stretch   stretch
Him out is what I said   stretch him out for millions
    Of light years.   His eye   his eye

    I'll make blue-white, so that the thing
Will cut and go deep and heal.   God, the *claws* that son-of-a-bitch

    Is going to get from You! The clock-spire is telling me
To lie
    for glory.   This is a poet talking to You
Like you talked to yourself, when you made all this up   while you conceived

    The Zodiac. From every tower in Europe:
    From my lifework and stupid travels and loneliness
      And drunkenness, I'm changing the heavens
    In my head. Get up there, baby, and dance on your claws:
      On the claws God's going to give you.
          I'm just before throwing up
  All over myself.   I've failed again.   My lobster can't make it
To Heaven.   He's right here in town.   It must be the DT's.

    You know, old lyre-picking buddy,
You in your whirling triangles, your terror of looking into a glass
    Beside a light, your waking from ancient new-math,
To say, "Wretches, leave those beans alone," and "Do not eat the heart,"
        You know   you know you've given me
Triangular eyes. You know that from the black death,
           of the forest of beast-
Symbols, the stars are beaten down by drunks

Into the page.
      By GOD the poem is *in* there   out there
    Somewhere   the lines that will change
    Everything, like your squares and square roots

Creating the heavenly music.
                                        It's somewhere,
Old great crazy thinker
                    ah
                                farther down
In the abyss.   It takes triangular eyes
                    To see Heaven.   I got 'em from you.
                                                All right,
I've got what I want, for now, at least.
                        The paper staggers
From black to white to black, then to a kind of throbbing gold
                And blue, like the missal he read as a boy. It's like something
                                He dreamed of finding
                In a cave, where the wellspring of creative blood
        Bubbles without death.
                            Where the hell *is* the light
Of the universe?   Gone out and around
                The world.   Oh my God

                You've got to look up
                            again: You've *got* to do it   you're committed
To it   look up   UP   you failed son of a bitch up MORE

                        There it is
            Your favorite constellation
                            the hurdling-deep Hunter

                            Orion

With dim Alnilam sputtering in the middle.
                                Well, but   quiet   why?
                    Why that one?   Why do you even remember
        The name?   The star's no good: not pretty,
    Not a good navigational aid.
                        Ah, but secret.

                                Ah, but central.

Let me explain it to you: that strange, overlooked, barely existing star

                    Is essential to the belt
Of the great, great Hunter.

                    Look.
                              Just look.   The sword hangs down
The dog star travels on   on like European Christian soldiers going on
Before.
            The whole thing's hacked out
      Like cuneiform.   All right, so Orion's not in
            The Zodiac.   We'll *put* him in, along with some other things.
      He should never've been blackballed, even by Pythagoras.
            All right, friend, my friend myself, feel friendly
      Toward yourself.   It's possible, you know.   One more *aquavit*
            And you'll be entitled to breathe.
                                        He breathes

Breathes deeply.
                        You know, like me, he says to the sideways
      Of the mobile,
                        the stars are gasping
                  For understanding.   They've *had* Ptolemy,
                  They've *had* Babylon
                              but now they want Hubbell
They want Fred Hoyle and the steady-state.
                              But what they really want   need
                              Is a poet   and
I'm going to have to be it.

      And all the time I'm sitting here the astronomers are singing

                  Dies Irae, to the Day of Judgment's horn.
                                                WHEN?

            In all this immensity, all this telescope-country,
            Why the microscopic searching
                              Of the useless human heart?

                              Why not die

                                    and breathe Heaven,
But not to have to *look* at it, not kill yourself trying to read it?

Except that there's relief   except
                        that there are birds.

There's one, a real *creature,* out there in a human city.
                  He's never seen a star
                  In his life, and if he has,

It didn't register.   There's no star-sound   star-silence
Around him.   He's in my main, starved winter tree,
He's the best thing I've got to my west.
                              When I look west I know
Everything's not over yet. I can always come back to earth.

But I want to come back with the secret
                              with the poem
That links up my balls and the strange, silent words
              Of God   his scrambled zoo   and my own words
                              and includes the earth

              Among the symbols.
                              Listen: you're talking to yourself
              About Time: about clocks   spires   wheels: there are times

                    There is Time
          That the time-bell can't hold back
                              but gives
                                        GIVES

Gives like vomit or diarrhea   but when it comes it is
                    The sound of new metal.
Well, all right.   Slowly the city drags and strays about in
                              Its wheedling darkness.

                    He looks up
          From his paper-scrap   his overworked script   and,

                    Work-beast-white, he wanders to the window,
          Getting himself brain-ready   ready for the pale-cell-game
                    He plays with the outside, when he turns his eyes down
                    Into trees, into human life,
                                        into the human-hair gray,
                    Man's aging-hair-gray
          Impenetrably thin   catching-up-with-and-passing the
                    never-all-there,
              Going-toward-blackness   thornless
              Thicket of twilight.

                              Words.

          How?

A clock smash-bongs.   Stun.   Stun.
A spire's hiding out in the sound   tower-sound and now
        Floating over him and living on the nerve

        Of the instant, vibrating like a hangover:

        Time.

He waits.   God, I'm going to ask you one question:
        What do *wheels* and *machinery* have to do with Time?

With stars?   You know damn well I've never been able to master
        A watch-maker's laugh.
                        Overhead in the midst of Nothing,
Is the very clock for a drunk man.   For the Lord also?
Is it some kind of *compass*?   Is direction involved, maybe,
        Or is it nothing but the valve-grinding
Human noise of duration?   Do the wheels shift gears?
        If they do, then Time shifts gears.

                —No; no:

Don't use that idea.
                It's simple enough, this town clock,
                The whole time-thing: after all
There's only this rosette of a great golden stylized asshole:

In human towns   in this one   in all of them—Ha! this is *our* symbol
        of eternity?
                Well, it's not good enough.

        Night.   Walking.   Time.
                                Nothing.
He goes on without anywhere to go. This is what you call Europe.
        Right?   The clock strokes pass
                Through him, aching like tooth-nerves, and he thinks

Our lives have been told, as long as we've had them,
                                that the Father
                Must be torn apart in the son.
                                Why?
                                He swings up

        Through his eyes, and God

Whirls slowly in men's numbers   in the gilded Gothic
Of thorn-spiked Time.   What the hell: Can't eternity *stand* itself?
       Men caught that great wild creature minute
              By shitty minute and smashed it down
       Into a rickety music box.
                      Stun.   Stun.   Stun.
       The new hour's here.   He stares, aging, at new Time.

I know God-damned well it's not what they say it is:
       Clock-hands   heart-rhythm   moon-pulses   blood-flow
                            of women—
No.
       Its just an uncreated vertigo
       Busted up by events.   Probably—now get this—
       The thing most like it is Cancer   both in and out

Of the Zodiac: everywhere existing in some form:
       In the stars   in works of art   in your belly,
       In the terrified breast of a woman,
       In your fate, or another's:
                      the thing that eats.

       If Cancer dies overhead,
It dies everywhere.   Now try *that* one out, you and your ideas
       For poems.   Every poet wants
       To change those stars around.
                    Look: those right *there*:
       Those above the clock.
                    Religion, Europe, death, and the stars:
I'm holding them all in my balls, right now.
And the old *aquavit* is mixing them up—they're getting to know—
       They're *crazy* about each other!
       Where God stood once in the stadium—I said this somewhere—
Of European history, and battled mankind in the blue air
       for domination, under the exploding Olympic-style flags
       Of dawn, I'd put something *else* now:
                    something overhead.

       God, at your best, you're my old—

You really *are* the water of life!   Look: here's what I'm going to do

       For you. I'm going to swirl the constellation Cancer

Around like rice in a bucket, and out of that'll come a new beast

For the Zodiac!
               I say right now, under the crashing clock, like a man
Bartending for God,
           What'll it be?
Do you want me to decide?   The stars are mine as well as yours,
              And don't forget it   and Christ
Would you tell me why my head keeps thinking
             Up these half-assed, useless images?
                            Whiskey helps.
But it does.   It does.   Swirl on, sky! Now, I'm working
With constellations.   What'll it be, Heaven? What new earthly creature

Would you like up there?   Listen, you universal son of a bitch
I've heard it all   I've said it all—
You're talking to poet now, so don't give me a lot of shit.
           You've got to remember that my old man
Was an astronomer, of sorts, and didn't he say the whole night sky's
             invented?
Well, I am now *inventing*. You've *got* a crab.   Right?

     How about a *Lobster* up there? With a snap of two right fingers
      Cancer will whirl like an anthill   people will rise
Singing from their beds and take their wheaten children in their arms,

           Who thought their parents were departing
        For the hammer-clawed stars of death. They'll live

And live.   A *Lobster!* What an idea!   An idea God never had.   Listen, My God,
        That thing'll be great!   He's coming into my head—
           Is he inside or out?   No, I can *see* him!
       The DT's aren't failing me: The light of Time shines on him
          He's huge   he's a religious fanatic
       He's gone wild because he can't go to Heaven
          He's waving his feelers   his saw-hands
          He's praying to the town clock   to minutes   millennia
       He's praying the dial's stations of the Cross   he sees me
          Imagination and dissipation both fire at me
       Point-blank   O God, no   NO   I was playing   I didn't mean it
       I'll never write it, I swear   CLAWS   claws   CLAWS

            He's going to kill me.

III

Hallucination fading.   Underseas are tired of crawling
In a beast   waving claws for a drunk
Under man's dim, round Time.   Weird ring
Of city-time.   Well, now:

night hits a long stride.
There's the last tower-tone.   You might know it.
Bronze.
He feels it. The thing hurts. Time hurts. Jesus does it.

Man,
God-damn it,
you're one *too*!   Man   MAN   listen to me
Like God listened when he went mad
Over drunk lobsters.   This is Time, and more than that,
Time in Europe

Son of a bitch.
His life is shot   my life is shot.
It's also shit.   He knows it.   Where's it all gone off to?
The gods are in pieces

All over Europe.

But, by God, not *God*—

He sees himself standing up—

Dawn-rights.   How the hell did he ever get home?
What home?   You call this white sty a *home*?
Yes, but *look* . . .

The vision's thorn-blue

between a slope
And the hot sky.

And now his travels begin to swarm
All over him.   He falls into clichés
Right and left, from his windows! That remembered Greek blue
Is *fantastic*!   That's all: no words
But the ones anybody'd use: the one from humanity's garbage-can
Of language.

A poet has got to do better . . . *That* blue
Jesus, look at *that* in your memory!
There   *there*   *that* blue   that *blue*
Over some Demetrian island   something that's an island
More or less, with its present hour smoking

Over it . . . It's worth it all   worth it and lifted
into memory
             he's lifted   he rises on the great, historical strength
Of columns.   Look, you son of a bitch, I know what peace is,
He says to his morning drink.   Peace, PEACE, you asshole . . .
Look at me, mirror.   My *eyes* are full of it, of the pale blue fumes
Of Mediterranean distance.   Isn't that *enough*?   The fresh stuff?
The old stuff . . .
             —but, damn it, forgetting keeps moving in   closer.

        It's that thing you might call death.
                              The walled, infinite
Peaceful-sea-beast-blue   moves in   in   it has a face

Bewildered, all-competent   everlasting   sure it will lie forever

Lie in the depths in distance-smoke: he's been there
        Among the columns:
                              among Europe. He can't tell Europe
From his own death, from his monstrous, peaceful   fierce
        Timelessness.   It follows like the images
        Of day-sleep.
                        Water-pressure   smoke   crabs
Lobsters.
        All RIGHT, reader, that's enough.   Let him go:
Let him go back to traveling   let him go on   in   onward   backward . . .

Ah, to hell with it: he can't quit.
                              Neither can you, reader.
He travels   he rises up
             you with him, hovering on his shoulders,
             A gas-fume reader   a gull a sleep and a smoke
        Of distance   a ruined column, riding him,
        His trapezius muscles in your deadly   your DT lobster's
        Your loving claws:
                        god-*damn*   it, he *can't* quit,

But—*listen* to me—how can he *rise*
                   When he's *digging*? Digging through the smoke
Of distance, throwing columns around to find   throwing
To find   throwing distance   swaying   swaying into his head . . .
He's drunk again.   Maybe that's all.   Maybe there's nothing maybe
There's a mystery   mystery nearly got-to

Now NOW
                    No.
                              I can't get it.   Ah,
         But now he can think about his grave.   It's not so bad;
It will be better than this.   There's something there for him—
              At least it'll be in Europe, and he won't be sick
              For the impossible: with other-world nostalgia,
              With the countries of the earth.   Holland is good enough
              To die in.   That's the place to lay down
              His screwed-up body-meat.   That's it.
                                        This is it.

         It's that thing you might call home.

I V

              He moves.
                         While he's going

He sees the moon white-out. But it maintains itself
              Barely, in   some kind of thing

              Vibrating faintly with existence,   inside a crown
              Of desperate trees.   Image of Spring,

Old Buddy. But where in this neon,
Where in *hell* am I *going*? Well, it looks like I've come to some kind of
                    Lit-up ravine—

Well, what on God's earth *is* it?   I can barely make out
              A black church.   Now come on now: are you sure?

I can't cross it.   It moves across me
              Like an all-mighty stone.   But is it *universal*?
              The thing's been lifted from the beginning
                         Into this night-black—
                                        Into the Zodiac.

Without that hugely mortal beast   animal   multi-animal animal
              There'd be no present time:
              Without the clock-dome, no city here,
              Without the axis and the poet's image   God's image
No turning stars   no Zodiac   without God's conceiving

         Of Heaven as beast-infested   of Heaven in terms of beasts
              There'd be no calendar   dates   seasons

No Babylon   those abstractions that blitzed their numbers
    Into the Colosseum's crazy gates   and down
                         down
    Into the woven beads that make the rosary
      Live   sing and swirl like stars

    Of creatures.

             Well, enough.   He loafs around
The square.   He might be a cock-sucker
Looking for trade.   He's got a platform   a springboard
For himself . . .
         Nobody sees him;
                nobody cares.

He thinks he's sending night-letters
To Mars, and yet he's looking straight
Into the Milky Way   right now he's liking the hang of it—
Now he's with Venus   he's getting a hard-on
        My God, look at that love-star   hammock-swaying
Moving like an ass   moving the sky along.

V

        Dark.

Bed-dark.   The night can get at him here   and it comes,
Tide after tide   and his nightmares rise and fall off him
      On the dry waves of the moon

      Thinking:
    The faster I sleep
  The faster the universe sleeps.
             And the deeper I breathe
The higher the night can climb
           and the higher the singing will be.
Bird, maybe?   *Night*ingale?   Ridiculous
           but over me
They're all one-eyed: the animals of light are in profile;
They're flat: God can't draw in depth
     When He uses constellations: the stars are beyond Him,
     Beyond his skill;   He can't handle them right.
      A child could do better.

At the moment I'm passing truly
                              into sleep, a single star goes out

In each beast.
                    Right.
                                The eye.
                                        The eye, but can it be
That from the creative movement of the first light
On the face of the waters   from Time   from Genesis

The orbiting story   the insane mathematics   the ellipsis
Of history: the whole thing: time art life death stars
Love blood till the last fire explodes into dark
The last image   the candlestick the book and the lamb's fleece
Flame in delight at the longed-for end of it all
            Will flame in one human eye?   Right or left?   Well, old soul,
            What is it?
What does it mean, poet?   Is all this nothing but the clock-stunned light
Of my mind, or a kind of river-reflection of my basic sleep
Breaking down   sleeping down into reprisal-fear of God:
            The Zodiac standing over, pouring into
            The dreams that are killing me?

V I

Dreams, crossing the body, in and out and around   crossing
                        Whatever is left of me. What does that include?   Images:

Monsters.   Nothing else.   Monsters of stars.
The moon dies like a beast.   Not a stone beast or a statue:

A *beast*.   But it can't fall: it's in a gully of clouds,
A shameless place, like the rest of nature is.

At this idea, one part of his brain goes soft
As cloud, so the Lobster can come.

Soft brain, but the spirit turns to fire
Pure cosmic tetanus.   The sponge of his brain drinks it up:
            In the place where the thing is   seethes

The sweat of thought breaks out.
                                        It crowns him like a fungus:
            Idea of love.
                        Love?

Yes, but who'll put a washrag on him?
It wouldn't matter; his whole skull's broken out with it.
There's no sponge, no rag—

Poet's lockjaw: he can't speak: there's nothing

Nothing for his mouth.

VII

O flesh, that takes on any dirt
  At all
    I can't get you back in shape—
It'd be better to go on being
What I was at one time or another: a plant
In the dead-black flaming flowing
Round flume of Time.

Words fade before his eyes
Like water-vapor, and the seed he thinks he's got available to give
  Some woman, fades back
  Deep into his balls, like a solar
  Phenomenon, like cloud
  Crossing the Goat—

He comes back, and some weird change comes on:
Our man may be getting double-sexed
  Or something worse
    or better—
      but either way
His children are already murdered: they'll never *be* until the Goat
 Shines blindingly, and Time ends. Then, no,
  Either. Nothing will ever be.

  He says from his terrible star-sleep,
  Don't shack up with the intellect:
  Don't put your prick in a cold womb.
  Nothing but walking snakes would come of *that*—

  But if you conceive with meat

  Alone,
    that child, too, is doomed.
  Look. The moon has whited-out the script
    Your hand drove into the paper.

This poetry that's draining your bones
Of marrow has no more life
Than the gray grass of public parks.

Leave it, and get out.   Go back to the life of a man.
Leave the stars.   They're not saying what you think.
God is a rotten artist: he can't draw
With stars worth a shit   He can't say what He should
To men   He can't say   speak   with   with
Stars what you want Him to
Ah, but the key *image*
Tonight   *tonight*
is the gully   gullies:

Clouds make them, and other Realities
Are revealed in Heaven, as clouds drift across,
Mysterious   sperm-colored:
Yes.

There, the world is original, and the Zodiac shines anew
After every night-cloud.   New
With a nameless tiredness   a depth
Of field I can't read   an oblivion with no bottom

To it, ever, or never.

VIII

Sun.   Hand-steadying brightness   Time
To city-drift leg after leg, looking Peace
In its empty eyes as things are beginning
Already to go twelve hours
Toward the other side of the clock, the old twilight
When God's crazy beasts will come back.
Death is twenty-eight years old
Today.   Somewhere in between sunrise
And dusk he'll be bumming around.
Now he walks over water
He's on a bridge.   He feels truly rejected
but as he passes,
Vacancy puts on his head
The claw-hammer hair of terror.
He moves along the slain canal

Snoring in its bronze
Between docks.
                    The fish, too,
          Are afraid of the sun
Under the half-stacked greens of the rotten bridge,
And light falls with the ultimate marigold horror:

          Innocence.
                    The fish fin-flutter   able
Unable to hide their secrets any longer: what they know of Heaven
          As stars come down   come effortlessly down   down
Through water.   The trees are motionless, helping their leaves hold back

          Breath   life-death-breath—BACK: it's not time—

From the transparent rippling
                    European story they've been told to tell
Themselves when everybody's dead
                                        they glitter the water.

          They shake with dawn-fear.

I X

Again, his stepping stops him.   No reason.   Just does.
He's right here.   Then he's drawn wavering into the fort
                    Where the old house stands
On the vine-stalking hill.   The town moat gets with the dawn,
                    The morning loses time
Under the elm-heavy night, and in lost time   drift the swans
                    On-down, asleep.
          He roams all the way round, one finger tracing
A house-size circle on the wall.   The stone trembles   scrambles—
                    Comes clear: here was his room

                    Here his mother twisted pain to death
                    In her left breast—
                    Above that wrung one window on the battle-tower
His father hauled, each night the Beasts had their one-eyes,
His telescope across the galleried desert-might of Heaven.
                    Far, far beneath the body
Of his boy   the cellar filled with rats. Their scrambling made his poor, rich youth
Shake all night, every night. His face and neck were like sponges

Squeezed, slick with the green slime
That gave the book-backs on his shelves
Leprosy itself, and broke them out like relief-maps.
The garden, he thinks, was here,
Bald   a few sparse elephant-head hairs

Where as a kid he'd ambled grumbling like a ghost
In tulip shadow,
The light humid cool

Of the family maze.

The garden where he hid the body—
His own—somewhere under the grape-roof—well,

Let him cry, and wipe his face on dead leaves
Over the little bitch who filled, with *his* hand,
His diary with dreadful verses.

Why didn't he *do* it? That thing that scared him limp
In daylight, that he did all night with himself?
He should have screwed her or killed her
And he did—both—a hundred times. So would you.
Sure, sure. He always put it off.   Nothing would happen.
Too late anyway.   Too shy.   She'd pass right by him in the street,
Still, even if she saw him, joking with that asshole
She married, who'd once been a school-god to him.

Over.   All that's left of her is the dark of a home

She never visited.   There's no one in it; the man outside—myself—
Is understanding he's in the business
Of doublecrossing his dreams.

The grave of youth?   HA!   I told you: there's nobody *in* it!

Why the hell did he come out here?

He lays his forehead on the salt stone-grains of the wall,
Then puts an ivy-leaf between. He turns his cheek.

Outrage. Bare moon-stone. His ear's there
And the rock prepares.   It stills   stills
With his mother's voice. He grinds his hearing
Into the masonry   it is   it is   it says

"Never come back here.
                     Don't wander around your own youth.
         Time is too painful here. Nothing stays with you
    But what you remember."   The memory-animal crouched
Head-down   a huge lizard   in these vines, sleeping like winter,
Wrapped in dead leaves, lifts its eyes and pulls its lips back

                Only at reunion.

       He looks toward the window
       Behind whose frozen glass he'd fucked
       The first body he could get hold of.

       Leaving skin, he tears himself off the wall.

Goodbye?
       You're goddamned right, goodbye: this is *the* goodbye.

       "You must leave here in every way," she'd said.
       "When you feel the past draw you by the small intestine

       You've got to go somewhere else.   Anywhere.
Somewhere no footstep has scrambled.   Go for the empty road."

       "There's not any road," he says to the ivy
Massing with darkness behind him   "that doesn't have tracks,
    Most of them men's.   They've always been there."
        He sees his mother, laid-out in space,
         Point to the moon. "That thing," she says,
    "Puts man-tracks out like candles."
            He gets all the way away

       At last winding a little more
   Than the garden path can wind.   He struggles in weeds,
         Cursing, passing along
       The piss-smell standing with the stable,
       And reads on the first and last door,
          Where his father's live
       Starry letters had stood, a new

Designation   of somebody once human and here,
        Now also moved away, dead, forgotten too,

       His long name harder than time.

X

Tenderness, ache on me,   and lay your neck
On the slight shoulder-breathing of my arm . . .
There's nobody to be tender with—
This man has given up
On anything stronger than he is.

He's traveled everywhere
But no place has ever done any good.
What does his soul matter, saved like a Caesar-headed goldpiece,
When the world's dying?

He goes to the window,
Hating everything, worn out, looking into the shook heart
Of the city.

Yet the stairwell hammers lightly
Alive: a young step, nimble as foxfire,
And the vital shimmer of a real face
Backs-off the white of the room.
He closes his eyes, for the voice.
"My head is paralyzed with longing—"

He is quiet, but his arm is with her   around
Her belly and tailbone.
His heart broods: he knows that nothing,
Even love, can kill off his lonesomeness.

Twilight passes, then night.

Their bodies are found by the dawn, their souls
Fallen from them, left in the night
Of patterns   the night that's just finished
Overwhelming the earth.

Fading   fading   faded . . .

They lie like the expanding universe.

Too much light.   Too much love.

XI

A big room, a high one;
His first time in somebody else's.

Past the window, wind and rain
Paper-chasing each other to death,

And in the half-light, framed, Kandinsky's blue pressure-points,
Against their will, turn red, and swirl
Art's drunken blood out of the wallpaper.
His friend's voice rolls in his brain,
Rolls over and over
Joyfully, rapid-fire.   The lamp seeps on;
He thaws, forge-red like the stove,
Going blue with room-smoke—
And he shakes free of two years of wandering
Like melting-off European snows.

He tells.

He polar-bears through the room.
When he turns, a great grin breaks out.
The bottle pops its cork, and talk rushes over   rushes into
Cheese and gin   women   politics—
All changed   all the same . . .
Getting darker,
And by God, there's the *fish* market, gleaming its billion scales
Upward to him through the window.
More lights go on.
Where was he this time last year? He sees it:
Sees himself for a second at the Tetuan Friday Market,
And the *chalif,* through a double shine of trumpets,
Go into the tiny mosque.   It's all in pictures
In his friend's drunk-book.   He feels his last year, and his back
To the foreign wall. He turns page after page
Of the world   the post-cards he's sent,

Eagerly, desperately, looking for himself,
Tired, yellow with jaundice as an old portrait,
and something—
That's it.   He's just heard an accordion:
Two squeezed-lung, last-ditch
First-ditch Dutch chords

And he's back home.

XII

A day like that.   But afterwards the fire
Comes straight down through the roof, white-lightning nightfall,
A face-up flash. Poetry. Triangular eyesight. It draws his
fingers together at the edge
Around a pencil.   He crouches bestially,
         The darkness stretched out on the waters
      Pulls back, humming Genesis. From wave-stars lifts
         A single island wild with sunlight,
         The white sheet of paper in the room.

He's far out and far in, his hands in a field of snow.
      He's making a black horizon with all the moves
      Of his defeated body. The virgin sheet becomes
   More and more his, more and more another mistake,

But now, *now*
               Oh God you rocky landscape   give me,   Give
Me drop by drop
            desert water at least.
      I want to write about deserts

      And in the dark the sand begins to cry
      For living water that not a sun or star
Can kill, and for the splay camel-prints that bring men,
   And the ocean with its enormous crooning, begs

      For haunted sailors   for refugees putting back
         Flesh on their ever-tumbling bones
            To man that fleet,
                           for in its ships
            Only, the sea becomes the sea.

      Oh my own soul, put me in a solar boat.
         Come into one of these hands
         Bringing quietness and the rare belief
      That I can steer this strange craft to the morning
   Land that sleeps   in the universe on all horizons
         And give this home-come man who listens in his room

      To the rush and flare of his father
      Drawn at the speed of light to Heaven
Through the wrong end of his telescope, expanding the universe,

The instrument   the tuning-fork—
He'll flick it with his bandless wedding-finger—
Which at a touch reveals the form
Of the time-loaded European music
That poetry has never really found,
Undecipherable as God's bad, Heavenly sketches,
Involving fortress and flower, vine and wine and bone,

And shall vibrate through the western world
So long as the hand can hold its island
Of blazing paper, and bleed for its images:
Make what it can of what is:

So long as the spirit hurls on space
The star-beasts of intellect and madness.

THE STRENGTH

OF FIELDS

Root-light, or the Lawyer's Daughter

That any just to long for
The rest of my life, would come, diving like a lifetime
Explosion in the juices
Of palmettoes flowing
Red in the St. Mary's River as it sets in the east
Georgia from Florida off, makes whatever child
I was lie still, dividing
Swampy states   watching
The lawyer's daughter shocked
With silver   and I wished for all holds
On her like root-light. She came flying
Down from Eugene Talmadge
Bridge, just to long for as I burst with never
Rising never
Having seen her except where she worked
For J. C. Penney in Folkston. Her regular hours
Took fire, and God's burning bush of the morning
Sermon was put on her; I had never seen it where
It has to be. If you asked me how to find the Image
Of Woman to last
All your life, I'd say go lie
Down underwater for nothing
Under a bridge and hold Georgia
And Florida from getting at each other   hold
Like walls of wine. Be eight years old from Folkston ten
From Kingsland twelve miles in the cleam palmetto color
Just as it blasts
Down with a body   red and silver buck
Naked with bubbles on Sunday   root
light explodes

Head-down, and there she is.

The Strength of Fields

. . . a separation from the world,
a penetration to some source of power
and a life-enhancing return . . . —*Van Gennep: Rites de Passage*

Moth-force a small town always has,

Given the night.

What field-forms can be,
Outlying the small civic light-decisions over
A man walking near home?
Men are not where he is
Exactly now, but they are around him   around him like the strength

Of fields.   The solar system floats on
Above him in town-moths.
Tell me, train-sound,
With all your long-lost grief,
what I can give.

Dear Lord of all the fields
what am I going to *do*?
Street-lights, blue-force and frail
As the homes of men, tell me how to do it   how
To withdraw   how to penetrate and find the source
Of the power you always had
light as a moth, and rising
With the level and moonlit expansion
Of the fields around, and the sleep of hoping men.

You?   I?   What difference is there?   We can all be saved

By a secret blooming. Now as I walk
The night   and you walk with me   we know simplicity
Is close to the source that sleeping men
Search for in their home-deep beds.

We know that the sun is away   we know that the sun can be conquered
By moths, in blue home-town air.
The stars splinter, pointed and wild. The dead lie under
The pastures.   They look on and help.   Tell me, freight-train,
When there is no one else
To hear.   Tell me in a voice the sea

Would have, if it had not a better one: as it lifts,
      Hundreds of miles away, its fumbling, deep-structured roar
        Like the profound, unstoppable craving
        Of nations for their wish.
                        Hunger, time and the moon:

  The moon lying on the brain
                      as on the excited sea   as on
    The strength of fields.   Lord, let me shake
  With purpose.   Wild hope can always spring
  From tended strength.   Everything is in that.
    That and nothing but kindness.   More kindness, dear Lord
Of the renewing green.   That is where it all has to start:
    With the simplest things.   More kindness will do nothing less
      Than save every sleeping one
      And night-walking one

  Of us.
      My life belongs to the world. I will do what I can.

Two Poems of the Military

I. HAUNTING THE MANEUVERS
           Prepared for death and unprepared
For war, there was Louisiana   there was Eisenhower a Lieutenant
          Colonel and there was I
    As an Invasion Force.   The Defenders were attacking
         And I was in the pinestraw
  Advancing   inching through the aircraft of the Home
      Force.   Sacks of flour were bursting
All over the trees. Now if one of them damned things hits you in the head
        It's gonna kill you just as sure as if
         It was a real bomb
     So watch it.   Yes Sir. I was watching
      It.   One sack came tumbling after
         Me no matter
    What. Not in the head,   though,
      I thought thank God at least
  Not dead.
         But I was dead.   The sergeant said go sit

Over there: you are the first man killed.   It's KP for you
For the whole rest of the war.   This war,
Anyway.   Yes Sir.   The Defenders had struck
The first blow: I was plastered.   I thought why this
Is easy: there's not a drop
Of blood there's only death
White on me; I can live
Through.
I lived through in the Hell
Of latrine duty, but mostly on KP, on metal
Trays that dovetailed to each other, stacked by the ton in the field
Kitchens. I moved them all at one time
Or other, and the Defenders
Ate   ate and went back to killing
My buddies with blanks and bread. But when I slept on that well
Defended ground   the pinestraw stirred   each needle pointed up
Into the dark like a compass, and white   whiter
Than my skin, edible, human-eyed through the pines,
Issued a great mass
Laugh   a great lecture-laugh by the chaplain's one
Dirty joke, I rose
Over the unprepared boys   over the war
Games the war
Within a war   over the trucks with mystical signs
On them that said TANK   over World War One
Enfield rifles filled with dud rounds   self-rising
Through the branches   driven up like a small cloud
Of the enemy's food   at the same time bread

And bomb, swanned out like a diver, I came
From my death over both sleeping armies,
Over Eisenhower dreaming of invasion.   Where are you,
My enemy?   My body won't work any more
For you: I stare down like stars
Of yeast: you will have to catch me
And eat me.   Where are you, invading
Friends?   Who else is dead?   O those who are in this
With me, I can see nothing
But what is coming   can say
Nothing but what the first-killed
Working hard all day for his vision

Of war says best: the age-old Why
In God's name Why
In Louisiana, Boys   O Why
In Hell are we doing this?

II. DRUMS WHERE I LIVE

So that sleeping and waking
Drum, drum, every day the first part of the sun,
Its upper rim
And rhythm, I live here. I and my family pass, in the new house,
Into the great light mumbling one
Two three four, marching in place like boys
Laid out, all voices of the living and the dead
To come and hovering
Between brought in
to cadence.   It is not
A heart, but many men.   Someone said it is
Comfort, comforting to hear them.   Not every
Sun-up, neighbor: now and then I wish I had a chance
To take my chances
With silence. More and more
They seem to be waiting
For the day   more and more as my son sighs all over the house
Intercom.   I know, I know: he is counting
His years.   When we rise, the drums
Have stopped. But I know from the jungle of childhood
Movies what that means. There is nothing in the grenades'
Coming-closer bursts to worry
Anyone; they are Expanding
The Range.   It is only in the morning
Paper that a trainee hangs himself
On the obstacle course.   And it is nothing but nerves
That make something human, a cry,
Float like a needle on the sunlight
From the stockade.   But every night I sleep assured
That the drums are going
To reach me at dawn like light
Where I live, and my heart, my blood and my family will assemble
Four barely-livable counts.   Dismissed,
Personnel.   The sun is clear

Of Basic Training.   This time, thís
Is my war and where in God's
Name did it start?   In peace, two, three, four:
In peace peace peace peace

One two

In sleep.

The Voyage of the Needle

The child comes sometimes with his mother's needle
And draws a bath with his hand.   These are your fifty years
Of fingers, cast down among
The hard-driven echoes of tile
In the thresholding sound of run water.   Here the sun divides light
From the Venetian sector of the dark
Where you sink through both,
and warmly, more slowly than being
Smoothed and stretched, your bodying barge-ripples die.
A gauze of thin paper upholds
The needle, then soaks like an eyelid
And falls, uncontrolling, away.
The hung metal voyages alone,
Like the trembling north-nerve of a compass,
On surface tension, that magic, like a mother's spell
Cast in sharp seed in your childhood, in scientific trickery rooted
And flowering in elation. It is her brimming otherworld
That rides on the needle's frail lake, on death's precarious membrane,
Navigating through all level latitudes,
Containing a human body
She gave, and saved to bear, by a spell
From physics, this fragile cargo.   "Mother," you say,
"I am lying in a transference
Of joy and glory: come to me
From underground, from under the perilous balance
Of a thicket of thorns.   I lie
As unmoving. Bring the needle to breathless harbor
Somewhere on my body, that I may rise
And tell. My sex is too deep,

My eyes too high for your touch. O let it reach me at the lips'
        Water-level, the thorns burst
Into rain on your wooded grave, the needle plunge
Through the skin of charmed water and die, that I may speak at last
        With up-bearing magic
    Of this household, weightless as love."

The Rain Guitar

—England, 1962—

        The water-grass under had never waved
      But one way.   It showed me that flow is forever
    Sealed from rain in a weir.   For some reason having
  To do with Winchester, I was sitting on my guitar case
Watching nothing but eelgrass trying to go downstream with all the right motions
    But one. I had on a sweater, and my threads were opening
      Like mouths with rain. It mattered to me not at all
        That a bridge was stumping
      With a man, or that he came near and cast a fish
      thread into the weir.   I had no line and no feeling.
        I had nothing to do with fish
  But my eyes on the grass they hid in, waving with the one move of trying
      To be somewhere else. With what I had, what could I do?
  I got out my guitar, that somebody told me was supposed to improve
     With moisture—or was it when it dried out?—and hit the lowest
      And loudest chord.   The drops that were falling just then
        Hammered like Georgia railroad track
      With E.   The man went into a kind of fishing
      Turn.   Play it, he said through his pipe.   There
    I went, fast as I could with cold fingers.   The strings shook
  With drops.   A buck dance settled on the weir.   Where was the city
        Cathedral in all this?
      Out of sight, but somewhere around.
        Play a little more
    Of that, he said, and cast.   Music-wood shone,
      Getting worse or better faster than it liked:
        Improvement or disintegration
        Supposed to take years, fell on it
      By the gallon.   It darkened and rang

Like chimes. My sweater collapsed, and the rain reached
My underwear. I picked, the guitar showered, and he cast to the mountain
Music.   His wood leg tapped
On the cobbles.   Memories of many men
Hung, rain-faced, improving, sealed-off
In the weir.   I found myself playing Australian
Versions of British marching songs.   Mouths opened all over me; I sang,
His legs beat and marched
Like companions.   I was Air Force,
I said.   So was I; I picked
This up in Burma, he said, tapping his gone leg
With his fly rod, as Burma and the South
west Pacific and North Georgia reeled,
Rapped, cast, chimed, darkened and drew down
Cathedral water, and improved.

Remnant Water

Here in the thrust-green

Grass-wind and thin surface now nearly
Again and again for the instant

Each other   hair-lined backwater barely there and it
Utterly:
                              this that was deep flashing—
Tiny grid-like waves   wire-touched water—
No more, and comes what is left

Of the gone depths duly arriving
Into the weeds belly-up:
                              one carp now knowing grass
And also thorn-shucks and seeds
Can outstay him:
                              next to the slain lake the inlet
Trembles   seine-pressure in something of the last
Rippling   grass in the slow-burning

Slow-browning dance learned from green;
A hundred acres of canceled water come down
To death-mud shaking

Its one pool   stomach-pool   holding the dead one diving up
Busting his gut in weeds   in scum-gruel glowing with belly-white
Unhooked   around him all grass in a bristling sail taking off back-
       blowing.   Here in the dry hood I am watching
Alone, in my tribal sweat   my people gone my fish rolling
                      Beneath me   and I die
                      Waiting   will wait out
                The blank judgment given only
In ruination's suck-holing acre   wait and make the sound surrounding NO
                Laugh primally: be
       Like an open-gut flash   an open under-
                water eye with the thumb
       pressure to brain the winter-wool head of me,
Spinning my guts with my fish in the old place,
       Suffering its consequences, dying,
                Living up to it.

Two Poems of Flight-Sleep

I. CAMDEN TOWN

—Army Air Corps,
Flight Training, 1943—

       With this you trim it.   Do it right and the thing'll fly
       Itself.   Now get up there and get those lazy-
       eights down.   A check-ride's coming at you
Next week.
       I took off in the Stearman like stealing two hundred and twenty horses
Of escape from the Air Corps.
                      The cold turned purple with the open
       Cockpit, and the water behind me being
The East, dimmed out.   I put the nose on the white sun
And trimmed the ship.   The altimeter made me
At six thousand feet.   We were stable: myself, the plane,
                The earth everywhere
                Small in its things with cold
       But vast beneath.   The needles on the panel
All locked together, and a banner like World War One
Tore at my head, streaming from my helmet in the wind.

I drew it down   down under the instruments
Down where the rudder pedals made small corrections
Better than my feet   down where I could ride on faith
And trim, the aircraft slightly cocked
But holding the West by a needle.   I was in
Death's baby machine, that led to the fighters and bombers,
But training, here in the lone purple,
For something else.   I pulled down my helmet-flaps and droned
With flight-sleep.   Near death
My watch stopped.   I knew it, for I felt the Cadet
Barracks of Camden die like time, and "There's a war on"
Die, and no one could groan from the dark of the bottom
Bunk to his haggard instructor, I tried
I tried to do what you said   I tried   tried
No;   never.   No one ever lived to prove he thought he saw
An aircraft with no pilot showing: I would have to become
A legend, curled up out of sight with all the Western World
Coming at me under the floor-mat, minute after minute, cold azures,
Small trains and warbound highways,
All entering flight-sleep.   Nothing mattered but to rest in the winter
Sun beginning to go
Down early.   My hands in my armpits, I lay with my sheep-lined head
Next to the small air-moves
Of the rudder pedals, dreaming of letting go   letting go
The cold   the war   the Cadet Program and my peanut-faced
Instructor and his maps.   No maps   no world   no love
But this.   Nothing can fail when you go below
The instruments.   Wait till the moon.   Then.   Then.
But no.   When the waters of Camden Town died, then so
Did I, for good.   I got up bitterly, bitter to be
Controlling, re-entering the fast colds
Of my scarf, and put my hands and feet where the plane was made
For them.   My goggles blazed with darkness as I turned,
And the compass was wrenched from its dream
Of all the West.   From luxurious
Death in uncaring I swung
East, and the deaths and nightmares
And training of many.

—New York, 1972,
St. Moritz bar—

Didn't we double!
Sure, when we used to lie out under the wing
Double-teaming the Nips near our own hole
In the ground   opening an eye

For the Southern Cross, and we'd see something cut the stars

Out into some kind of shape, the shape of a new Widow

Black Widow
and all over the perimeter the ninety millimeters would open

Up on Heaven   the sirens would go off
And we'd know better than not to dive
for the palm logs,
The foxhole filled with fear-slime, and lie there,
Brains beating like wings
our new wings from Northrop,
The enemy looking for the aircraft
We slept under.
Well, we knew what we wanted,
Didn't we?
To get out from under our own wings,
To let them lift us
together
lift us out of the sleep
With a hole in it, and slot back fresh windows and climb in the squared-off cool
Of the Cross.
Angels, Observer!
Nine thousand angels,
Pilot! The altitude of the Heavenly Host

In the Philippines is that completely air-conditioned
Nine *thousand feet!*
I couldn't wait to fool with the automatic pilot,
And I went absolutely crazy over Howard Hughes' last word
In radar!
Remember?
We were pulling convoy cover.

By my figures we were seven hundred miles south of base, my eyes brilliant sweeps
Of electronic yellow, watching the spinner painting-in the fleet,
The arranged, lingering images of the huge fortunes
Of war   the great distances and secret relationships
Between tankers and troopships   and on my screen, God's small, brilliant chess-set
Of world war, as we sat
      Circling
                  relaxing in all the original freshness
                  Of the Cross, comfortable and light
                  And deadly: night-cool of nine thousand angels
                  Over the fleet.
                        You called back with clear, new
                  Electricity: Hey, Buddy, how're you liking this?
            What a war! I said.   The scope just pulses away
Like a little old yellow heart.   The convoy comes in, the convoy goes out
            And comes right back in for you and me
            And Uncle Sam.
                              It was easy,
            Right?   Milk run?   Why, by God, we flew on milk!
            I cut-in the automatic pilot and leaned back
In the cool of those southern stars, and could have spent the rest of my life
                  Watching the gyros jiggle the wheel
            With little moves like an invisible man   like a ghost
            Was flying us.   The next thing I knew the intercom busted in
            With YOU   I looked down and out
                              I looked the radar down
            To the depths of its empty yellow heart.   I didn't have a ship
            To my name.
                        And I said where in Hell
      Are we?   Jesus God, I was afraid of my watch   afraid to look
            Afraid the son of a bitch had stopped.   But no,
                  Four hours had gone to Hell
      Somewhere in the South Pacific.   Our engines were sucking wind,
            Running on fumes, and I started calling everything that had a code
Name south of our island.   Nothing.   But I thought of the five boys
            From our squadron   all volleyball players
                  With no heads, and all but one
Island south of us was Japanese.   I thought I could hear the sword swish,
                  But it was a wisp arriving
            In my earphones   an American spirit crackling

That we were over Cebu.   They had one strip and no lights,
          Lumps and holes in the runway and the moon
Almost gone.   I said to the Seabees get me a couple of things
          That burn;   I'll try to come down between 'em.

     —Can you hold out for fifteen minutes?—

     Just about.

          They doubled.   Two pairs of lights came running.
Together   then split   stopped and gave us five thousand devilish feet
     Of blackness laid out maybe on the ground. I said hold on,
          Buddy;   this may just be it.   We drifted in   full
Flaps   nose-high   easing   easing   cleared the first lighted jeep

               Hit and

               Bounced   came down again hit a hole
          And double-bounced   the great new night-
     gathering binoculars came unshipped and banged me in the head
               As I fought for hot, heavy ground,
               Trying to go straight for the rest of my life
                    For the other jeep,
               Doing anything and everything to slaughter
                    The speed, and finally down   ·
               Got down to the speed of a jeep   down
          Down and turned off into the bushes that'd been pouring
               By   pouring with sweat and killed
     The engine.   Man, was I shaking!   I couldn't even undo the hatch.
               You pounded at me
From underneath.   I'm all right, I said, drawing in the stuffed heat of life,
          Of my life. I climbed down, rattling the new black
California bolts of the wings.

                         Buddy, would you sit there and tell me
     How we got over Cebu?   Why, it was the wrong goddamned *island*!
               Why didn't you give me a course
     Correction?   Our million dollar Black Widow bird like to've carried us off
          And killed us!   How come you didn't say a thing
          For four hours?
                    I'm sorry, Pilot, but that Southern Cross
                    Had the most delicious lungs
                    For me.   We'd jumped out of our hole

On wings   the heat was off   and weight, and I could breathe
At last.   I was asleep.
　　　　　　　　　Well, for the Lord's sake,
　　　　Observer　　Navigator　　Miracle
　　　　Map-reader　　second half of the best
　　Two-man crew in night-fighters, as we sit here
　　　In Central Park, where on earth in that war
Have we *been?*
　　　　　　　　　I don't know.   I told you I was asleep.

　　　Well, Old Buddy, the ghosts had us
For sure, then.　　Ghosts and angels.　　Nobody else.
I guess, in Central Park, I can tell you, too, after all
　　　　These years.　　So was I.

For the Death of Lombardi

　　　I never played for you.　　You'd have thrown
　　　　Me off the team on my best day—
　　　No guts, maybe　　not enough speed,
　　　　　Yet running in my mind
　　　　As Paul Hornung, I made it here
　　With the others, sprinting down railroad tracks,
　　　Hurdling bushes and backyard Cyclone
Fences, through city after city, to stand, at last, around you
　　　　Exhausted,　　exalted, pale
　　　As though you'd said "Nice going":　　pale
　　　As a hospital wall.　　You are holding us
Millions together:　　those who played for you, and those who entered the bodies
　　Of Bart Starr, Donny Anderson, Ray Nitchke, Jerry Kramer
　　Through the snowing tube on Sunday afternoon,
　　　　　Warm, playing painlessly
　　In the snows of Green Bay Stadium, some of us drunk
On much-advertised beer　　some old　　some in other
　　　　Hospitals—most, middle-aged
　　And at home.　　Here you summon us, lying under
　　The surgical snows.　　Coach, look up:　　we are here:
　　　　　We are held in this room
　　　Like cancer

The Crab has you, and to him
And to us you whisper
Drive, *Drive*.   Jerry Kramer's face floats near—real, pale—
We others dream ourselves
Around you, and far away in the mountains, driving hard
Through the drifts, Marshall of the Vikings, plunging   burning
Twenty-dollar bills to stay alive, says, still
Alive, "I wouldn't be here
If it weren't for the lessons of football." Vince, they've told us:
When the surgeons got themselves
Together and cut loose
Two feet of your large intenstine, the Crab whirled up   whirled out
Of the lost gut and caught you again
Higher up.   Everyone's helpless
But cancer.   Around your bed the knocked-out teeth like hail-pebbles
Rattle down   miles of adhesive tape from hands and ankles
Writhe in the room like vines   gallons of sweat blaze in buckets
In the corners   the blue and yellow of bruises
Make one vast sunset around you.   No one understands you.
Coach, don't you know that some of us were ruined
For life?   Everybody can't win.   What of almost all
Of us, Vince?   We lost.   And our greatest loss was that we could not survive
Football. Paul Hornung has withdrawn
From me, and I am middle-aged and gray, like these others.
What holds us here?   It is that you are dying by the code you made us
What we are by.   Yes, Coach, it is true: love-hate is stronger
Than either love or hate.   Into the weekly, inescapable dance
Of speed, deception, and pain
You led us, and brought us here weeping,
But as men.   Or, you who created us as George
Patton created armies, did you discover the worst
In us: aggression   meanness   deception   delight in giving
Pain to others, for money?   Did you make of us, indeed,
Figments   over-specialized, brutal ghosts
Who could have been real
Men in a better sense?   Have you driven us mad
Over nothing?   Does your death set us free?

Too late.   We stand here among
Discarded TV commercials:
Among beer-cans and razor-blades and hair-tonic bottles,

Stinking with male deodorants: we stand here
Among teeth and filthy miles
Of unwound tapes, novocaine needles, contracts, champagne
Mixed with shower-water, unraveling elastic, bloody faceguards,
And the Crab, in his new, high position
Works soundlessly.   In dying
You give us no choice, Coach,
Either.   We've got to believe there's such a thing
As winning.   The Sunday spirit-screen
Comes on   the bruise-colors brighten   deepen
On the wall   the last tooth spits itself free
Of a line-backer's aging head   knee-cartilage cracks,
A boy wraps his face in a red jersey and crams it into
A rusty locker to sob, and we're with you
We're with you all the way
You're going forever, Vince.

False Youth: Autumn   Clothes of the Age

[for Susan Tuckerman Dickey]

Three red foxes on my head, come down
There last Christmas from Brooks Brothers
As a joke, I wander down Harden Street
In Columbia, South Carolina, fur-haired and bald,
Looking for impulse in camera stores and redneck greeting cards.
A pole is spinning
Colors I have little use for, but I go in
Anyway, and take off my fox hat and jacket
They have not seen from behind yet.   The barber does what he can
With what I have left, and I hear the end man say, as my own
Hair-cutter turns my face
To the floor, Jesus, if there's anything I hate
It's a middle-aged hippie.   Well, so do I, I swallow
Back: so do I   so do I
And to hell.   I get up, and somebody else says
When're you gonna put on that hat,
Buddy?   Right now.   Another says softly,
Goodbye, Fox.   I arm my denim jacket
On and walk to the door, stopping for the murmur of chairs,

And there it is
                    hand-stitched by the needles of the mother
Of my grandson   eagle riding on his claws with a banner
        Outstretched as the wings of my shoulders,
            Coming after me with his flag
        Disintegrating, his one eye raveling
            Out, filthy strings flying
    From the white feathers, one wing nearly gone:
            Blind eagle but flying
    Where I walk, where I stop with my fox
Head at the glass to let the row of chairs spell it out
    And get a lifetime look at my bird's
One word, raggedly blazing with extinction and soaring loose
In red threads burning up white until I am shot in the back
    Through my wings   or ripped apart
            For rags:

                    Poetry.

For the Running of the New York City Marathon

                    If you would run

    If you would quicken the city with your pelting,
        Then line up, be counted, and change
Your body into time, and with me through the boxed maze flee
    On soft hooves, saying   all saying in flock-breath
        Take me there.
                    I am against you
            And with you: I am second
Wind and native muscle in the streets   my image lost and discovered
        Among yours: lost and found in the endless panes
    Of a many-gestured bald-headed woman, caught between
        One set of clothes and tomorrow's: naked, pleading in her wax
            For the right, silent words to praise
            The herd-hammering pulse of our sneakers,
        And the time gone by when we paced
River-sided, close-packed in our jostled beginning,
        O my multitudes.
                    We are streaming from the many to the one

At a time, our ghosts chopped-up by the windows
Of merchants;   the mirroring store-fronts let us, this one day,
Wear on our heads feet and backs
What we would wish.   This day I have taken in my stride
Swank jogging-suits rayed with bright emblems
Too good for me: have worn in blood-sweating weather
Blizzard-blind parkas and mukluks, a lightning-struck hairpiece
Or two, and the plumes of displayed Zulu chieftains.

Through the colors of day I move as one must move
His shadow somewhere on
Farther into the dark.   Any hour now   any minute
Attend the last rites
Of pure plod-balance!   Smoke of the sacrificial
Olympic lamb in the Deli!   O swooping and hairline-hanging
Civic-minded placement of bridges!   Hallelujas of bars!
Teach those who have trained in the sunrise
On junk-food and pop, how to rest   how to rise
From the timed city's never-die dead.   Through the spattering echo
Of Vulcanized hundreds, being given the finish-line hot-foot,
I am lolloping through to the end,
By man-dressing mannequins clad   by flashes of sun on squared rivers
As we breast our own breathless arrival: as we home in,
Ahead of me   me   and behind me
All winning over the squirrel-wheel's outlasted stillness, on the unearthly pull and
Of our half-baked soles, all agony-
smiles and all winning—

All winning, one after one.

Exchanges
(Phi Beta Kappa Poem, Harvard, 1970)

—being in the form of a dead-living dialogue with
Joseph Trumbull Stickney (1874–1904)—
(Stickney's words are in italics)

Under the cliff, green powered in from the open,
Changed   and she
And I crouched at the edge
Five hundred feet above the ocean's suicide in a bubble

And horizon of oil.   Smog and sweet love!   We had the music for the whale-
        death of the world.   About us the environment crumbled
                In yellow light.   There was no forth-
            coming of wave-silver, but silver would flash now
        And then through, turning side-on in many mullet
                To the sun to die, as I tuned
            The wild guitar.   This won't get any worse
                Until tomorrow, I said
        Of Los Angeles, gazing out through "moderate eye
        damage"   twisting the pegs   and under the strings

            —The gray crane spanned his level, gracious flight

                Knowing better than to come
                To rest on anything, or touch
                Zuma Point here and now.

                                        —O sea

                Of California, thou Pacific,
            For which the multitude of mortals bound
            Go trembling headlong and with terrific
        Outcry are drowned:
                                Day-moon meant more
    Far from us   dazing the oil-slick with the untouched remainder
        Of the universe   spreading   contracting
                Catching fish at the living end
            In their last eye   the guitar rang moon and murder
    And Appalachian love, and sent them shimmering from the cliff

                —The burning season shone
                On the vast feather-shapes of the open
                    Sea tranquilized by off-
                shore drilling
                            where gulls flapped in black
                        Gold   black
                        Magic of corporations—

            —So here did mix the land's breath and the sea's:
                Among the beautiful murders
                Showering down ballad
            After ballad on the rainbows of forever lost
            Petroleum that blew its caps and turned on

All living things, we sang and prayed for purity, scattered everywhere
Among the stones
Of other worlds   and asked the moon to stay off us
As far as it always had, and especially far
From L.A.   I playing from childhood also
Like the Georgia mountains   the wind out of Malibu whipped her
Long hair into "Wildwood Flower"   her blue eye   —*whose eye*
Was somewhat strangely more than blue
Closed
—and if we lived
We were the cresting of a tide wherein
An endless motion rose exemplified.

                                                                                    In

—The gentle ecstasy of earth
And ruination, we lay on the threatened grass
Of cliffs, she tangled in my strings, her dark hair tuned
To me, the mountains humming back
Into resolution, in the great low-crying key
Of A.
—I saw the moon and heard her sing.
I saw her sing and heard the moon.

O vibrating mountains and bronze
Strings, O oil-slicks in the moderately damaged eye
And the sides of fish flashing out
One more time   birds black with corporations, turn me over to those

—Maddened with hunger for another world:
She lies in Glendale,
In Forest Lawn,
                                                            O astronauts,
Poets, all those
Of the line of wizards and saviors, spend your lives
And billions of dollars to show me
The small true world
Of death, the place we sang to
From Zuma.   I read and imagine everything
I can of the gray airless ground
Of the moon   sphere cracked and bombarded
By negation   pure death, where death has not
Yet come

                    —where yet no God appears:
                                        Who knows?
              There might be some unknown
              Consolation in knowing California
              Is not the deadest world of all
        Until tomorrow: might be some satisfaction
              Gone spatial   some hope
        Like absolute zero, when the earth can become

                    —The last of earthly things
              Carelessly blooming in immensity
                                        and live men ride
Fleeing outward
                    —a white flame tapering at the core of space   their hatches
              —Firm-barred against the fearful universe   until
              In the easy-leaping country
        Of death, beings——*still armored in their visionary gold*
Do human deeds.
              What deeds?
                                        Will Los Angeles rise from the Sea
              Of Tranquillity, on a great bubble
              Of capped breath and oil?   Not yet;
              The first men will see that desolation
              Unimproved, before the freeways
              Link it to Earth. Ah, to leap or lie
              On some universal ruin
        Not ruined by us!   To be able to say—*Am I dead*
              That I'm so far?
                                        But where I stand,
              Here, under the moon, the moon
              —Breaks desperate magic on the world I know,

On Glendale.   *—All through the shadows crying grows, until*
        The wailing is like grass upon the ground.
                                        It is I

Howling like a dog for the moon, for Zuma Point no matter what
        The eye-damage   howling to bring her back note
              By note like a childhood mountain
        In the key of A   or, lacking that, howling
     For anything   for the ultimate death   pure death
        For the blaze of the outer dark   for escape

From L.A. smoldering and eye-
burning along the freeways   from the rubber-smoke
And exhaust streaming *into the endless shadow*
Of my memory.   *—Let me grind alone*
And turn my knuckles in the granite
Of the moon
                        where underfoot the stones
—*wild with mysterious truth*
                              lie in their universal
            Positions, in a place of no breath
    And one machine
                        and for these reasons and many
        Another I was quartered and drawn
To Cape Canaveral, with my tangled dream of Los Angeles
And death and the moon, my dead girl still tuned to me
In my tangled guitar.   The environment crumbled
        In red light, and raised up by dawn
Almighty buildings.
                        I felt a time-like tremor in my limbs.
        I wished to be bound that morning
For the true dead land, the land made to sustain
No life at all, giving out the unruined light
That shines on the fish-slicks of Zuma.
                              —Are we the people of the end?
                                          Before us all
            The sun burst
From a machine   timed   slowly   tilting   leaning
    Upward   drawn moonward inch by inch   faster
        Faster   a great composite roar battered
            Like a board at the very bone
            Marrow, and in the hardshell case
        I sat on, the strings vibrated not with
    Mountains   but made the shapeless and very
            Music of the universal
    Abyss
                —and all the air
        Was marvelous and sorrowful
                              as we beheld,
Exploding with solitude   blasting into the eyes and body,
        Rising   rising in dreadful machine-

pain as we prayed   as the newsmen fell to their knees   as the quality of life
              And death changed forever
        For better or worse
               —Apollo springing naked to the light.
          Nothing for me
       Was solved.   I wandered the beach
        Mumbling to a dead poet
      In the key of A, looking for the rainbow
         Of oil, and the doomed
    Among the fish.
              —Let us speak softly of living.

*HEAD-DEEP IN
STRANGE SOUNDS:
FREE-FLIGHT
IMPROVISATIONS
FROM THE
UNENGLISH*

Purgation

—Po Chü-yi—

Beyond the eye, grasses go over the long fields.
Every season it happens, as though I—no; I and you,
Dear friend—decreed it.   It is what we would like to have,

And it is there.
                    It is the season for wildfire,
And it will come, but will never quite get every one
Of the grasses.   There is some green left, this year as last,

For us.   Once more they are tall
In the April wind.   They make the old road *be*

The road, where you and I go toward the old, beetle-eaten
City gate.   Oh, fire, come *on*!   I trust you.

My ancient human friend, you are dead, as we both know.
But I remember, and I feel the grass and the fire
Get together in April   with you and me, and that
Is what I want   both age-gazing living and dead

        both sighing like grass and fire.

The Ax-God: Sea Pursuit

—after Alfred Jarry—

On the horizon, through the steam of exhausted blast-furnaces   fog   Yes
Pure Chance blows, as though it were really itself   blows
Not very well, and moans and shakes bells.

These are the sounds that invented salt.   But, listen,
Waves, we are among the arced demons you are hiding

In the visiting green gullies of your mountains.
Where the shoreline clamps a lost quivering over all
Of us, a huge and shadow-cast shape looms over muck.
We crawl round his feet, loose as lizards,

While, like a filthy Caesar on his chariot,
Or on a marble, leg-crossing plinth,
Carving a whale-boat from a tree-trunk, he . . .

Well, in that branching boat, he'll run
Us down, league for league   down   down to
The last of the sea's center-speeding
Center-spreading and ropeless knots.   Green   blue   white
Time space distance: starting from the shore

His arms of unhealable, veined copper   over us
Raise to Heaven a breathing blue ax.

Nameless

(near Eugenio Montale)

Sure.   All the time I come up on the evil

                        of just living:

It's been the strangled creek that still tries
To bubble like water   it's been the death-rattling leaf
Dried out for no reason
                    and the tripped-sprawling horse.

As for anything good: you find it for me
And I'll look at it.   All I can come up with
Is an enclosure: the religion-faking sun-blasted rack
Of divine Indifference.   As I say, Sure:

It's the statue in its somnolescence
Of primitive, hectored stone.   It's noon

And cloud   and the falcon in circles,
Who planes, as high as he can get,

                For nothing.

Math

—*Lautréamont*—

Numbers who can't ever hear me
                I'll say it anyway
All the way from my age-old school.   You're still in my heart,
    And I can feel you go through there

Like a clean sea-wave.   I breathed-in, instinctively,
From the one-two, one-two counts
        Of the soft-rocking cradle

      As drinking from a universal spring
                              older than the sun:

Numbers.   There is this wave of matched, watched numbers
In my school-soul.   Sometimes it is like smoke: I can't get through it.
Sometimes I believe that you've put   put in place of my heart
Inhuman logic.   Coldness
                          beyond bearing.   And yet . . . because of you
My intelligence has grown far beyond me
                              from the frozen, radiant center
Of that ravishing clarity you give: give to those
      Who most truly love you   and can find you: *Listen,* ever-deaf numbers.
                                Hail!   *I* hail you
            Arithmetic!   Algebra!   Geometry!

                  Triangle gone luminous!

Judas

—*Georg Heym, resurrected from under the ice*—

Mark.   Hair, one strand of it, can curl
Over your forehead like a branding-iron.
And meaningless winds   and many voices can be whispering
Like creek-flow, staying and going by.

But he runs close to His side like a mongrel,
And in the sick mud he picks up everything said
To him, and weighs it in his quivering hands.
                              It is dead.

Ah, most gently in the swaying dusk,
The Lord walked down
Over the white fields.   Ear by ear, green by green,
Yellow by yellow, the corn-ears, the stalks, the sheer *growing*
Glorified.   His feet were as small as houseflies, as they were perpetually being

Sent-down step by step
            From the golden hysteria of Heaven.

Small Song

—from the Hungarian of Attila Jozsef,
head crushed between two boxcars—

I'm laughing, but being very quiet about it.
I've got my pipe and my knife:
I am quiet, and laughing like hell.

All hail, Wind!   Let my song fall in jigsaw fragments!
Nobody is my friend except the one who can say
"I take pleasure in his misery."

I am of shadow and of sun   of the sun
                    Returning always,

And I laugh, silently.

Undersea Fragment in Colons

—Vicente Aleixandre—

Swordfish, I know you are tired: tired out with the sharpness of your face:
        Exhausted with the impossibility of ever
Piercing the shade: with feeling the tunnel-breathing streamline of your flesh
        Enter and depart   depart
                                    spirit-level after level of Death
                        Tamped flat, and laid
Where there is no hillside grave.
                        Take this as it settles, then: word
        That behind your incomparable weapon chokes and builds,
            Blocked and balanced in your sides
                Instinct with meridians: word: the x-mark of certain world-numbers
                    Blood-brothering   rising blade-headed
To an element as basic as the water
                                    unraveling in layers from around you:
                    Strata trapped and stitched
By your face like tapestry
                            thinning   exploding
            The depth-imploded isinglass eye
                                    west of Greenwich and shocked
        Into latitude   into the sea-birds' winged sea   tonnage of shifting silence now

Freed to the unleashed Time
And timing of coordinates: all solid-light:

Pierceable sun   its flash-folded counterpart beneath
By the billion: word: in one leap the layers,

The slant ladder of soundlessness: word: world: sea:
Flight partaking of tunnels   fins, of quills and airfoils:
Word: unwitnessed numbers   nailed noon   enchanted three minutes
Of the sun's best effort of height   this space   time   this
Hang-period   meridian passage:
Sing.

Mexican Valley

—homage and invention, Octavio Paz—

The day works on
works out its transparent body.   With fire, the bodiless hammer,
Light knocks me flat.
Then lifts me.   Hooked on-
to the central flame-stone, I am nothing but a pause between
Two vibrations
of pressureless glow: Heaven
And trees.   Tlaloc help me
I am pure space:
One of the principle future-lost battlefields
Of light.   Through my body, I see my other bodies

Flocking and dancing   fighting each other
With solar joy.   Every stone leaps inward, while the sun tears out my eyes
And my Heaven-knifed, stone-drunken heart.
Yes,
But behind my gone sight is a spiral of wings.
Now   *now*
My winged eyes are fetched-back and singing: yes singing like buzzards
From the black-feathered crown-shifts of air
That have always wished to be singing
over this valley.
And I lean over my song
Within trees, God knows where,

                                    in Mexico.
No matter what they say, it is not bad here.   No, it is good:
It is better than anything the astronomers can dream up
With their sweaty computers.   I've shaved my chest off to be
         Slowly-nearer and now without junk-hair
That is not really me   instantaneously nearer
         Soft universal power!   It is warm, it is maybe even a little
Too hot, but glorious, here at the center   all the center there is
Before history . . . I send you a searing Yes
From the thousand cross-glittering black-holes of obsidian:
              I am like the *theory* of a blade
         That closes rather than opens   *closes:*
         That sends something back
Other than blood.   Among leaves, I have torn out the heart of the sun
              The long-lost Mexican sun.

Low Voice, Out Loud

   —*Léon-Paul Fargue*—

A good many times I've come down among you.
I've brought down my mountains, and washed them, just as a cloud would
                                                            have done
But you   YOU   cannot even begin to guess the *space*
Of the great shadows that've just gone past us.
                                    But, look:
I come out of you!
                   I was your hands   your life-work
Your bleeding eyes   your red cubby-hole!   And that guitar:
To you, one touch of E minor is suicide!
I need you.
              I have lifted the anchor.
                             For the thousandth time
I have smelled your shoes.
                             There I have done it, close to you and me:
I have lifted the anchor.
                   Whoever loves well
Punishes well.   But don't go
Against my rhythm.
                   It is by you that the man   in this case myself

Limits himself to being   his own being
A man: Identity blind, deaf
And indivisible!
                    I am tired of existing
As an animal of intelligence—

Don't try to name what is nameless.

Nothing.   Everything.   Nothing.
                      Rest easy, love.   It is best:
Let us go back into the immense and soft-handed, double

Fire-bringing ignorance.

Poem

—*from the Finnish of Saima Harmaja*—

O death, so dear to me,
Do you remember when someone loved you?

Let all our blood-kin come back, into
Your soft, embalmed half-shadow.

Look.   I'm making no gestures.
I like and don't like
Your diligent work.   I try not to pay attention.
Other troubles I can stand.   Not yours.

Free my soul
            and open your blinding jail.

O my sweet, owned death,
Lift the used-up one,
The soul half-opened as a wound
                  and let him fly.

When

—Pierre Reverdy—

A prisoner in this space perpetually narrow
With my left-over hands left on my eyelids
With none of the words that reason can bring itself

To invent
        I play the hell-game
That dances on the horizon.   Space in darkness makes it better,

And it may be there are people passing through me—
There may even be a song
               of some kind

      The cloud fills itself full of hovering holes

      The needle loses itself
      In clothes-covered sharpness

      The thunder stops short—
A few more minutes
            I'll start to shake:
It's too late   too late ever to act   to act at all:

This is the thing as it will be.
All around, chains are gritting on each other
Like blackboard chalk   every tree
In the world is going to fall.

The window opens to summer.

A Saying of Farewell

—homage, Nordahl Grieg—

You've dressed yourself so white for it!   And you poise
As on the edge of an undersea cliff, for departure.
We two are the only ones who know that this lost instant
      Is not lost, but is the end
        Of life.

"It's as though we were dying, this calm twilight."

No;   only you.   I hang on watch,
High up in Time.   Step off and fall as the wind rolls the earth

Over you like a wave.   I am left on duty with the heart
    Going out over everything, no sleep

      In sight   braced,   monster-eyed,
    Outstaring the shaken powder of fatigue   mist—
      By your clothes and mine white-bled

    Raging with discovery like a prow
       Into the oncoming Never.

Three Poems with Yevtushenko

I. I DREAMED I ALREADY LOVED YOU

I dreamed I already loved you.
I dreamed I already killed you.

But you rose again;   another form,
A girl on the little ball of the earth,
Naive simplicity, curve-necked
On that early canvas of Picasso,
And prayed to me with your ribs
"Love me," as though you said, "Don't push me off."

I'm that played out, grown-up acrobat,
Hunchbacked with senseless muscles,
Who knows that advice is a lie,
That sooner or later there's falling.

I'm too scared to say I love you
Because I'd be saying I'll kill you.

For in the depths of a face I can see through
I see the faces—can't count them—
Which, right on the spot, or maybe
Not right away, I tortured to death.

You're pale from the mortal balance. You say
"I know everything;   I was all of them.
I know you've already loved me.
I know you've already killed me.

But I won't spin the globe backwards
We're on: Love again, and then kill again."

Lord, you're young.   Stop your globe.
I'm tired of killing.   I'm not a damn thing but old.

You move the earth beneath your little feet,
You fall, "Love me."
It's only in those eyes—not similar—you say
"This time don't kill me."

II. ASSIGNATION

No, no! Believe me!
                    I've come to the wrong place!
I've made a god-awful mistake!   Even the glass
In my hand's an accident
                    and so's the gauze glance
Of the woman who runs the joint.
                              "Let's dance, huh?
You're pale . . .
                    Didn't get enough sleep?"
And I feel like there's no place
To hide, but say, anyway, in a rush
"I'll go get dressed . . .
                    No, no . . . it's just
That I ended up out of bounds . . ."
And later, trailing me as I leave:
                         This is where booze gets
                              you . . .
What do you mean, 'not here'? *Right* here! Right here every time!
You bug everybody, and you're so satisfied
With yourself about it.   Zhenichka,
You've got a problem."
                         I shove the frost of my hands
Down my pockets, and the streets around are snow,
Deep snow.   I dive into a cab.   Buddy, kick this thing!   Behind the Falcon
There's a room.   They're supposed to be waiting for me there.
She opens the door
                    but what the hell's wrong with her?
Why the crazy look?
                    "It's almost five o'clock.

You sure you couldn't come a little later?
Well, forget it.   Come on in.   Where else could you go now?"
Shall I explode
                    with a laugh
                                    or maybe with tears?
I tell you I was scribbling doggerel
                                    but I got lost someplace.
I hide from the eyes.   Wavering I move backwards:
"No, no!   Believe me!   I've come to the wrong place!"
Once again the night
                    once again snow
and somebody's insolent song
and somebody's clean, pure laughter.
I could do with a cigarette.
In the blizzard Pushkin's demons flash past
And their contemptuous, bucktoothed grin
Scares me to death.
                    And the kiosks
And the drugstores
                    and the social security offices
Scare me just as much . . .
                            No, no!   Believe me!   I've ended up
In the wrong place again . . .
                            It's *horrible* to live
And even more horrible
                    not to live . . .
                                    Ach, this being homeless
Like the Wandering Jew . . . Lord!   Now I've gotten myself
Into the wrong century
                    wrong epoch
                                    geologic era
                                            wrong number
The wrong place again
                    I'm wrong
                            I've got it wrong . . .
I go, slouching my shoulders like I'd do
if I'd lost some bet,
                    and Ah, I know it . . . everybody knows it . . .
I can't pay off.

When you throw your dancing shoes out, back over your shoulder,
And lose yourself, you find yourself twisting on the stage,
                                    dancing,
                                        dancing,
                                            dancing—
let that pink boy whip you around—I can tell you:
Life doesn't dance this way—
            That way dances death.
Thighs
            shoulders
                    breasts:
                                they're all in it!
Inside you, dead drunk,
                    wheezes of air are dancing
Somebody else's ring
                    dances on your hand,
And your face by itself
                    doesn't dance at all
Flying, lifelessly, above all the body's life
Like a mask taken off your dead head.
And this stage—
                is only one part of that cross
On which they once
                    crucified Jesus;
The nails shot through to the other side, and you began
To dance on them,
                    sticking out.
                            And you dance
On the nails
            nails
On sandals red as rust
                    on the thorn-points of tears: Listen,
Because I once loved you, tiresomely, gloomily,
I also hammered the crooks of my nails
                            into this page.
Ah, bestial, beastly music,
                    do you keep on getting stronger?
No one can see the blood
                    ooze from your foot-soles—

To wash the steps with clean water,
I'd rather you'd do it, Mary Magdalene,

                                   not Jesus.

I'll wash all their days, their yesterdays, not like a brother would
For a sister,

                but like a sister for a sister.

I'll kneel down and pick up your feet
And hold them quietly, and with kisses try to do something
About their wounds.

SIX FROM
PUELLA

Veer-Voices: Two Sisters Under Crows

Sometimes are living those who have been seen
Together   those farthest leaning
With some dark birds and fielded
Below them   countercrying and hawing in savage openness
For every reason.   Such are as we, to come out
And under and balance-cruise,

Cross-slanting and making long, raw, exhaustless
Secret-ballot assertions   feeding and self-
supporting our surround

By all angles of outcry; it seems to lift and steady us
To the ground.   If I were to say to you
From a stand-off of corn-rows—
Say to you just as I entered
Their shifting, bi-lingual rasping,
The crows' vector-cloud
And parable, my sister, this is where we eat

The last of our dawn-dust hanging
Stranded and steady behind us   shall say
We should have known we would end up in full
Health here   end up pilfering

A crossroads and passing out
One kind of voice in skinned speeches
All over the place   leaning and flying
Passing into
              flying in and out
Of each other
                    with nothing to tell of
But the angles of light-sensitive dust
Between fences leaded with dew,
You might say back,
                    Come with me
Into the high-tension carry
Of these fences: come in a double stand-down
From the night-mass of families—
Rooms of world-wearying order, our stifled folk—
And bring them forth with us,

Stalk-standing, space-burning, to call
All over, to hear
These wires—thumb-echo of the harp
Pronged with herding whispers, cross-handed
Fingered—and all
Of us would be then

Veer-crying and straining like wire
Redoubling its prongs, and could contrive to praise
Sufficiently, and counterpraise
Barbed wire and these crows:
Their spirit-shifting splits
Of tongue, their cry of unfathomable hordes.

Springhouse, Menses, Held Apple, House and Beyond

Nothing but one life: all stands:
I go out with my main ear in each stone

End-stopping a creek: territorially

Listen, and beyond the live seepage of rock
Is a window cleanly blinded with an orchard.
Everything the world has made
This day, through sheen and rock
Can pierce   through stone and glass
And air, I hear.
My hand inertially rounding,
I love far in and far from me:
The stalled tightening of distant fruit, the wasp's delaying
Uncontested spasm at the pane.

Sealed and sweeping depth
Is part of me now, and I ride it, gone bright inside in the dark
Of the raised, rounded quarry and its cool;
I am reined-in and thriving with the wasp:
I meet now vibrantly with him
And unbearably at the broad window:
When he gives up the glass, I shall rise and walk out through all
the walls

Of my father's house   holding, but not at bay,
High-energy cloth where I scotched it
Like iron between my legs
                              and go

Whole-hearted and undoctored toward the hillside
Beaming its distances, the fruit in my hand
Encompassing, crackling with vitality
Like a burning basket
                              the day-moon stronger

In me than on me   outdoing what is left of the wasp's
Smattering and hard-nosed abandon
And pick up his rifling thread
Where it lays out my wandering for me
Center-boring through fields of ray-flowers:
I help it   I ride it   I invent it
To death and follow down   shameless with energy

From the closed river flowering,
Upgathered and delighted in the hive's
High-risk and conglomerate frenzy:

        One life
                              brought to bear
On what I require:

A stone house, a father, a window,
The wasp's holocaust of location,
The bees' winnowed over-stressed time-zone,
Far orchards blazing with slant.

Deborah as Scion

I
WITH ROSE, AT CEMETERY

                Kin: quiet grasses.   Above,
Lace: white logic   fretted cloud-cloth.
                              In steady-state insolence
                I bring up a family
Look: a look like sword-grass, that will leave on anything human

A swirl-cut, the unfurling touch of a world-wound
Given straight out
Of my forehead, and having all the work and tide-
pull of the dead, from their oblong, thrilling frame-tension
Filled here with sunlight.

God give me them,
God gave them me, with a hedgerow grip on a rose
And black brows: in over-sifted, high-concentrate cloth
And a high-fashion nudity, that shall come
Of it, when the time comes.
                              Now at any good time
Of this struck eleven o'clock, I can look forth on you
Or anyone, as though you were being grazed
Forever by a final tense of threads,
The inmost brimming feather-hone of light.

The dead work into a rose
By back-breaking leisure, head-up,
Grave-dirt exploding like powder
Into sunlit lace, and I lie and look back through their labor
Upon their dark dazzle of needles,
Their mineral buckets and ore-boats
Like millwheels, pinnacling, restoring lightly
All over me from the green mines
And black-holes of the family plot.
                              I am one of them

For as long as we all shall die
And be counted.   I am the one this late morning
Pulled-through alive: the one frame-humming, conveying
                              the tension,
Black-browed from the black-holes
Of family peace.   My uncle's brows are still
As they were, growing out in mine,
                              and I rest with good gut-
feel in the hand-loomed bright-out
In the dead's between-stitches breathing,
And am watchful as to what I do
With the swirl-cut of my straight look,
And of whom among the living it shall fix
With trembling, with unanswerable logic,

With green depth and short deadly grasses,

With my dead full-time and work-singing.

II
IN LACE AND WHALEBONE
Bull-headed, big-busted,
Distrustful and mystical: my summoned kind of looks
As I stand here going back
And back, from mother to mother: I am totally them in the
eyebrows,

Breasts, breath and butt:
You, never-met Grandmother of the fields
Of death, who laid this frail dress
Most freshly down, I stand now in your closed bones,
Sucked-in, in your magic tackle, taking whatever,

From the stark freedom under the land,
From under the sea, from the bones of the deepest beast,
Shaped now entirely by me, by whatever
Breath I draw.   I smell of clear
Hope-surfeited cedar: ghost-smell and forest-smell
Laid down in dim vital boughs

And risen in lace
and a feeling of nakedness is broadening
world-wide out

From me ring on ring—a refining of open-work skin—to go
With you, and I have added
Bad temper, high cheek-bones and exultation:
I fill out these ribs

For something ripped-up and boiled-down,
Plundered and rendered, come over me
From a blanched ruck of thorned, bungled blubber,
From rolling ovens raking-down their fires

For animal oil, to light room after room
In peculiar glister, from a slim sculpt of blown-hollow crystal:
Intent and soft-fingered
Precipitous light, each touch to the wick like drawing
First blood in a great hounded ring
the hand blunted and gone

Fathomless, in rose and ash, and cannot throw
The huddled burn out of its palm:

It is all in the one breath, as in the hush
Of the hand: the gull stripped downwind, sheering off
To come back slow,
                        the squandered fat-trash boiling in the wake,
The weird mammalian bleating of bled creatures,

A thrall of ships:
                        lyric hanging of rope
(The snarled and sure entanglement of space),
Jarred, hissing squalls, tumultuous yaw-cries
Of butchery, stressed waves that part, close, re-open
Then seethe and graze: I hold-in my lungs
And hand, and try-out the blood-bones of my mothers,
And I tell you they are volcanic, full of exhorted hoverings:
                                                This animal:
            This animal: I stand and think

Its feed   its feel   its whole lifetime on one air:
            In lightning-strikes I watch it leap
And welter   blue wide-eyes   lung-blood up-misting under
            Stamped splits of astounding concentration,
But soundless,
                        the crammed wake blazing with fat
And phosphor,
                        the moon stoning down, Venus rising,

            And we can hold, woman on woman,
This dusk if no other
                        and we will now, all of us combining,
            Open one hand.
                        Blood into light
Is possible: lamp, lace and tackle   paired bones of the deep
            Rapture
                        surviving   reviving, and wearing well
            For this sundown, and not any other,
                        In the one depth

            Without levels, deepening for us.

Doorstep, Lightning, Waif-Dreaming

Who can tell who was born of what?
I go sitting on the doorsteps of unknowns
And ask, and hear nothing
From the rhythmical ghosts of those others,
Or from myself while I am there, but only
The solid shifts of drumming made of heart.
I come always softly,
My head full of lingering off-prints

Of lightning—vital, engendering blank,
The interim spraddling crack   the crowning rollback
Whited-out *ex nihilo*
and I am as good as appearing
The other time: I come of a root-system of fire, as it fires
Point-blank at this hearthstone and doorstep: there is
A tingling of light-sensitive hairs
Between me: my clothes flicker
And glow with it, under the bracketing split
Of sky, the fasting, saint-hinting glimmer,
The shifting blasts of echo, relocating,
And of an orphaning blaze

I have been stressed, and born, and stamped
Alive on this doorstep.   I believe it between cloud
And echo, and my own chosen-and-sifted footstep
Arriving,
engendered, endangered, loving,

Dangerous, seeking ground.

From Time

Deborah for Years at the Piano

My hands that were not born completely
Matched   that struck at a hurt wire upward
Somewhere on the uncentered plain
Without cause: my hands that could not befriend
Themselves, though openly fielded:

That never came out

Intercepting: that could get nothing back
Of a diamonded pay-off, the whole long-promised
Harmonic blaze of boredom never coming—
                                              now flock
In a slow change like limitless gazing:
From back-handed, disheartening cliff-sound, are now
A new, level anvilling of tones,
Spread crown, an evening sprinkle of height,
Perfected wandering.   Here is

The whole body cousinly: are
Heartenings, charged with invented time,
A chord with lawn-broadness,
Lean clarities.
                    With a fresh, gangling resonance
Truing handsomely, I draw on left-handed space
For a brave ballast shelving and bracing, and from it,
                                              then, the light
Prowling lift-off, the treble's strewn search and wide-angle glitter.

How much of the body was wasted
Before I drew up here!   Who would have thought how much music
The forearms had in them!   How much of Schumann and Mozart
In the shoulders, and the draining of the calves!
I sit, as everlasting,
In the overleaf and memory-make of tedium,
Bach and his gist freely with me, four hands
Full in the overlook. You bet. The dead at their work-bench altars

Half-approving
                    time-releasing.

Tapestry and Sail

She imagines herself a figure upon them

A wrong look into heavy stone
And twilight, wove my body,
And I was snowing with the withering hiss of thread.
My head was last, and with it came
An eyesight needle-pointing like a thorn-bush.
I came to pass
slant-lit, Heaven-keeping with the rest
Of the museum, causing History to hang clear of earth
With me in it, carded and blazing.   Rigidly I swayed

Among those morningless strings, like stained glass
Avertedly yearning: here a tree   a Lord
There a falcon on fist   an eagle
Worried into cloud, strained up
On gagging filaments   there a compacted antelope
With such apparent motion stitched to death
That God would pluck His image
Clean of feathers if I leapt   or breathed
Over the smothered plain:
the Past, hung up like beast-hides,
Half-eaten, half-stolen,
Not enough.
Well, I was not for it:
I stubborned in that lost wall
Of over-worked dust, and came away
in high wind,
Rattling and flaring
On the lodge-pole craze and flutter of the sail,
Confounding, slatting and flocking,
On-going with manhandled drift, wide-open in the lightning's

Re-emphasizing split, the sea's holy no-win roar.
I took the right pose coming off
The air, and of a wild and ghostly battering

Was born, and signed-on
                    and now steady down
To movement, to the cloth's relationless flurries,
Sparring for recovery   feather-battling   lulling,

   Tautening and resolving, dwelling slowly.

THE EAGLE'S MILE

Eagles

If I told you I used to know the circular truth

Of the void,
                that I have been all over it building
    My height
                  receiving overlook

And that my feathers were not
Of feather-make, but broke from a desire to drink
    The rain before it falls
                    or as it is falling:

If I were to tell you that the rise of any free bird
    Is better

              the larger the bird is,

And that I found myself one of these
Without surprise, you would understand

That this makes of air a thing that would be liberty
    Enough for any world but this one,
    And could see how I should have gone

        Up and out of all

              all of it

      On feathers glinting

Multitudinously as rain, as silica-sparks around
One form with wings, as it is hammered loose
    From rock, at dead
    Of classic light: that is, at dead

      Of light.

      Believe, too,
While you're at it, that the flight of eagles has
    For use, long muscles steeped only
      In escape,
              and moves through
    Clouds that will open to nothing

But ít, where the bird leaves behind
All sympathy: leaves
The man who, for twenty lines
Of a new poem, thought he would not be shut
From those wings: believed

He could be going. I speak to you from where

I was shook off: I say again, shook
Like this, the words I had
When I could not spread:

When thát bird rose

Without my shoulders: Leave my unstretched weight,
My sympathy grovelling
In weeds and nothing, and go
                              up from the human down-
beat in my hand. Go up without anything

Of me in your wings, but remember me in your feet

As you fold them. The higher rock iś
The more it lives. Where you take hold, Í will take

Thát stand in my mind, rock bird alive with the spirit-
life of height,
                    on my down-thousands
Of fathoms, classic

Claw-stone, everything under.

Gila Bend

Where aerial gunnery was, you think at first a cadaver

On foot might get through

Forty years after. Shots of space pelter back

Off the dead bullets; walking, you should brand, brand
The ground but you don't: you leave

Not a thing moving on a sand mountain
Smashed flat by something that didn't know

What else to do.
                    This silver small-stone heat
          No man can cross; no man could get

          To his feet, even to rise face-out

Full-force from the grave, where the sun is down on him

          Alone, harder than resurrection

               Is úp: down harder

                              harder

          Much harder than that.

Circuit

          Beaches; it is true: they go on   on
          And on, but as they ram and pack, foreseeing

     Around a curve, always   slow-going headlong

          For the circle
                         swerving from water
But not really, their minds on a perfect connection, no matter
          How long it takes. You can't be
          On them without making the choice
          To meet yourself no matter

          How long. Don't be afraid;
          It will come   will hit you

     Straight out of the wind, on wings or not,
          Where you have blanked yourself

     Still with your feet. It may be raining

          In twilight, a sensitive stripping
     Of arrow-feathers, a lost trajectory struck
Stock-stilling through them,
                              or where you cannot tell
          If the earth is green or red,

     Basically, or if the rock with your feet on it

Has floated over the water. As for where you are standing

Nów, there are none of those things; there are only
In one shallow spray-pool   thís one

Strong horses circling. Stretch and tell me, Lord;
Let the place talk.

This may just be it.

Night Bird

Some beating in there

That has bunched, and backed
Up in it out of moonlight, and now
Is somewhere around. You are sure that like a curving grave

It must be able to fall

and rise

and fall and that's
Right, and rise

on your left hand

or other

Or behind your back on one hand

You don't have and suddenly there is no limit

To what a man can get out of
His failure to see:

this gleam

Of air down the nape of the neck, and in it everything
There is of flight

and nothing else,

and it is

All right and all over you
From around

as you are carried

In yourself and there is no way
To nothing-but-walk—

No way and a bidden flurry
And a half-you of air.

Daybreak

You sit here on solid sand banks trying to figure
What the different is when you see
The sun and at the same time see the ocean
Has no choice: none, but to advance more or less
As it does:
waves
Which were, a moment ago, actual
Bodiless sounds that could have been airborne,
Now bring you nothing but face-off

After face-off, with only gravitational sprawls
Laid in amongst them. To those crests
Dying hard, you have nothing to say:
you cannot help it

If you emerge; it is not your fault. You show: you stare

Into the cancelling gullies, saved only by dreaming a future
Of walking forward, in which you can always go flat

Flat down where the shallows have fallen
Clear: where water is shucked of all wave-law:
Lies running: runs

In skylight, gradually cleaning, and you gaze straight into

The whole trembling forehead of yourself
Under you, and at your feet find your body

No different from cloud, among the other
See-through images, as you are flawingly
Thought of,
but purely, somewhere,

Somewhere in all thought.

Two Women

Alone here. Beach, drum out
What you want to say: a dolphin,
Sockets, sword-flats. Seething landscape of hilts, no limits are set

On you. Sand, sand,
Hear me out: Hear me out with wind
Going over, past
All sound but sand. Listen,

Clean vastness, I am alone here.
I should be, for I have
No mark.
Woman, because I don't love you,
Draw back the first

Of your feet, for the other will fall
After it, and keep on coming. Hold back

A little, your printed pursuit, your

Unstemming impurity.

Early light: light less
Than other light. Sandal without power
To mark sand. Softly,
Her hair downward-burning, she walks here, her foot-touch

The place itself,

Like sand-grains, unintended,

Born infinite.

Immortals

Always as it holds us in one place, the earth
Grows as it moves, exhaling
Its rooted joy. I stand in tracks
Where nothing starves. Vegetation, green blush,
You and I sail today
Through newly infinite
Space on this surfeited hillside. Complacency has its own force

Leafed-out with renewal. I cannot be anything
But alive, in a place as far

From the blank and the stark, as this.

Air, much greater than the sea—
More basic, more human than the sea: all that air
Is calm:
        unpeopled, wearing the high lucidity

Of vigil. Maybe one day the mere surface
Of the earth will feel you. But the air
You can never keep doesn't know
When it lived in your chest:

Mindless, nerveless, breathless,
The air glitters
All the outside, and keeps carrying

You from within.

Who told you that the sea said something,
Something toward the beaches?
Let it spread more, belligerent with light,
Saying one thing, resounding,

Up front for all of us!

To the Butterflies

—homage, Central America

Open windows; we always have them, háve
to have them. We widen

Them all, and butterflies come in, and come

To rest on our mirrors, breathing with their wings

Almost like light,
Or better, almost like flight,

And then leave. Others come,
Háve to come, and some of the time this happens
We are singing, trying hard,

But it comes out a croak
From dryness, and when we move it is like
Moving muscles of powder, but
Really no muscles are on us; they are all gone
Into sweat. Every light the hand turns on
Hurts the eyes, and there is nowhere on earth
That the heels of the feet
Are so hot, and they cannot be cooled.
I love to know nothing

Of the sun; I love to feel

That I float, forgotten,
with two warm rivers
That cannot touch me, on a stream come down
Between them from a mountain
Of frozen rain. We all have wanted,

Too long, not to have our tears,
Our salt-showing tears, dry before anyone
Can see them, dry
Before we can feel them,
Or find out what they really have
To do with grief. To say that I am not true
To fever is to say I am not
Loyal to my green country,
not true, not real

Myself,
so I say it in secret

In steam: Forgive me, butterflies:
I know you have to have
All this heat for your colors,
but you are breathless, too,
In spite of your breathing

Wings and God help me I must say it before I melt
Into the sugar-sick ground:
If we could do it

Without dimming the butterflies, we should find some way
To get on the good side of North: Yes North and enough

Cold: Yes cold

And snow! I've heard of it! Flakes lilting onto us!

Life light on the common grave

Shapeless with swelter! Every tongue of us out
To be new to that taste! Mountains of rain
Gone into feather-fall
Floating us out of it! But not dimming   not fading
The butterflies
or the hats and handkerchiefs.
Let the wings on our mirrors

In whatever falls

Keep breathing   Keep burning

and us, Lord, please—

And us in the dresses and shirts.

The One

No barometer but yellow
Forecast of wide fields that they give out
Themselves, giving out they stand
In total freedom,

And will stand and day is down all of it

On an ear of corn. One. The color one:
One, nearly transparent
With existence. The tree at the fence must be kept

Outside, between winds; let it wait. Its movement,

Any movement, is not

In the distillation. Block it there. Let everything bring it
To an all-time stop just short of new
Wind   just short
Of its leaves;
its other leaves.

One.

Inside.

Yellow.

All others not.

One.

One.

The Three

I alone, solemn land

clear, clean land,

See your change, just as you give up part
Of your reality:
a scythe-sighing flight of low birds
now being gone:
I, oversouling for an instant

With them,
I alone
See you as more than you would have

Bé seen, yourself:
grassland,

Dark grassland, with three birds higher
Than those that have left.
                                    They are up there
With great power:
                    so high they take this evening for good
                    Into their force-lines. I alone move

Where the other birds were, the low ones,
            Still swaying in the unreal direction
            Flocking with them. They are gone

And will always be gone; even where they believe
            They were is disappearing. But thése three
            Have the height to power-line all

Land: land thís clear. Any three birds hanging high enough
                From you trace the same paths
        As strong horses circling
                            for a man alone, born level-eyed

            As a pasture, but like the land
        Tilting, looking up.

                    This may be it, too.

The Six

When you think strong enough, you get something
                    You don't mean
            And you dó: something prized-out,
            Splintered, like a rock quarry going
                Through you and over you
                Like love, and past and on

        Like love: whatever arms, legs, head,

Breastbone, whatever feet and hands you love most,
                Most want to live
            And die with, are given out as flying
                Related rock; are charged
                    With the life that lives
By means of stone. The body of your lover tries to form and be

Those six stones. For some reason

They are hurtling, and if you meet them head-on
You will know something nobody means

But her. She is moving at the speed of light

Some place else, and though she passes
Through you like rock-salt, she is still six
And not one.

But neither is the rain
Single, blotting number and stone
With vibrancy; neither is the rain, I tell you,
Man riddled with rocks
And lust:

The rain putting out
Your wretched, sympathetic
Stone-jawed poetic head, its allotted
Fresh bodies falling as you stand

In amongst, falling and more
Than falling   falling more

Falling   now falling

More than now.

Weeds

Stars and grass
Have between them a connection I'd like to make
More of—find some way to bring them

To one level any way I can,
And put many weeds in amongst. O woman, now that I'm thinking,
Be in there somewhere! Until now, of the things I made up
Only the weeds are any good: Between them,

Nondescript and tough, I peer,
The backs of my hands

At the sides of my face, parting the stringy stalks.

Tangible, distant woman, here the earth waits for you
          With what it does not need
          To guess: with what it truly has
          In its hands. Through pigweed and sawgrass

          Move; move sharply; move iń
Through anything,
                    and hurt, if you have to. Don't come down;

          Come forward. A man loves you.

Spring-Shock

                    All bubbles travelling

          In tubes, and being lights: up down and around
          They were: blue, red and every man uncaught

                    And guilty. Prison-paleness
          Over the street between strobes
          Unfailingly. But no light
          On top of anything moving, until
          The last, one:
                    one. Whoever it was switched it

Dead when he saw me. Winter; not dreamlike but a dream and cars
          Of that. I took my stand where they were called
          By absent law to stop, obstructedly raging

          And I could not get in. All their windows
          Were sealed and throbbing
          With strobe, red and blue, red and blue

          And go. One pulled out of the flight
          Of others; pulled up and may have had back-road
          Dust on it   red dust in a last shot
          Of blue. A man in a cowboy hat rolled down

          The window on my side. His voice
          Was home-born Southern; Oklahoma, Texas,
          Could have been. Manhandling my overcoat, I slid
          Iń there with him. Central Park South, I said,
          A war-safety zone; the St. Moritz.

He turned up

One of the streets with no lights. Into the seat
I settled; black buildings thickened
Around us, high tenements flattening
Into squares; warehouses now,
They were; maybe docks. I watched. No birds.
No trash-cans. The car died

Between two alley walls

And froze, and a voice at last, still
Out of Oklahoma, said "I want your money."
We were present
In silence. A brought-on up-backward thock

Took place, and on the fresh blade
A light alive in the hand
New-born with spring-shock. It was mine
At sixty. "I want your car," I said.

The Eagle's Mile

for Justice William Douglas

The Emmet's Inch & Eagle's Mile —*Blake*

Unwarned, catch into this
With everything you have:
the trout streaming with all its quick
In the strong curve   all things on all sides
In motion   the soul strenuous
And still
in time-flow as in water blowing
Fresh and for a long time

Downhill   something like air it is
Also and it is dawn

There in merciless look-down
As though an eagle or Adam
In lightning, or both, were watching uncontrollably
For meat, among the leaves. Douglas, with you
The soul tries it one-eyed, half your sight left hanging in a river

In England, long before you died,

And now thát one, that and the new one
Struck from death's instant—
Lightning's: like mankind on impulse blind-
siding God—true-up together and ride
On silence, enraptured surveillance,

The eagle's mile. Catch into this, and broaden

Into and over

The mountain rivers, over the leaf-tunnel path:

Appalachia, where the trail lies always hidden
Like prey, through the trembling south-north of the forest
Continent, from Springer Mountain to Maine,
And you may walk

Using   not surpassing

The trout's hoisted stand-off with the channel,
Or power-hang the same in the shattered nerves
Of lightning: like Adam find yourself splintering out
Somewhere on the eagle's mile, on peerless, barbaric distance
Clairvoyant with hunger,

Or can begin   can be   begin to be
What out-gentles, and may evade:
This second of the second year
Of death, it would be best for the living
If it were your impulse to step out of grass-bed sleep

As valuably   as cautiously

As a spike-buck, head humming with the first male split
Of the brain-bone, as it tunes to the forked twigs
Of the long trail

Where Douglas you once walked in a white shirt as a man
In the early fall, fire-breathing with oak-leaves,
Your patched tunnel-gaze exactly right
For the buried track,
                    the England-curved water strong
Far-off with your other sight, both fresh-waters marbling together

Supporting not surpassing

What flows   what balances

In it. Douglas, power-hang in it all now, for all
The whole thing is worth: catch without warning
Somewhere in the North Georgia creek like ghost-muscle tensing
Forever, or on the high grass-bed
Yellow of dawn, catch like a man stamp-printed by God-
shock, blue as the very foot
Of fire. Catch into the hunted
Horns of the buck, and thus into the deepest hearing—
Nerveless, all bone, bone-tuned
To leaves and twigs—with the grass drying wildly
When you woke   where you stood with all the blades rising
Behind you, and stepped out
                                        possessing the trail,
The racked bramble on either side shining
Like a hornet, your death drawing life
From growth
                        from flow, as in the gill-cleansing turn
Of the creek
                        or from the fountain-twist
Of flight, that rounds you
Off, and shies you downwind
Side-faced, all-seeing with hunger,

And over this, steep and straight-up
In the eagle's mile
Let Adam, far from the closed smoke of mills
And blue as the foot
Of every flame, true-up with blind-side outflash
The once-more instantly
Wild world: over Brasstown Bald

Splinter uncontrollably whole.

Daughter

Hospital, and the fathers' room, where light
Won't look you in the eye. No emergency
But birth. I sit with the friend, and listen

To the unwounded clock. Indirectly glowing, he is grayer,
Unshaven as I. We are both old men
Or nearly. He is innocent. Yet:
What fathers are waiting to be born
But myself, whom the friend watches
With blessed directness? No other man but a worker

With an injured eyeball; his face had been there
When part of an engine flew up.
                        A tall nurse blotted with ink
And blood goes through. Something written
On her? Blood of my wife? A doctor with a blanket
Comes round a blind corner. "Who gets this little girl?"
I peer into wool: a creature
Somewhat strangely more than red. Dipped in fire.

No one speaks. The friend does not stir; he is innocent
Again: the child is between
Me and the man with one eye. We battle in the air,
Three-eyed, over the new-born. The doctor says,
"All right, now. Which one of you had a breech baby?"
All around I look: look at the possible
Wounded father. He may be losing: he opens his bad eye.
I half-close one of mine, hoping to win
Or help. Breech baby. I don't know. I tell my name.
Taking the doctor by his arms
Around her, the child of fire moves off. I would give one eye for her

Already. If she's not mine I'll steal her.
The doctor comes back. The friend stirs; both our beards
Quicken: the doctor is standing
Over me, saying, "This one's yours."
                        It is done: I set my feet
In Heavenly power, and get up. In place of plastic, manned rubber
And wrong light, I say wordlessly
Roll, real God. Roll through us. I shake hands

With the one-eyed man. He has not gained
A child, but may get back his eye; I hope it will return
By summer starlight.
                        The child almost setting
Its wool on fire, I hold it in the first and last power

It came from: that goes on all the time
There is, shunting the glacier, whirling
Whole forests from their tops, moving

Lava, the flowing stone: moving the hand
Of anyone, ever. Child of fire,
Look up. Look up as I lean and mumble you are part
Of flowing stone: understand: you are part of the wave,
Of the glacier's irrevocable
Millennial inch.
                    "This is the one," the friend repeats
In his end-of-it daze, his beard gone
Nearly silver, now, with honor, in the all-night night
Of early morning. Godfather, I say

To him: not father of God, but assistant
Father to this one. All forests are moving, all waves,
All lava and ice. I lean. I touch

One finger. Real God, roll.

Roll.

The Olympian

—False Youth: Spring—

Los Angeles back-yarding in its blue-eyed waters
Of empty swim, by my tract-house of packaged hard-candy
I lay in wait with the sun
And celebrity beer
                    for the Olympian,
Now my oldest boy's junior
High school algebra teacher, who had brought back the black-magic gold
Of the East, down the fast lane,
Freewaying, superhuman with rubberized home-stretch,
The four hundred meters from Tokyo
To Balboa Boulevard, leaving in his wake
All over the earth, the Others, the nation-motley doom-striped ones,
Those heart-eating sprinters, those Losers.
With Olympia Beer I was warming

Warming up with the best chill waters
Of the West Coast, cascading never-ending
Down out of Washington State. Now is your moment of truth
With me at last, O Champion! for I had laid a course as strange
To him as to me. Steeplechase! I had always leapt into water
Feet first, and could get out
Faster than in. I was ready for the Big One:
For the Water Jump in the corner
Of the lax, purfled pool, under the cemented palm
Where at night the shrewd rat climbed
And rustled and ruled the brown fronds over the underlit
Blue oval, surveying Sepulveda,
And in its color and kind, suffered
World recognition.
                        With a slide-rule in his shirt-pocket,
His bullet-proof glasses drawing
Into points—competitive points—and fish-eye-lensing,
Crossflashing on my hogged, haggard grassplot
Of slapped-down, laid-back Sepulveda, just after he'd Won It All,
He came lankily, finely drawn
Onto my turf, where all the time I had been laying
For him, building my energy-starches,
My hilarious, pizza-fed fury. My career of fat
Lay in the speed-trap, in the buckets and tools of the game-plan,
The snarls of purified rope. Then dawned the strict gods of Sparta,
The free gods of Athens! O lungs of Pheidippides collapsing in a square
Of the delivered city! O hot, just hurdlable gates
Of deck-chairs! Lounges! A measured universe
Of exhilarating laws! Here I had come   there I'd gone
Laying it down   confusing, staggering
The fast lane and the slow, on and over
And over recliners, sun-cots, cleaning-poles and beach-balls,
Foiled cans of rusty rat-poison   bowing, split casks
Of diatomaceous earth   corks spaced-out like California
On blue-and-white dacron cords   lost-and-found swim-fins
Unmatched and pigeon-toed   half-hearted air
In blazing rings   doughnuts and play rafts   dragons and elephants
Blown-up by mouth, now sighing most of life
Away   the lawful No-Running signs
Turned to the wall. And all the time, all the time,

Under the brown-browed, rose-ash glower
Of the smog-bank, the crows, long gone
Gray with the risen freeways, were thronging and hawing
To be Doves of Peace   to be turned
Loose, displaying and escaping, over the jolted crowds
Of Unimart, the rammed Victory Stand,
                                        and in the rose-ash
Of early dusk, we called our wives, gray as crows
In their golf-hats, to the secret Olympics, laid down in my laws
Within laws, where world champions, now mad with the moon
Of moonlighting, sold running shoes. This so, we insisted
On commercials, those all-comers'
Career-dreams of athletes: "We are brought to you by the Bringers of the Flame,
The double-dry double martini," those women said. "Get set!
Get set! You're being born
Again, in spite of everything!" James Bond and my smallest boy
Blazed with one cap-pistol together. We hove like whales from the line.

Twice around

    We were going for, cursing and cruising like ghosts, over dog-food bowls,
Over sprinklers passed-out from their spin-off
Of rainbows and I was losing
But not badly, and even gained a little, coming out
Of the water-jump and over the jump-rope, and out of him or maybe
Me   surely me   burst a mindless deep
Belching blindsiding laugh down the backstretch
Of earth-kegs and dirty cleansing-tools that skinned the dust
From the under-blue, and for one unsettling moment left it
Blazing and mattering. I blazed I felt great I was a great
Plaster stadium-god   lagging   lolloping   hanging
In there with the best: was running pale and heavy
With cement-dust   from two wives running
Then coming around   coming back
Down the slow lane   lurching   lorry-swaying:
Now toward two wives making up for   —making
The gelatin-murmur of crowds, I pounded, wet and laboring,
And then, half a pool
Behind, went into the bell-lap.
                                        I was holding my own
Back there, as we rounded

Past the stands   he a long first and I
A world-class second and counting
On my finish or something   Yes! My finish to come
From the home turf like an ascension   all-seeing
World-recognized   poison-proof   smoke-proof   time-proof
Out of the pool, a rat's climb grappling
Half-a-lap half-a-lap   still alive
In mid-stride, louring, lumbering, crow-hopping
Behind the athlete's unhurried
Slack, unearthly footling lope:
                                            I stepped low and heavy
Over the last light rope, smashed water with my sole
Flat   climbed, lurched, legged it and duck-footed
For home   a good not shameful
Second   this was all right and everything
But no! My weave   my plan   the run
Of my knots had caught up with him   caught
Him where he lived
                              —in his feet—
                                            and he was down
In styrofoam, and on a bloated blessèd doughnut-ring
Of rubber rolled: the finish-line leapt   exploded
Into Reality, shot-through with deathless flame, crossed with white paper:
Swam illicitly, aboundingly
Like wind-aided glory. With courage to do credit
To any rat, I cornered and turned
It on. He came back instantly, but instantly was not soon
Enough, for I charged past like a slow freight
All over the earth, and had got it
And gone   long gone   and burst

Through the living tissue: breasted and blanked
The Tape and can feel it

Bannering, still, on my chest
Like wing-span, that once was toilet-paper, torn epically
Where the true Olympian slurred
His foot and fell, and I felt my lungs collapsing in a square
Of the City, like Pheidippides dying of the sheer
Good of my news.
                              Far off, still rising at rose dusk

And night, free under the low-browed smoke, and grayer
Than any fake peace-bird,
Like a called crow I answer
Myself utterly, with a whole laugh   —that body-language one-world
One word of joy   —straight into the ruining tons
Of smoke that trash my head and doom it
And keep it recognized
in the age
And condition of my kind, and hear also, maybe not entirely
From myself, the Olympian's laugh
Coming from somewhere
Behind, blindsidedly, getting the point
At last, sighing like ghosts and like rubber, for fat
And luck, all over the earth, where that day and any and every
Day after it, devil hindmost and Goddamn it

To glory, I lumbered for gold.

The Little More

JBTD

I

But the little more: the little more
This boy will be, is hard
For me to talk of
But harder for him. Manhood is only a little more,
A little more time, a little more everything than he

Has on him now. He would know, if he could go forward
From where he puts down his ball,
His top, his willow spear,
that he will face into the air
Where the others his age will be breaking, or be
About to break,
and he will watch them grow pale
With the warnings of doctors,
And all their balloons, and parents and the other
Dead will be floating

Away from them, over the mountains.

This is where the quiet

Valley comes in, and the red creek
Where he will row with no other,
The water around each blade
Explosive, ablaze with his only initials,
Joy set in the bending void
Between the oars
and swung,
As the last balloon disappears, needing
Color no more. Yes! This is when the far mountain
Will come to him, under his feet
Of its own wish
when he steps up

From water, and in the wind he will start
To hear the enormous resonance
Children cannot make out: of his own gigantic
Continuous stride over all ferocious rocks

That can be known.

II

From the ones who have grown all they can
Come and stop softly, boy,
On the strong side of the road

That the other side does not see. Then move.
Put your feet where you look,
and not

Where you look, and none of your tracks
Will pass off, but wander, and for you

Be fresh places, free and aggressive.

Boy who will always be glanced-at
and then fixed

In warm gazes, already the past knows
It cannot invent you again,

For the glitter on top of the current

Is not the current.
                No, but what dances on it is
        More beautiful than what takes its time
        Beneath, running on a single unreleased
              Eternal breath, rammed
        With carry, its all-out dream and dread

                Surging bull-breasted,
                Head-down, unblocked.

For a Time and Place
A South Carolina inauguration of Richard Riley as governor

        May we be able to begin with ourselves
                Underfoot and rising,
Peering through leaves we have basketed, through tendrils hanging
            Like bait, through flowers,
        Through lifted grave-soil: peering
            Past the short tree that stands
      In place for us, sawed-off, unbendable: a thing
                Pile-driven down
      And flowering from the impact—such weaving
      Consuming delicacy in the leaves, out of such
      Up-wedged and pineappled bark! We look alive
Through those petals in the censer-swung pots: through
    That swinging soil, and the split leaves fountaining out
        Of the mauled tree, to the east horizon vibrant
With whole-earth hold-down, past a single sail pillowing
                From there on out.

            We peer also from the flat
        Slant sand, west from estuary-glitter,
        From the reed-beds bending inland
    At dawn as we do, to the high-ground hard-hurdling
Power of the down-mountain torrent: at a blue-ridged glance
            From the ocean, we see all we have
    Is unified as a quilt: the long leaves of the short tree,
  The tough churchly feathers, dance rice-like this side of
            The far-out wave-break's lounging

Curved insolent long sparking thorn, and
The gull's involving balance, his sweeping-through shuttle-run
Downwind; his tapestry-move
Is laid on our shoulders, where the unspilled dead
Are riding, wild with flowers, collision-colors
At the hairline, tended, sufficient, dead-level with us
From now on out.

What visions to us from all this lived
Humidity? What insights from the blue haze alone? From kudzu?
From snake-vine? From the native dog-sized deer
From island to island floating, their head-bones
Eternal and formal,
Collisionless? We are standing mainly on blends
Of sand, red-rooted, in dark
Near-fever air, and there is a certain weaving
At our backs, like a gull's over-the-shoulder
Peel-off downwind. Assuming those wings, we keep gazing
From goat-grass to the high
Shifts, splits, and barreling
Alcohol of the rocks, all the way from minnows flashing whole
The bright brittle shallows, waiting for our momentum
From here on out.

It is true, we like our air warm
And wild, and the bark of our trees
Overlapping backward and upward
Stoutly, the shocks of tough leaves counter-
balancing, with a flicker of lostness. Beside the dead,
The straw-sucking marsh, we have stood where every blade
Of eelgrass thrilled like a hand-line
For the huge bass hanging in the shade
Of the sunken bush, and have heard the unstuffed moss
Hiss like a laundry-iron. This point between
The baskets and the tree is where we best
Are, and would be: our soil, our soul,
Our sail, our black horizon simmering like a mainspring,
Our rocky water falling like a mountain
Ledge-to-ledge naturally headlong,
Unstoppable, and our momentum

In place, overcoming, coming over us
And from us
from now on out.

Vessels

When the sound of forest leaves is like the sleep-talk
Of half-brothers; when it trembles   shorts itself out
Between branches, and is like light that does not cost
Itself any light, let me turn: turn right thén,

Right as it happens and say: I crave wandering
And giving: I crave

My own blood, that makes the body
Of the lover in my arms give up
On the great sparking vault of her form,
when I think instead
Of my real brother, who talks like no leaf
Or no half,
and of the road he will be on
As my body drops off
And the step he takes from me
Comes kicking,
and he feels the starry head that has hovered

Above him all his life

come down on his, like mine

Exactly,

or near enough.

Sleepers

There is a sound you can make, as if someone asked you
To sing between oar strokes, or as though
Your birth-cry came back, and you put it into sails
Over water,
or without vocal cords, like a torso,

Said what it meant, regardless. That is the voice
For sleepers; find it—
Use it and you can join them, that assault-force

Without a muscle, fighting for space

To lift in planned rows over graveyards
Like full battalions. Not one can give you the location
Of his stump-stillness, or even one

Of his edges; none knows where his body will end,
Or what it is stamped with
This moment: agate,

Nova-burst   earthworm
Owl feather.
Sound off, sleepers,
Headless singers. One.
One, two: Sound off.
Not knowing where your tombs
Already lie, assemble, sail through

The lifted spaces, unburied.

Meadow Bridge

There might be working some kind of throwaway

Meditation on Being, just
From what I am looking at
Right here. I can't tell, myself. But it may already have happened
When I batted my eye—

a new fix

Of sun lined out, squaring off: a fresh
Steel bridge,
exactly true
To a crosscut of starkness
And silver.
Tell me: why do I want
To put over it, the right hand drawing

Inexhaustibly drawing

out of the left, a vibration

Of threads? This also, beholders,
Is a fact: gauze
Burns off,
keeps coming: the bridge breaks through anything
I can pull from my hand. No matter how I brim, there is

No softening.

Field, what hope?

Tomb Stone

This place named you,
And what business I have here
Is what I think it is
And only that. I must ask you, though, not to fall

Any farther,
and to forgive me
For coming here, as I keep doing,
as I have done
For a while in a vertical body
That breathes the rectangular solitude

Risen over you. I want time to tell the others
Not to come, for I understand

Now, that deep enough
In death, the earth becomes
Absolute earth. Hold all there is: hold on
And forgive, while I tell thém as I tell
Myself where I stand: Don't let a breast

Echo, because of a foot.

Pass, human step.

To Be Done in Winter

in memoriam, T.C.

What you hold,
Don't drink it all. Throw what you have left of it
Out, and stand. Where the drink went away
Rejoice that your fingers are burning
Like hammered snow.

He makes no sound: the cold flurries, and he comes all the way
Back into life; in the mind
There is no decay. Imagine him
As to behold him, for if you fail
To remember, he lies without
What his body was.
His short shadow
Is on you. Bring him in, now, with tools
And elements. Behold him

With your arms: encircle him,
Bring him in with the forge and the crystal,

With the spark-pounding cold.

Moon Flock

No, don't ask me to give you
What happened in my head when the dark felt
It should change: when the black ploughblade
Went through and dissolved. That was bad enough,

But if you want to understand

Frustration, look up while the moon, which is nothing

But a wild white world,

Struggles overhead: fights to grow wings
For its creatures but cannot get
Creatures to have them. It is known: nothing can be put

Up on a wind with no air;
No wing can lift from stones

Lighter than earth-stones, where a man could leap

Leap till he's nearly forever

Overhead: overhead floating.

                                No wings,
    In all that lightness. You want to understand:

All right. You don't have to look up, but can look straight

                    Straight

        Straight out   out over the night sea
            As it comes in. Do that.
Do it and think of your death, too, as a white world

            Struggling for wings. Then
        All the water your eyesight will hold
        While it can, will not be lost

        And neither will the moon
            As it strains and does nothing
    But quiver
                    when the whole earth places you
            Underfoot
                    as though suspended
    For good. You deserve it. Yóu should be

    That moon flock; and not, as you will be,
        A moveless man floating in the earth

        As though overhead, where it is not
            Possible to wave your arms
        At something, or at nothing: at a white world

        Or at your mother, or at the ocean
        In shock, that I told you about, all insanity
    And necessity when it sees you, and is right at you

                Coming
                    hair-tearing

        Hair-tearing and coming.

Snow Thickets

Helplessly besieging: it is dim,

Unity wavering

Wavering on us, the land in canceling flak. From inside, you and I
Are watching gravity come down

In monotonous awe
each flake a part

Of it, or not. With no blinking, we do
As the snow does

eyes burning   thorns hooding   our tongues

Being born: we watch, under the bush

Being bound, those all-whites yearning
For anvil-points, for contact,
still holding
The airborne embattlement:

Offered and cutthroat   lost
Very great winning hand

Down-dealt to the upthrust.

Expanses

Enjoyable clouds, and a man comes;

It's true, he's alive, but from this distance
No one could tell he is breathing.
You want to be sure he knows, though,
Not to confuse the sea
With any kind of heart: never to mix blood with something

As free as foam. The color white is wing, water, cloud;
It is best as sail.

Sail.

Drawn always off, off the sea
To the chopped soft road, your look

Goes willingly yonder, to and through
The far friendly mountain

                    then

Back over earth level-jawed   shoulder-energy widening
From water, everywhere there is land,

          Brother: boundless,
Earthbound, trouble-free, and all you want—

          Joy like short grass.

DOUBLE-TONGUE: COLLABORATIONS AND REWRITES

Lakes of Värmland

with André Frénaud

Under the terrible north-light north-sea
Light blue: severe smile of a warrior who sleeps in chain-mail
Like a child: sleeps for the many, in water turned to brass
By the dumped cannon of Charles the Twelfth—
                                        leave them at their level,
            O Sweden, like the ultimate weapons
      Like the last war-dead
                        steeped in the angles of your just light—

A single pine tree standing for my heart, I wish to gather near them
      Anything that grows; myrtle, this stuff could be,

                  Or bilberry; whatever.

Form

with André Frénaud

I

            Pull out the pissed-on clinkers,
      Rake down the ashes of my bed, and come in

            And let's do it, as cold as we can get,

            Calving into the void like glaciers
      Into the green Northern Sea. Give me a cliff-shudder
      When you're finishing, before you split off
Unheard, almost booming: cliff-shudder   child-shudder

      That ends it. We have been here before, as you know.

II

      We have been here again, humped-up and splintering
            Like ice-junk: here it has happened
      But we missed it, and dead birds from many migrations
      Float eye-up between us,
                              between bergs, Carrara-piles

Where we chopped and hacked, shattering glass, searching jaggedly
For the radiant nude ice-sculpture
That never showed   never shaped itself free

Of us   was never anything
But chip-chaff and gentian-blue zero
and, as before,
The glorious being we froze together
To bring forth, that we chiseled toward closer and closer,
Whinging and ringing, weeping

For discovery: that together we have annihilated
But not found, is now no more

Than our two hostile cadavers, together.

Heads

with Lucien Becker

I

There is no longer any reason to confuse
My breath with the room's. Sleep empties the pillow;
The world looks into various windows
Where human beings are unfinished,

Like blueprints; no substance has come.
Meadow-saffron dries, tenses. Morning pulverizes it
With a single vague foot, heavy as with
All the sleepless eyelids that there are.

The wellsprings are gray as the sky;
The smoky wind, a wind for headless people,
Flees with the thousands of voices
That solitude waits for, like tide-slack.

Above the roofs everything is empty;
Light cannot get all the way up
To where it was, stalled in dim lamp-bulbs
And bottles drunk dry to hold it down.

Beyond the sill the day has started and quit.
The sheet has cut off my head; my mirror's
   Still deep with the whole night,
  And the road has made great progress

   Into the wall. A fly goes all around
In a big balance. I used to lie here, darling,
With unimproved light: I took it from your brow
   To mine, a glimmer over well-springs,

  Not zoned, not floor-planned for death.
But a building you can see through is rising:
   They are settling and dressing the stones
That pain from everywhere, so long as human,

Fastens onto like clothespins. Lie still, though;
  We're not hanging. You are always covered
  By your smooth forehead and your eyelids;
   You are grazed by no tissued humming

Of razor wire, or by the shadows that come out
Framing, scraping, hosing-down sides of glass,
   And leave for a specified time
  The sides of their heads against banks.

Farmers

a fragment
with André Frénaud

There are not many meteors over the flat country

Of the old; not one metaphor between the ploughblade
  And the dirt
        not much for the spirit: not enough
   To raise the eyes past the horizon-line
Even to the Lord, even with neck-muscles like a bull's
For the up-toss. The modest face has no fear

   Of following a center-split swaying track
     Through grain and straw
   To the grave, or of the honor of work

With muck and animals, as a man born reconciled
With his dead kin:

When love gives him back the rough red of his face he dares

To true-up the seasons of life with the raggedness of earth,
With the underground stream as it turns its water
Into the free stand of the well: a language takes hold

And keeps on, barely making it, made
By pain: the pain that's had him ever since school,
At the same time the indivisible common good
Being shared among the family
Came clear to him: he disappears into fog

He reappears he forces out his voice

Over the field   he extends his figures

With a dead-right clumsiness,
And the blazon that changes every year
Its yellow and green squares, announces at each moment
What must be said: the justice that the power of man installs
In exhausted fresh-air coupling with the earth.

Slogger—

Figure of glory

Less and more than real, fooled always
By the unforeseeable: so nailed by your steps
Into the same steps   so marked by wisdom calamitously come by,
And always uncertain, valiantly balancing,
So stripped, so hog-poor still, after a long day
In the immemorial, that I cannot say to you
Where you will hear me,
Farmer, there will be no end to your knowing

The pastures drawn breathless by the furrow,
The fields, heartsick, unquenchable   arid

avid,
The forgivable slowness, the whispered prophecies of weather:
Winter   spring, the season that always comes through
For you, and never enough,

But only dies, turning out

In its fragile green, its rich greens,
To be nothing but the great stain of blankness
Changing again—

Gravedigger

On Sunday, you come back Monday to the laying-out
In squares, of your infinite land
the furs of snow do not reach us
When they should
the moon has troubled the sown seed . . .

Craters

with Michel Leiris

Roots out of the ground and ongoing
The way wé are, some of them—

Spokes   earth-slats   a raft made of humped planks
Slung down and that's right: wired together
By the horizon: it's what *these* roads
Are growing through: fatal roads,
No encounters, the hacked grass burning with battle-song—

Then when we get *our* voices together,
When we mix in that savage way, in the gully of throats
Where the fog piles up, and we turn our long cadences loose
Over the grooved pastures, the running fence of song

Will flap and mount straight up for miles

Very high, all staring stridulation,
Softer than beer-hops:
one of the days when the wind breathes slackly,
Making the lightest perches tremble
Like hostile stems interlacing,
As in the heart a lock of blond hair knots on itself
Suicidally, insolubly
someone will plough-out a door,
A staircase will dig itself down, its haunted spiral

Will blacken and come out

Where the ashes of those who were once turned to Pompeian lava
Will abandon their smouldering silkworks,
Their velvet slags, and take on the courtliness
Of ghosts: then, then the sky will be gone from us
Forever, we wretched ones who can love nothing
But light.
Such will the craters tell you—any crater
Will tell you, dry-heaving and crouching:
will tell us we've stumbled
Onto one:
we're iń one, dry-heaving and crouching.

Attempted Departure

with André du Bouchet

I come back

hoping to leave

From these planks; for farewell and for lift-off I am lighting
Four walls of a fire, here. Blank plaster comes alive
On me in square gold: my shadow goes giddy with dimension, dropping off
The outflanked pious hunger of the flat;
The damn thing can come at me now
Like death, from anywhere

but while I stand
No side protected, at home, play-penned
With holocaust
the slashes disappear from this flayed back, like
My step on the rammed road,

the only thing fleeing.

Poem

through a French poet, Roland Bouhéret, and my running father

For having left the birds that left me
Better streaks on my eyes than they can make

On any sky alive:
                    for having broken loose new stars
          By opening to the storm a deaf window

At the moment the summer park closed:
                         for having rubbed out,
          From cliffs not dangerous enough, or cold enough
               For you,
                         the name of the dead,
          I hear the sound of fresh steps seeding toward me,
               Steps I could take.

                    Gene,

               Dead in the full of July
          Ten years ago, I have learned all the tracks
Of the stars of that month: they give me more body-authority
     Than a beast-birth in straw. Believe me I have kept

     The old river that ran like something from a crock,
     Through the cow-battered weeds: that runs over us
               As baptismal water always;
          I believe I could be walking there

               Like high valleys crossing,
          In the long laconic open-striding fullness

     Of your muscular death. In whole air your form
     Takes up with me best, giving more than it could
          In the hospital's mirror-blanked room
     Where you leaned toward the grim parks under you

          Before they closed,
                         and out of the rattling rails
     Of your cocked bed, talked about mowing, nothing
          But mowing, of all weird, unearthly
               Earthly things: like a shower of grassblades
Talked, tilted and talked,
                         and shivered, down past you, the gaunt
     Traffic-islands into green; from that time on, I saw them
     As blocked fields, part of elsewhere.

                         But we are advancing
               By steps that grew back to my door,

And if I set your long name in the wind
And it comes back spelling out
The name of a far port-of-call,
                                    the place we never got to,
    That is all right.
                        And yet, with the ashy river
        Running like a soul where I'm headed,
    Even with the names of harbors that swarmed all over me
        When I hit the open, when I paced myself exactly
        With the current—these and the birds, the old cows,

    Have stubborned here
                            stalled   no matter how I increase
            My leg-beat, or stretch and find myself
Calling out in mid-stride. You are motionless, you are in the middle
        Of elsewhere, breathing the herd-breath
        Of the dead—singled and in-line breathing

        Among so many—looking in the same direction
    As the rest of them, your long legs covered with burrs
        And bent weeds, splinters of grassblades:
        Squared off, power-bodied, pollen-lidded

        You are: green-leggèd, but nailed there.

Purgation *(second version)*

homage, Po Chü-yi

        Before and after the eye, grasses go over the long fields.
        Every season they walk on
                                    by us, as though—no; I and you,
            Dear friend—decreed it. One time or another

        They are here. Grass   season . . .   yet we are no longer the best
            Of us.
                        Lie stiller, closer; in the April I love

        For its juices, there is too much green for your grave.
            I feel that the Spring should ignite with what is
    Unnatural as we; ours, but God-suspected. It should come in one furious step,
        and leave

Some—a little—green for us; never quite get every one of the hummocks
    tremoring vaguely

Tall in the passed-through air. They'd make the old road *be*
The road for old men, where you and I used to wander toward
The beetle-eaten city gate, as the year leaned into us.
        Oh fire, come *on*! I trust you!

My ancient human friend, you are dead, as we both know.

But I remember, and I call for something serious, uncalled-for
By anyone else, to sweep, to *use*
           the dryness we've caused to become us! Like the grasshopper

I speak, nearly covered with dust, from the footprint   and ask
Not for the line-squall   lightning:
                the cloud's faking veins—Yes! I catch myself:
    No; not the ripped cloud's open touch   the fireball hay
      Of August
             but for flame too old to live
    Or die, to travel like a wide wild contrary
    Single-minded brow over the year's right growing
    In April
           over us for us   as we sway stubbornly near death
        From both sides   age-gazing

        Both sighing like grass and fire.

Basics

      Who has told you what discoveries
      There are, along the stressed blank
      Of a median line? From it, nothing

      Can finally fall. Like a spellbinder's pass
      A tense placid principle continues

      Over it, and when you follow you have the drift,

      The balance of many compass needles
      Verging to the pole. *Bring down your arms, voyager,*

And the soul goes out
Surrounding, humming
                                    standing by means

Of the match-up in long arm-bones

Dropped:
                        held out and drawn back   back in
Out of the open
                                    compass-quivering and verging
            At your sides, as median movement

Lays itself bare: a closed vein of bisected marble, where

                        Along the hairline stem
Of the continuum, you progress, trembling
With the plumb-bob quiver of mid-earth,
                                                with others in joy
                        Moving also, in line,

                        Equalling, armlessing.

II. SIMPLEX

        Comes a single thread
                                    monofilament coming

            Strengthening   engrossing and slitting
                Into the fine-spun life

            To come, foretold in whatever
Ecstasy there's been, but never suspected, never included
    In what was believed. The balance of the spiral
            Had been waiting, and could take

    What was given it: the single upthrust through
    The hanging acid, the helix spun and spellbound

By the God-set of chemistry, the twine much deeper
        Than any two bodies imagined
        They could die for: insinuate, woven
            Single strand, third serpent
Of the medical wood, circling the staff of life

            Into the very body

            Of the future, deadly

But family, having known from the beginning

Of the sun, what will take it on.

III. WORD

Heat makes this, heat makes any
Word: human lungs,
Human lips. Not like eternity, which, naked, every time
Will call on lightning
To say it all: No after
Or before. We try for that

And fail. Our voice
Fails, but for an instant
Is like the other; breath alone
That came as though humanly panting
From far back, in unspeakably beautiful

Empty space

And struck: at just this moment
Found the word "golden."

ACKNOWLEDGMENTS

Many of the previously unpublished poems in *Summons* are used courtesy of the Washington University Libraries.

Three sections in this volume were previously published as three books, *The Eye-Beaters, Blood, Victory, Madness, Buckhead and Mercy*; *The Zodiac*; and *The Strength of Fields*. They are published by arrangement with Doubleday & Company, Inc.

The poem "The Strength of Fields" originally appeared in *A New Spirit, a New Commitment, a New America* by the 1977 Inaugural Committee, published by Bantam Books, copyright © 1977 by James Dickey.

"I Dreamed I Already Loved You," "Assignation," and "Doing the Twist on Nails," translated by James Dickey, are all from *Stolen Apples* by Yevgeny Yevtushenko. Translation copyright © 1971 by Doubleday & Company, Inc. Reprinted by permission of the publisher.

"Purgation," "The Ax-God: Sea Pursuit," "Nameless," "Math," "Judas," "Small Song," "Undersea Fragment in Colon," "Mexican Valley," "Low Voice, Out Loud," "Poem," "When," and "A Saying of Farewell" originally appeared in *Head-Deep in Strange Sounds: Free Flight Improvisations from the Unenglish*, by James Dickey, published by Palaemon Press, Ltd. Copyright © 1979 by James Dickey. Reprinted by permission of the publisher.

Many of the poems collected herein first appeared in the following publications: *American Poetry Review, The Amicus Journal, The Atlantic Monthly, Beloit Poetry Journal, The Bulletin* (Sydney, Australia), *Charleston Magazine, Chicago Choice, Choice, Commentary, Encounter, Esquire, False Youth* (Pressworks Publishing, Inc.), *Gentleman's Quarterly, Harper's, Hastings Constitutional Law Quarterly, Hudson Review, Impetus, Kenyon Review, Mutiny, The Nation, New World Writing, The New Yorker, The New York Times Book Review, Night Hurdling* (Bruccoli Clark, Inc.), *North American Review, Paris Review, Partisan Review, Poetry, Poetry Dial, Proceedings, Quarterly Review of Literature, Saturday Evening Post, Saturday Review, Sewanee Review, Shenandoah, Southern Magazine, Southern Review, Southport, Texas Quarterly, Transatlantic Review, Värmland* (Palaemon Press, Ltd.), *Verse, Virginia Quarterly, Wormwood Review,* and *Yale Review.*

UNIVERSITY PRESS OF NEW ENGLAND publishes books under its own imprint and is the publisher for Brandeis University Press, Brown University Press, University of Connecticut, Dartmouth College, Middlebury College Press, University of New Hampshire, University of Rhode Island, Tufts University, University of Vermont, and Wesleyan University Press.

Library of Congress Cataloging-in-Publication Data

Dickey, James.
The whole motion : collected poems, 1945–1992 / by James Dickey.
   p.   cm. — (Wesleyan poetry)
ISBN 0–8195–2202–3
I. Title. II. Series.
PS3554.I32A17 1992
81 1'.54—dc20   91–50811

∞